Exploring Depth Psychology and the Female Self

Exploring Depth Psychology and the Female Self: Feminist Views from Somewhere presents a Jungian take on modern feminism, offering an international assessment with a dynamic political edge which includes perspectives from both clinicians and academics.

Presented in three parts, this unique collection explores how the fields of gender and politics have influenced each other, how myth and storytelling craft feminist narratives and how public discussion can amplify feminist theory. The contributions include some which are traditionally theoretical in tone, and some which are uniquely personal, but all work to encounter the female self as an active entity. The book as a whole offers a multi-faceted and interdisciplinary approach to feminism and feminist issues from contemporary voices around the world, as well as a critique of Jung's essentialist notion of the feminine.

Exploring Depth Psychology and the Female Self will offer insightful perspectives to academics and students of Jungian and post-Jungian studies, gender studies and politics. It will also be of great interest to Jungian analysts and psychotherapists, and analytical psychologists

Leslie Gardner, PhD, is a Fellow in the Department of Psychosocial and Psychoanalytic studies at the University of Essex, UK.

Catriona Miller, PhD, is a Senior Lecturer at Glasgow Caledonian University, UK, where she teaches television script writers and media students.

Exploring Depth Psychology and the Female Self

Feminist Themes from Somewhere

Edited by

Leslie Gardner
and Catriona Miller

Routledge
Taylor & Francis Group

LONDON AND NEW YORK

First published 2021
by Routledge
2 Park Square, Milton Park, Abingdon, Oxon OX14 4RN

and by Routledge
52 Vanderbilt Avenue, New York, NY 10017

Routledge is an imprint of the Taylor & Francis Group, an informa business

British Library Cataloguing-in-Publication Data
A catalogue record for this book is available from the British Library

Library of Congress Cataloging-in-Publication Data
A catalog record has been requested for this book

ISBN: 978-0-367-33064-4 (hbk)
ISBN: 978-0-367-33065-1 (pbk)
ISBN: 978-0-429-31783-5 (ebk)

Typeset in Times
By Deanta Global Publishing Services, Chennai, India

Disclaimer: All names and places of clients/patients mentioned in case
studies have been made anonymous and any similarity to living persons is
completely inadvertent.

Contents

Notes on contributors

Lene Auestad (PhD in Philosophy from the University of Oslo) writes and lectures internationally on ethics, critical theory and psychoanalysis. Books include *Respect, Plurality, and Prejudice: A Psychoanalytical and Philosophical Enquiry into the Dynamics of Social Exclusion and Discrimination* (2015) and *Shared Traumas, Silent Loss, Public and Private Mourning* (2017). In 2010 she founded the international and interdisciplinary conference series Psychoanalysis and Politics (www.psa-pol.org), which continues to this day.

Emma Buchanan is a PhD candidate at the School of Philosophy and Religion at Bangor University. She completed her undergraduate degree at the University of Sheffield in 2013, in Modern Languages (German, Russian and Dutch), and she has worked as a secondary school teacher since. Her PhD is on gender roles and Jungian archetypes *in The Walking Dead*.

Mary Gayle Certeza-Narcida is a graduate of Engaged Humanities and the Creative Life with Emphasis on Depth Psychology in Pacifica Graduate Institute. She is an advertising entrepreneur, author and publisher, as well as a board member of the *Carl Jung Circle Center of the Philippines* and member of *the Jungian Society for Scholarly Studies* in the United States. Her country of residence is the Philippines.

Martyna Chrzescijanska is Lecturer at London Metropolitan University, UK. She completed her PhD in Psychosocial and Psychoanalytic Studies at University of Essex. Her research focuses on the role of space in psychotherapy. She published in *International Journal of Jungian Studies*.

Terence Dawson has recently retired, after teaching English and European literature at both the top universities in Singapore for the best part of thirty years. He has a special interest in both music and the visual arts. With Polly Young-Eisendrath, he co-edited *The Cambridge Companion to Jung* (1997; 2nd ed. 2008). He is the author of *The Effective Protagonist in the Nineteenth-Century British Novel: Scott, Brontë, Eliot, Wilde* (2004), and articles on wide-ranging topics. He also serves as an associate editor of *The International Journal of Jungian Studies*.

Betty Sue Flowers, PhD (University of London), is a Distinguished Alumnus of the University of Texas, is a writer, editor, and international business consultant, with publications ranging from poetry therapy to human rights, including two books of poetry and four television tie-in books with Bill Moyers.

Leslie Gardner is co-editor of this volume, and last year, co-editor with Frances Gray, and author of chapter 'Explorations in the poetics of the feminine pronoun' in *Feminist Views from Somewhere* (2017); earlier books *Rhetorical Investigations: GB Vico and CG Jung* (2015); *The Ecstatic and the Archaic: an Analytical Psychological Inquiry* (2018) co-edited with Paul Bishop; *House: the Wounded Healer on Television* (2010) co-edited with Luke Hockley, upcoming *Narratives of Individuation* co-edited with Raya Jones, with two authored chapters 'Autobiography as agenda: Augustine, Vico, Jung' and 'Affectivity and *Narratio*' and other chapters and articles. She is a Visiting Fellow in Department of Psychosocial and Psychoanalytic Studies, University of Essex where she gained her PhD. She is director and founder of the international literary agency Artellus Limited.

Phil Goss is a Jungian Analyst (AJA, London) and Director for Counselling and Psychotherapy at the University of Warwick. Phil is author of *Men, Women and Relationships, A Post-Jungian Approach: Gender Electrics and Magic Beans* (2010), as well as of *Jung: A Complete Introduction* (2015). His other publications include chapters in the edited collections *Education and Imagination: Jungian Approaches* and *Dreaming the Myth Onwards* (2008). His interest in gender is reflected in his paper 'Discontinuities in the male psyche' in the *Journal for Analytical Psychology* (2006), and in his chapter on clinical themes and the masculine in the 'Psychotherapy and Alchemy' (2014) edited collection. Phil's paper 'Wordsworth, Loss and the Numinous' (2012) was published from the conference he organised at the Wordsworth Trust, Grasmere, in 2011. He also helped organise the Notion of the Sublime Jung-Lacan conference in Cambridge (2014).

Frances Gray holds a PhD in Philosophy and Women's Studies from Australian National University. She was Honorary Senior Research Fellow in the School of History Philosophy Classics and Religion, University of Queensland. She is the author of many volumes including *Jung, Irigaray, Individuation: Analytical Psychology and the Question of the Feminine* (2007), *Cartesian Philosophy and the Flesh: Reflections on Incarnation in Analytical Psychology* (2012) and *Jung and Levinas: An Ethics of Mediation* (2015) all published by Routledge. Her articles, chapters in books, and reviews have appeared internationally. Her current research is in hierarchical relations in religious systems and the ontological implications of belief.

MJ Maher is a group analyst in private practice in London. She teaches trainee counsellors in London and also teaches on a Foundation Course and an Intermediate Course in Group Analysis in Rwanda. MJ facilitates experiential groups for trainee counsellors and university students. She has over 28 years' experience of working in the NHS as a community psychiatric nurse and a group psychotherapist, she specialised in Drug and Alcohol Rehabilitation, worked in Therapeutic Community for people with a Personality Disorder diagnosis and now is engaging in further focused work on suicide. MJ presents at national and international conferences and symposiums. She is the author of *Racism and Cultural Diversity: Cultivating Racial Harmony through Counselling, Group Analysis and Psychotherapy* (2012). Her response to an international keynote address by Professor Elisabeth Rohr on *World in Motion – The Emotional Impact of Mass Migration* (2018) at a Berlin symposium of over 400 group analysts was published in the journal *Group Analysis*.

Catriona Miller is co-editor of this volume and is a Senior Lecturer at Glasgow Caledonian University where she teaches television script writers and media students. She has a PhD from the University of Stirling and publishes in the field of film and television studies, with a particular interest in horror, cult TV and science fiction genres from a Jungian perspective, publishing an article on slasher movies for the *International Journal of Jungian Studies* in 2014. Her chapter 'A Jungian Textual Terroir' opens *The Routledge International Handbook of Jungian Film Studies* (2018). She is author of *Cult TV Heroines* (2020).

Susan Rowland is Chair of MA Engaged Humanities and the Creative Life at Pacifica Graduate Institute, California. As writer on Jung, literary theory, gender and the arts, she published *Jung: A Feminist Revision* (2002) and other books including *Jung as a Writer* (2005) and *The Ecocritical Psyche: Literature, Complexity Evolution and Jung* (2012), and *Remembering Dionysus* (2016) among other works. She was founding Chair of the *International Association for Jungian Studies* (2003–2006), and now teaches Shakespeare, gender theory, *The Red Book*, ecocriticism and Jung. Recent projects include a book on goddesses in mystery fiction and another on literary theory in James Hillman and Jung.

Sulagna Sengupta is a postgraduate in English Literature and an independent scholar of Jungian Studies, based in Bangalore, India. She is the author of *Jung in India*, published in 2013 by Spring Journal Books, USA.

Laura Camille Tuley, PhD, is a Jungian analyst in private practice in Madison, Wisconsin. She has contributed to the *New Orleans Review*, *Mothering in the Third Wave*, *Art Papers*, *Hypatia*, the APA Newsletter on Feminism and

Philosophy and *Iris* and is the co-editor of *Mother Knows Best: Talking Back to the Experts* (2009).

Huan Wang is a PhD candidate at the University of Essex, and her research is on the femininity and masculinity in romantic relationships in contemporary China. Her study is mainly from Jungian and post-Jungian perspectives, and focuses on how young Chinese couples have been affected by traditional values, Westernization and the one-child policy. She was a psychotherapist for five years in the clinic department of a hospital in Wuhan, China, and has collected many clinical materials on couple issues from previous work. At the present, her research interests mainly focus on the effects of political interventions on relationships within families, and how to address the individual position in a collectivism.

Heba Zaphiriou-Zarifi is a Jungian Analytical Psychologist, a registered member of GAP, UKCP and IAAP, and in private practice in London and Greece. She consults on psychosocial projects in the Middle East and has devised a process of building resilience in adverse conditions. She has contributed to a pilot project for The British Refugee Council. Heba read Philosophy at The Sorbonne – Paris IV to doctorate level and has a Master's in Dance. She founded the Central-London Authentic Movement Group and is a Leader in Bodysoul Rhythms© at The Marion Woodman Foundation.

Preface

In the dark, on land resistant to human cultivation, three transgender figures await the victorious warrior and his best friend. Marginalized by poverty and ostracized by their religion, these outcasts know what the warrior does not, that his triumph will lead him into unbearable temptation. As a feted patriarchal conqueror, he has all the privilege denied to these so-called women with beards and wild attire (Shakespeare 1606: Act 1, sc. 3, 1. 40–45: 776). They gather to dissolve all the divisions and hierarchies of order in their nasty pot of human and animal parts. The warrior too is fresh from dismembering bodies. His violence not only sanctioned but, as he is about to learn, rewarded.

Within the teeming cauldron of destroyed identities, this victorious male finds his own mirror image. In fact, he so fatefully weds his inner being to these vagrants that he will return to summon their powers of chaos again: "I conjure you, by that which you profess" (Act IV, sc. 1, 1.50: 689). From then on, the witches' annihilation of boundaries becomes this warrior's project of apocalyptic destruction: "though the treasure/of nature's germens tumble all together/even till destruction sicken." (ibid.: 1. 58–60: 690). And yet, what he hears in both encounters is not the truth they tell. That is why he finds their seduction irresistible.

The witches in Shakespeare's play *Macbeth* remain at the heart of feminism, not least in their refusal to be unambiguously women. In fact, these characters who perform the deconstruction of identity, remain radical to all four terms in this rich book's title: Depth Psychology, Female Self, Feminist Themes and Somewhere. Depth psychology designates psychologies that place the unknown psyche as an important yet mysterious contributor to being. That which resists rational knowing cannot be cast out without terrible consequences. Just so the weird women are dangerous because there is no rational context for the hero to process the desires they arouse.

As female selves, the witches conform to no recognizable social dress or body standards. Possessed of 'beards' and 'wild attire', they were, of course, first performed on stage by boys. Here is the performance of gender as its most un-placeable, most toxic and most overpowering to the dominant patriarchy personified in the successful warrior. Of course, Macbeth the great successful subordinate in King Duncan's wars, cannot find it in his heart to treat the sovereign with love for a father. Hailed as future monarch by these 'female' selves, he hears only Oedipal urgings to replace Duncan as lord of the Mother's body, the land itself.

'Feminist themes' is a potent conjuring of interwoven enquiry. For feminist themes serves to open up that contested term, 'Feminism' to the contests of the twenty-first century. Feminism has a history of struggle against the rule of the father. In theological and political terms, father-rule in Western Christianity produced cultures of dominion that moulded sons into warriors. Women were only visible as the flesh and wombs to generate more of them. Women did not *matter*, they simply enacted it on behalf of father-rule. Hence the struggle to liberate women was one condensed out of patriarchy's relentless binary structures. Feminism was about the necessary liberation of women who would be freed from being abjected (made repulsive and meaningless) through their bodies (Kristeva 1982).

Step forward Shakespeare's witches as those very abjected women. They figure the horror of all that is repressed from warrior patriarchal culture to form its norms. Yet today, these very same characters sponsor of twenty-first-century feminist themes of questioning binaries such as women versus men, heterosexuality versus LGBTQ, even machine versus natural. Feminism has long understood that oppression must be apprehended, understood and combatted in its multiple locations. Women and men of colour suffer together what some white women never apprehend. Class, sexual, religious and geographical status may manifest in ways that crush being.

Fortunately, depth psychology is a knowing of human potential which no oppression can magic away. Unfortunately, the radical potential of depth psychology has not yet been accepted fully established. This book of diverse essays is predicated on the notion that the depth psychology unconscious, particularly in the work of C. G. Jung, contains the seeds of creativity so innate that they can never be entirely obliterated by oppression or exterior circumstances. It is this psyche that contains the 'nature's germens' invoked by Macbeth. Despite his scorched earth reign, strong shoots of regeneration dominate the last moments of the play. Ultimately the undaunted witches on the heath are answered by the dauntless spirit of the survivors.

'Somewhere' reminds us that the heath of those witches is as fundamental as their dark practices. In fact, the witches embody that wilderness of earth as nature, including psychic nature, that cannot be tamed. Perhaps more significant for the Climate Emergency of today, the heath speaks through the barely human beings to the men whose war has both destroyed and fertilized (with blood) more clement ground. The witches in the play are the Anthropocene, a term signifying that no part of this planet is untouched by human industry (particularly of Western industrialization). They are the Anthropocene as the untameable both inside humans (as unconscious) and outside as the climate that is changing in ways, we can neither wholly predict nor control.

The witches are Anthropocene because they are uninhabitable wilderness *made so* by the human world that celebrates the warrior. They are the deep psyche as that which has been repressed and that which can never be known. Repression makes them dangerous; unknowability makes them generative. In Macbeth, they germinate regicide leading to the darkest kind of father-leader; one who controls by more killing. In the dominant Western culture, the witches/Anthropocene births the monstrous Climate Emergency we face today. What exiles them, masculinity warped into killing machines, is precisely that structure behind the rape of the earth and the subjection of it to warrior-capitalism.

Yes, the witches are from 'somewhere' indeed, and from some specific inscription upon place. The essays in this book explore the 'somewhere' evoked in their feminist themes and how it may provide hope and meaning to female selves through depth psychology. For just as this book's scope can be understood through the lens of a play of the seventeenth century, so too are new directions in the academy such as quantum consciousness, comparable to Jung's own delve in the past (such as alchemy) for ways to re-imagine present and future. Here Karen Barad, from physics and philosophy, speaks of a new materialism characterized by agential realism. "Barad's work has focused on the way our inquiries are onto-logically generative – they create realities as opposed to describing them" (Rosick 2018: 637).

The world of matter is that of nonhuman agency, she finds. Witchcraft is everywhere and may not even require witches. There is no subject/object divide; knowing intervenes in being in ways we cannot fully trace nor comprehend. Barad explores what this means for research and ethics:

> Ethics is therefore not about right responses to a radically exteriorized other, but about responsibility and accountability for the lively relationalities of becoming, of which we are a part. Ethics is about mattering, about taking account of the entangled materializations of which we are a part, including new configurations, new subjectivities, new possibilities. … Responsibility, then, is a matter of the ability to respond. Listening for the response of the other and an obligation to be responsive to the other, who is not entirely separate from what we call the self.
>
> (Barad 2012: 69)

Radical, counter-cultural connectedness links witchcraft, feminism, depth psychology and now new materialism. For decades feminism has argued that scholarship, research and knowing are interventions that require ongoing ethical exploration. Shakespeare's witches demonstrate the necessity for a feminist theme of such ethics. It is, of course, my own perversity that sees the modern feminist as a witch (of any gender and none). Whatever emerges in the struggles of this time will be from somewhere, sustained by depth psychology and tender to the female self: that is my feminist theme.

Susan Rowland

References

Barad, K., 2012, 'Interview with Karen Barad'. In: R. Dolphijn and I. van der Tuin eds., *New Materialism: Interviews and Cartographies*, pp. 48–70. Ann Arbor, MI, Open Humanities Press.

Kristeva, J., 1982, *Powers of Horror: An Essay on Abjection*, New York: Columbia University Press.

Rosick, J., 2018, 'Art, Agency, and Ethics in Research: How the New Materialisms Will Require and Transform Arts-Based Research'. In: P. Leavy ed., *Handbook of Arts-Based Research*, pp. 632–648. New York & London: The Guilford Press.

Shakespeare, W., 1606/2011, '*Macbeth*'. In: R. Proudfoot, A. Thompson and D. S. Kastan eds., *The Arden Shakespeare Complete Works*, pp. 773–800, London: Bloomsbury.

Introduction

Leslie Gardner

Feminisms purposively and relentlessly evolve. Grounded in 'situated knowledges', as Donna Haraway (1988) called it, feminism has come a long way since its renewed modern-day iteration in the early twentieth century, and it further broadened its scope recently in the language and scholarship of the field, influenced by American, French, Italian, Asian, Australian and South American writers. Haraway noted that knowledge is not a "view from above, from nowhere" (Haraway, 1988, p. 589), that is 'objective', but a 'joining of partial views and halting voices ... within [living] limits and contradictions – of views from somewhere" (p.590). This collection of essays offers a range of such recognisably situated voices conversing with the female self within the frame of depth psychology. Some are traditionally theoretical in tone, some are uniquely personal, but all work to encounter the female self as an active entity.

'Situated knowledge', together with Karen Barad's (1998) explanation of 'agential realism', exposing the underlying subjectivity of 'objectivity' with their commitment to unconscious 'algorithms' (to use digital language metaphorically) and the impact of regarding female as a performative enterprise from Judith Butler's work (1990 and 1993), includes angles explored in Spivak's ideas (2010) about the subaltern's form of colonial communications, subverting meanings and Drucilla Cornell's (1992 and 1993) focus on transformative and 'deviant' language, based in part on Luce Irigaray's innovative albeit problematic and essentialist approaches (see 1985 and 1987). These writers, working to unpick male bias inherent in mainstream ideologies around gender, referred to psycho-analytic theory for their precepts and guidelines, and theoretical analysis also naturally spread to Jungian theorists, as well as to therapeutic practice and critiques on the practice of therapy on individuals, exploring and questioning subjectivity and the very notion of the 'individual'.

As contemporary feminists in philosophy and education – Audre Lorde, bell hooks, Haraway – point out, the collective and particular coincide in personality as contexts shift. Each self-presentation, multi-faceted and complex is worn when needed, without compromising a basic integrity. Deviance, given a difficult-to-pierce patriarchal world, is an inevitable resource as Drucilla Cornell points out.

Her efforts at ending of apartheid in South Africa did much to heal and set out liberating pathways in that beleaguered country.

Crafting language that circumvents its phallocentric frameworks requires 'thinking outside'. As such, feminist politics and law, as collaborative endeavours, contemplate the person on her specific home ground – the battered wife who seeks to exonerate her abuser is respected, as is the single mother giving up her child for adoption, and the feisty warrior represented on epic television, or the subservient handmaiden. The master/slave formula, as Lorde (1984/2007) tells us, is a tangle of objectives, and survival is the name of the game. Spivak (2010) recommends making discourse a strategic deployment of power positions. These issues are tackled in a variety of ways in this volume reflecting aspects of feminisms.

Helene Cixous questions how women can be free to write in the language of the prison, articulation under siege, overcoming fears of being ostracised, unread, accused of unreadability, and, finally, unaccountably, women 'let out a scream' in her essay 'We Who Are Free, Are we Free?' (1993). We propose here to release different responses to the constraints and contexts in themes of depth psychology, to open up discussion further into the twenty-first century.

Feminists of Jungian orientation have also sought to unpick gender bias evident in the theory, in order to overcome its namesake's anomalous practices and theories. In these pages too we question the notion of the 'feminine', which Jung distinctively nominated as the inferior 'anima' archetype, applied to the non-rational, feeling-based way of approaching the world. He contrasted these traits to those of the 'masculine': the 'animus' (about which he wrote more) as an 'opposite' – ideas which have been blown up in years since he wrote. As he set it out, the notion that it is possible to designate a feminine attribute in cultural and social habits of behaviour and thought is recognisably oppressive and distorting. Post-Jungian theorists have quashed his ideas in this realm, while utilising other Jungian theories of the persona, individuation, and transformation that he made part of analytical psychology. Language and semiotics are constrained by patriarchal patterns embedded deeply in communication, the imagination, psyche and thought, and the writers in this volume explore these modalities eschewing many of the futile ideas of depth psychology at its inception.

The Jungian perspective and its depth psychology allied orientations are where we focus in this volume with contributors from around the world, from theoreticians and clinical practitioners, but depth psychology is under tension at the moment, and we purposively include perspectives from throughout the field. Kleinian, Winnicottian and Lacanian ideas as well as reference to Freudian theories are among theories we also include. We are able to arrive at a positive formula of multiple personalities, alluding to Jungian notions of emergent aspects of the psyche in the moment, thriving together as the agent/individual seeks to steer in the world successfully.

This present collection follows on from an earlier book, *Feminist Views from Somewhere* (2017), which itself arose from an online colloquy of Jungian analysts and commentators. As Susan Rowland refers to it in the Preface, we follow on from that earlier volume with 'feminist themes from somewhere' and, like that earlier group of essays, we do not leave out those scholars who identify as male.

One of the most commented on parts of the earlier volume was the appendix, 'Voices'. In that section, we collected comment and interchanges from a forum belonging to the International Association for Analytical Psychology, an organisation open to academics and analysts, and therapists of all persuasions, but which is primarily Jungian. 'Voices' included exchanges which were rarely righteous or indignant – rather, participants were sympathetic not only to each other in allowing differences to be appreciated and acknowledged, but also in presenting pragmatic approaches to the patriarchal world even as it is a frustrating world. We follow up here with a similar exchange from a depth psychology forum, the International Association for Jungian Studies. But as Haraway insisted on the embodiment of vision, we insist upon the embodiment of the voices in this volume, which offer stories, experiences and specific points of view from around the world.

The female selves who emerge throughout are more difficult to pin down – they are not 'nice' or necessarily compassionate figures – like the bawdy Baubo from Greek mythology, and the ancient and modern representations of raucous warrior women; they include females who grab power with both fists, as in *House of Cards* (Netflix, 2013–2019) or in the myths of the devious and strong figures of Indian myth or the 'modern ancient' practices of the belligerent characters in Philippines origin stories (not to speak of the Sumerian power house goddesses)— they seek power or riches in sometimes ugly, brutal ways which can be read as 'aggressive' in derogative way only because it is female agency.

These chapters expand and reflect a similar sense of clearing-the-decks to focus on ways to accommodate themes from particular places and you will sense collaborative sensibilities which are the hallmarks of feminist groups, scholarly and in action. We have expanded the strong presence of voices to point up what may seem paradoxical, a universal set of differences. Where you are as a scholar/ writer in space and time (Western and patriarchal notions in themselves that require attentive self-awareness from the writer) wholly impacts on themes and observations – how your voice articulates ideas, including feeling and situated perspective provides the impetus for points of view. Depth psychology depends on awareness of the distinctions of consciousness and unconsciousness in culture and in personal 'interiors'. How do these elements combine in the moment and in the place?

Feminist theory has contributed to discourse around LGBT and gender, artificial intelligence and technology globally, and has entered into the mainstream as more nuanced discussion has taken place across social media. Feminism has become feminisms. As noted above, the Jungian orientation itself has been informed by problematic originary stories, and questionable notions of so-called 'archetypal' notions of femininity and masculinity ('archetype' itself a much over-used word), which on closer examination quickly break down from supposed universal characteristics, to those of a particular cultural time and place. However, these terms present an easily surmountable hurdle – although we include here chapters that find these designations useful as guidelines (if only to be dismissed), many of the chapters include backdrops of women's mythic behaviour which Jung saw as amplifications of psychological tropes, indeed his typology evolved from his creative use of important cultural tropes. We add to what is a burgeoning psychosocial field dealing here with feminism and depth psychology (see our *Select Bibliography* for some sources which have been influential in this area, may not be otherwise referenced in individual chapters).

What this new volume offers is a collective and multi-faceted approach from around the world, emerging from what became an international annual event at Amnesty International in London UK with the title 'Feminist Views from Somewhere'. Voices which this time were scholarly, poetic and specifically culturally based as we contemplated together, and later, what is here set out in writing, varied perspectives from different locations but also from differing senses of perceptions of the world and across the depth psychology field additionally to orientations enumerated above: relational psychology is reflected on with frequent reference to Jessica Benjamin's work. It is in that collaborative spirit that this new set of essays has emerged and while the contributors are predominantly clinicians, a scholarly interpretive approach also has a strong presence.

To differentiate the various aspects we pursue in this volume, we have divided papers into several sections, reflecting perspectives first on gender and politics; then on stories that expose feminist concerns in the analysis of their cultural impact; and finally a presentation of more personal voices, set in specific contexts that illuminate feminist concerns.

First up, in her insightful Preface, Susan Rowland, a long-time writer on feminist issues, draws our attention to Macbeth's witches – possessed of 'beards' and 'wild attire' – a pointed, and appropriate launch into the essays of the book.

In the opening section on gender as politics, Betty Sue Flowers uses samples of the stories of Texan women in their posture as strong 'male' figures despite otherwise female physical attributes – evoking female warrior figures of Elizabeth I or Joan of Arc. Laura Tuley adds the plaints and solutions of clients working through dilemmas of desire to achieve wholeness and health with humour, exploring Baubo's ancient presence as consoler and bawdy commentator. Martyna Chrzescijanska looks at the therapeutic space itself as a focus of political language and feeling – briefly, its history and attempts at liberation. Lene Auestad follows in a recounting a catastrophic event in Oslo tracking a neo-Nazi group and its impact on same-sex 'traitors' as a reflection of the political issues that are recognisable globally. Phil Goss uses controversial discussions of gender to try to parse out problematics of power distinctions in gender politics – how to identify yourself, if you need to do so at all – and draws on different psychosocial theses to orient such exploration.

Opening up the next section, 'Stories': Catriona Miller, co-editor of this volume, explores narrative sequences of 'becoming a queen' in a contemporary story –

House of Cards (Netflix, 2013–2019) – and contrasting that with the ancient Sumerian myth of Inanna and her political rise to power; the differences and similarities are illuminating. Terence Dawson proposes a fresh narrative analysis of the Antigone story as told by Sophocles – her radical departures reflect an attitude to hierarchy that has changed over the many years since her story was told. Sulagna Sengupta brings the ecological concerns she finds in Jungian psychology to light exploring Indian earth narratives that lean on feminist action in ancient tales. Gayle Certeza-Narcida uses the story of the 'modern ancients' in her home in the Philippines to disclose an underlying cultural foundational originary myth – with characteristic gender equality as building blocks toward implementing feminist precepts. Huan Wang uses tales of the Great Mother especially as revealed in the Chinese classic opera 'The Peony Pavilion' to show the way female desire is deployed as powerful jolt into action for romance and cultural equanimity. Emma Buchanan looks at similar foundations revealed in the contemporary American television series, *The Walking Dead* (AMC, 2010–on-going), hunting for female redemption in a fiercely apocalyptic tale of the living dead.

And, finally, the 'Voices' section includes distinctive pleas in affective essays: first, Heba Zaphiriou-Zarifi recounts stories of female survivors of war, and their heroic and metaphoric approaches, such as a re-enactment of Aristophanes play *Lysistrata,* to overcoming difficulties in violent ways that a female might use, including silence. MJ Maher issues a colourful, deeply humane exposure of that wholly vital person in female life – the mother of your mother – calling on the before-your-own-past to find yourself. Then philosopher Frances Gray's deeply moving voice, reflecting the earth and its tortures and relationship to women world over, before we finish with excerpts from the online discussion 'Let's talk about our mothers', which functions as a robust sign-off.

References

Barad, K., 1998, 'Getting real: Technoscientific practices and the materialisation of reality', *Differences: A Journal of Feminist Cultural Studies*, 10(2), pp. 87–128.

Butler, J., 1990, *Gender Trouble*, Abingdon: Routledge.

Butler, J., 1993, *Bodies That Matter: On the Discursive Limits of "Sex"*, London: Routledge.

Cixous, H., 1976, 'The laugh of the medusa' (trans. K. Cohen and P. Cohen) *Signs*, 1(4, Summer), pp. 875–893.

Cixous, H., 1993, 'We who are free, are we free?' (trans. C. Miller) *Critical Inquiry*, 19(2, Winter), pp. 201–219.

Cornell, D., 1992, *The Philosophy of the Limit*, New York: Routledge.

Cornell, D., 1993, *Transformations: Recollective Imagination and Sexual Difference*, New York: Routledge.

Gardner, L. & Gray, F. (eds.), 2017, *Feminist Views from Somewhere: Post-Jungian Themes in Feminist Theory*, Abingdon: Routledge.

Haraway, D., 1988, 'Situated knowledges: The science question in feminism and the privilege of partial perspective', *Feminist Studies*, 14(3, Autumn), pp. 575–599.

Irigaray, L., 1985, *Speculum of the Other Woman*, Hoboken, NJ: Cornell University Press.
Irigaray, L., 1987, 'Le sujet de science est-il sexue? / Is the subject of science sexed?' (trans. C. Mastragelo Bove), *Hypatia*, 2(3), pp. 65–87.
Lorde, A., 1984/2007, 'The master's tools will never dismantle the master's house' In: *Sister Outsider: Essays and Speeches*, Berkeley, CA: Crossing Press, pp. 110–114.
Spivak, G. C., 2010, 'Can the subaltern speak?' In: Morris, R.C. (ed.) *Can the Subaltern Speak?: Reflections on the History of an Idea*, New York: Columbia University Press, pp. 21–78.

Selected bibliography

Austin, S., 2005, *Women's Aggressive Fantasies: A Post-Jungian Exploration of Self-Hatred, Love and Agency*, Hove: Routledge.
Barad, K., 2007, *Meeting the Universe Halfway: Quantum Physics and the Entanglement of Matter and Meaning*, Durham, NC and London: Duke University Press.
Benjamin, J., 1988, *The Bonds of Love: Psychoanalysis, Feminism and the Problems of Domination*, New York: Pantheon Books.
Brinton Perera, S., 1981, *Descent of Inanna: A Way of Initiation for Women*, Toronto: Inner City Books.
Chodorow, N., 1999, *The Reproduction of Mothering: Psychoanalysis and the Sociology of Gender*, Berkeley, CA: University of California Press.
Covington, C., 2015, *Sabina Spielrein: Forgotten Pioneer of Psychoanalysts*, Hove: Brunner-Routledge.
Cowan, L., 2002, *Tracking the White Rabbit: A Subversive View of Modern Culture*, Hove: Brunner-Routledge.
Douglas, C., 1990, *The Woman in the Mirror: Analytical Psychology and the Feminine*, Boston, MA: Sigo Press.
Gray, F., 2008, *Jung, Irigaray, Individuation: Philosophy, Analytical Psychology and the Question of the Feminine*, London: Routledge.
Hannah, B., 2011, *The Animus: The Spirit of Inner Truth in Women Volume 1*, Asheville, NC: Chiron Publications.
Harding, M. E., 1970, *The Way of All Women*, New York: Puttnam.
hooks, b., 2004, *The Will to Change: Men, Masculinity, and Love*, New York: Atria Books.
hooks, b., 2015, *Ain't I a Woman: Black Women and Feminism*, New York: Routledge.
Jung, E., 1969, *Animus and Anima: Two Papers*, New York: Spring Publications.
Kast, V., 1986, *The Nature of Loving: Patterns of Human Relationship* (trans. B. Matthews), Wilmette, IL: Chiron Publications.
Kristeva, J., 1982, *Powers of Horror: An Essay on Abjection*, New York: Columbia University Press.
Kristeva, J., 1989, *Black Sun: Depression and Melancholia*, New York: Columbia University Press.
Lauter, E., 1984, *Women as Mythmakers: Poetry and Visual Art by Twentieth-Century Women*, Bloomington: Indiana University Press.
Lauter, E. & Rupprecht, C. (eds.), 1985, *Feminist Archetypal Theory: Interdisciplinary Re-Visions of Jungian Thought*, Knoxville: University of Tennessee.
Paris, G., 2016, *Wisdom of the Psyche: Beyond Neuroscience*, London and New York: Routledge.

Pratt, A., 1981, *Archetypal Patterns in Women's Fiction*, Bloomington: Indiana University Press.

Rowland, S., 2002, *Jung: A Feminist Revision*, London: Routledge.

Von Franz, M.-L., 2002, *The Anima and Animus in Fairy Tales*, Toronto: Inner City Books.

Wehr, D. S., 1987, *Jung & Feminism: Liberating Archetypes*, Boston, MA: Beacon Press.

Woodman, M., 1990, *The Ravaged Bridegroom: Masculinity in Women*, Toronto: Inner City Books.

Young-Eisendrath, P., 1997, *Gender and Desire, Uncursing Pandora*, Austin, TX: Texas A&M University Press.

Part 1

Gender in politics/politics in gender

Chapter 1

Empowered by myth

Persona, politics, and Texas women

Betty Sue Flowers

A personal (persona-l?) note to the reader

I wanted to write something about what a true act of the self it is to consciously create a persona and the bravery of women who do this in public ... especially a couple of decades ago. The three Texas women I focus on here were very different from each other. But what they all had in common was a *beautiful* sense of humor. By 'beautiful,' I mean that it operated in that higher level where you only make fun of the powerful – or of yourself ... where you look down on the whole human comedy without bitterness, although often with indignation. So even though I'm talking about political personas, I wanted you to know from the very beginning that these were large-souled women whom I feel grateful to have known.

The Texas myth

As a girl growing up in Texas, I knew that Texans were different – that is, they thought of themselves as different from folks in other states. We were the only state that had formerly been an independent nation. We had the Texas rangers, and we had our own navy (well, sort of), and the terms of our entry into the United States allowed us to choose, at any time in the future, to break into five states. We started the school day singing 'Texas, Our Texas,' not 'The Star-Spangled Banner.' And every Texas schoolchild had to spend a whole year of history class learning Texas history. We had that much history. Heck, we didn't just have a history – we had a *myth* (see Flowers, 2003).

Basically, the Texas myth is the hero myth on steroids. 'One riot, one ranger,' as the saying goes. 'Can do,' as anyone who worked for President Johnson learned to say in response to any request. We were equally proud of the Alamo hero Davy Crockett saying that Texas was "the garden spot of the earth" and the Yankee General Sheridan saying, "If I owned Texas and Hell, I would rent out Texas and live in Hell." And we quoted John Wayne, the quintessential Texan (that he was named 'Marion' and born in Iowa was a nonessential detail), who said, "Courage is being scared to death but saddling up anyway," and "A man's gotta do what a man's gotta do" (which academics can't find in *Stagecoach* (John Ford, 1939) or any of his other films, but then Texans don't pay much attention to academics).

Our parents taught us that as Texans we could be anything we wanted to be. I decided I would be a boy and was devastated when nature eventually reminded me I didn't get to choose. Actually, I didn't mind dresses and dolls and girl things *as a child* – I just didn't want to grow up to be a *woman*. I wanted to be powerful, a hero. Therefore, I wanted to be a man. All real Texans were men. And only men seemed to be powerful political leaders.

When I was seventeen, I met a truly powerful Texas female political leader for the first time – Barbara Jordan, who had just been defeated in her initial attempt to become a Texas state legislator but who was going to try again and win, becoming the first black woman to be elected to the US Congress from the South. Later I came to know Molly Ivins, an influential Texan journalist, and Ann Richards, the governor of Texas. All three were politically powerful – and all three achieved that power not by pretending to be men, as women sometimes have done in order to fight in wars (as the ex-slave Cathy Williams did when she served with the Buffalo soldiers) or travel safely when alone, but by *performing* parts of the Texas macho hero myth.

To be successful, this performance has to be *seen* as a performance and not as a pretension. How does this performance work? What does it take for a woman to be empowered by a myth that traditionally operates against her power? How does a woman create a public *persona* that augments rather than undercuts her authenticity and consequently, her political power?

Persona creation

Jung had many wise and inspiring words to say about the Self – the psyche as a whole – and the journey to realize it. One of the necessary steps along this journey is the creation of a persona, which he defines as

> a complicated system of relations between individual consciousness and society, fittingly enough a kind of mask, designed on the one hand to make a definite impression upon others, and, on the other, to conceal the true nature of the individual.

> (Jung, 1966, p.190)

In other words – *not* 'who you truly are'.

But artists seem to have a distinctly different attitude towards the persona. For many of them, especially actors and writers, the creation of a persona, or mask, is the truest expression of who they are. The poet W. B. Yeats said that happiness "depends on the energy to assume the mask of some other self" and that "all joyous or creative life is a rebirth as something not oneself" (Jones, 1967, p.313). This seems true of politicians, too.

Like writers and actors, politicians craft a persona for their audience, or voters. Traditionally, elected leaders have presented themselves as heroes returning from a journey with a gift for their community. Indeed, many elected officials in the United States have been military officers, even if not military heroes in the mold of George Washington.

And even if, as with President Trump, bone spurs or some other unfortunate barrier has prevented the candidate from serving in the military, he can still present himself as a hero with a gift to give to the community – the expertise from having run a business, for example. "I alone can fix it," as Trump proclaimed. The archetypal persona for someone aspiring to be a leader is created from elements of the hero myth.

So, what about women who aspire to be candidates for public office?

Power and the hero myth

On the most obvious level, the hero myth is an obstacle to any woman wishing to assume political leadership. The archetypal activity of the hero is competition, particularly in battle. The hero leaves home to go to war or to fight a dragon. Then he returns home with trophies and a story of his adventure.

Meanwhile, women stay home to mind the hearth and the children and take care of the endless round of sowing, growing, and harvest. In relation to the hero myth, women, like animals, live in the natural repetitive cycles that support biological life. They have no story because, unlike the repetitive round of daily life, a story has a linear quality – a beginning, a middle, and an end. (For a brilliant exposition of the role of the community in the heroic culture of Greece, see Arendt (1958).)

A woman who leaves home to go on an adventure is perceived as abandoning something or someone. A working mother is much more likely than a working father to be asked about who is taking care of the children. A man on a quest is brave; a woman on a quest is unnatural. Whether married or not, a woman who aspires to a position of political leadership is often accused of being a lesbian (formerly thought to be 'unnatural') – as Jordan, Richards, Ivins, and Hillary Clinton all were.

Pathways to power

In western cultures, women traditionally followed one of three pathways to power. The first consisted of the exercise of power in the household. Women in charge of a large estate, with servants and layers of authority, exercised a great deal of power over the lives of quite a few people, even if only in a limited sphere. In Great Britain, in 1891, it was estimated that one in three women between the ages of fifteen and twenty were in domestic service (see Clarke, n.d.). Even middle-class households had domestic servants. In the slavery economy of the antebellum South, this power sometimes included life-and-death decision-making.

Ironically, the advent of household technology, like washing machines and dishwashers, and the growing freedom of women to work outside the home have diminished the need for this kind of power. And as more and more people crowd into cities, living alone or with small families in ever smaller apartments, the 'space' of the household is shrinking. Hiring a cleaning service to come in once a week to wash clothes and vacuum is not so much an exercise of power as a chore.

The second traditional pathway to power came through inheriting a role that would normally be given to a man. Queen Elizabeth and Queen Victoria inherited the crown in the absence of male heirs. Occasionally, and again in the absence of a male alternative, a woman might inherit her father's or her deceased husband's company, or be elected to public office when her husband died, or, like 'Ma' Ferguson, the first woman governor of Texas, when her husband was impeached. When Pa Ferguson was no longer allowed to put his name on the ballot, Ma ran instead, saying that if she was elected, "she would follow the advice of her husband and that Texas thus would gain 'two governors for the price of one'" (Huddleston, n.d.). Without assuring voters that she would be a mere stand-in for Pa, it's doubtful she would have been elected.

The third and now much-traveled pathway involves checking the boxes in a meritocratic setting. Of course, glass ceilings still exist. But even so, in the last decade, women in the United States have helped redefine traditional power roles simply by occupying them, from Speaker of the House to CEO of General Motors. And in parliamentary democracies, where women who rise to the top of their parties also rise to the top of the power structure, women have also served as heads of government.

But women who attempt to stand and run on their own, without inheriting an estate or a crown, or standing on a conveyor belt that automatically tends to take high performers higher have a difficult time because they are competing not only against other people but also against a myth – the myth of the hero.

Women have usually assumed power in relation to communities or groups, not by striking out for adventure on their own. Every man running for president of the United States is undertaking a hero's journey. Every woman doing the same is perceived as *performing* a male role – and thus miscast from the beginning. When Bill Clinton ran for president, he pointed to his very able wife, who had graduated ahead of him in Yale Law School, and promised the electorate that if they voted for him as a political leader, they would be getting two for the price of one. Had Hillary Clinton said that when she ran for president, her perceived power would have been undercut. Like Ma Ferguson, she would have been seen as pointing to the real power behind the curtain.

Politics, performance, and the hero myth

Charisma, in electoral politics, is the capacity to evoke heroic projections. Voters want a champion – someone who can fight the dragons arrayed against them and win. That's a key reason why Christian evangelicals voted for Trump in the

2016 election, even though he seemed to be a rather deficient embodiment of Christian virtue. (For a fuller exploration of the primacy of authenticity over character, see Flowers, 2016). And the capacity to look as if you could fight a dragon and win may be one reason tall men are preferred over short ones when it comes to political and executive leadership. The challenge of eliciting a hero projection when you are short and in a skirt and high heels makes it very difficult for women to win statewide or national offices – even though, as Ann Richards famously said in her 1988 Democratic National Convention speech, "If you give us a chance, we can perform. After all, Ginger Rogers did everything that Fred Astaire did, but in high heels and backwards." (The quote was originally from a Bob Thaves *Frank and Earnest* newspaper cartoon strip, published in 1982.)

In the early days of the United States, you very seldom knew the candidate – but as a property-owning male, you did know your state representative, who chose the elector, who went up to Washington and chose the candidate in the electoral college. You trusted the man you knew to make a good choice.

These days, we still don't know the candidates – but we see them performing. When a candidate says, 'I alone can fix it,' we make a gut decision about whether that statement fits the character. It's not that we believe every promise the candidate makes but that we look for the *fit* between performance and what we intuit about the nature of the person. Even with very little information, humans make quick, gut-level decisions about this fit – about whether someone is authentic.

Voters value authenticity over truth and vote for their hero projections, not policy positions. In the 2016 US election, Trump told many more lies than Hillary Clinton – but he was an *authentic* liar, contradicting obvious facts without shame. What you saw was what you got. Clinton, on the other hand, held so tightly to her competent, truth-telling persona that many voters began to distrust it. She was, after all, a politician – so what was she hiding? Clinton promised to do a good job on behalf of traditional American values; Trump promised to fight the deep state (slay the dragon, like St. George), to drain the swamp (clean the Augean stables, like Hercules), and make America great again (bring back Camelot, like the return of Arthur).

Hero projections and heroic actions

Here it's important to state the obvious: while running for office requires coming to terms with the hero myth, Texas woman can perform heroically in other spheres without embodying the hero myth at all. In 2010, with a typical 'can do' Texas spirit, Shannon Davis, who ran a small foundation in San Antonio, created an alliance of public, private, military, and humanitarian organizations to capture Joseph Kony, head of the Lord's Resistance Army (LRA), which had been responsible for 100,00 deaths and the kidnapping of 30,000 children in four African countries over twenty-five years (see Sedgwick Davis, 2019). Her foundation paid for establishing and training a special unit of the Ugandan army, and she set up a communications system among the remote African villages in the area. After several years, Kony was still at large – but then, Davis switched to another tactic. Using a helicopter donated to her effort by Warren Buffet's son Howard, her team dropped leaflets over the jungle where the LRA was thought to be hiding, promising reintegration into society for those who would leave the LRA and broadcasting recordings from loudspeakers of mothers and other people LRA members would know. Gradually, LRA members began walking out of the jungle, undercutting Kony's power. In the year 2010, the LRA had killed 800 civilians. Four years later, after mass defections from the LRA, the yearly count was thirteen, and Davis closed down her project.

An interesting aspect of this story of heroic action is that its success depended on changing from the 'kill-the-dragon' hero myth goal of capturing Kony to a focus on what the real aim was – to decrease deaths and kidnappings. Davis failed to capture Kony; but by changing tactics, she succeeded in her humanitarian aim.

What if all our military and humanitarian goals as a nation focused on relieving suffering and increasing well-being rather than on heroic 'winning' over the enemy of the day? But I digress.

Building a political persona within the hero myth

So while women can perform heroic actions, they cannot fully perform the hero myth without calling attention to their gender – between the hero that voters desire to project on their candidate and the female actor attempting to embody that role.

One way women have traditionally attempted to narrow that gap between the heroic male projection and the female reality is by appropriating symbols of the military hero. It's not surprising that so many female armed forces veterans are running for office by airing videos of themselves in uniform or standing in front of the fighter jets they flew.

At Tilbury in 1588, before the expected invasion of the Spanish Armada, Queen Elizabeth I rode out to speak to her troops on a white horse wearing a plumed helmet and a steel cuirass over a white velvet gown. She was compared to Pallas Athena (always depicted with a helmet and shield) and to an Amazonian princess. Joan of Arc also wore armor. Like Elizabeth, wearing a costume to make a point, Secretary of State Madeleine Albright wore a series of large pins to make subtle points – such as the serpent pin she wore in response to a comparison of her to a serpent that appeared in the Iraqi press (Albright, 2009, p.17).

But each of these powerful women also explicitly expressed their awareness of the gap between the symbol of the hero they were wearing – the persona they were adopting – and the reality of the female self under the mask. And then, they went one step further to point to, rather than actively create, a third level of reality, a Self that was neither male nor female, but participated in both. Elizabeth created this third space by riding out in armor (the hero mask); declaring that "I know I have the body of a weak and feeble woman" (the female self); and then adding, "but I have the heart and stomach of a king – and of a king of England too, and think foul scorn that Parma or Spain, or any prince of Europe, should dare to invade the borders of my realm" (British Library, n.d.). The Self she proclaims is of the spirit, calling on her identity as her father's daughter in the long line of English kings, divinely chosen by God.

Athena, too, proclaims this tie with the masculine, having been born not from a woman but from the forehead of Zeus. Joan of Arc called attention to herself as a woman – 'the Maid' – as a way of deflecting her very real military prowess in favor of a greater source of Self – God, who directed her. Without this 3-layer performance – hero mask/persona, woman reality, and a *proclamation* of a Self that also 'channels' greater male power – women acting powerfully are likely to elicit Medusa projections.

Medusa was a witch, killed by the hero Perseus with the help of a polished shield that Athena gave him – an alliance of the power of the hero and the power of a father's daughter overcoming the power of an independent female (unnatural, evil, witch). It was Perseus, also, who rescued the princess Andromeda, who was chained to a rock, from the ravages of a sea monster and married her after using Medusa's head to turn Andromeda's fiancé to stone. The permutations of male and female power in this story point to the complexity inherent in the subject – even so, it's not surprising that there are so many famous paintings of the powerful hero rescuing the helpless, chained, beautiful, naked girl (see Flowers, 2011). That is the fundamental, archetypal image that women politicians have to struggle against.

Women, power, and the Texas myth: Molly Ivins

Molly Ivins came from a wealthy neighborhood in Houston, attended private schools and later Smith, Columbia, and Sciences Po, spoke French fluently, could sail her father's yacht, and worked for the *New York Times*. When she returned from a year in Paris, she was a tall, slender, beautiful, expensively dressed, sophisticated woman. But she became a best-selling author and influential voice in politics through her adoption of a Texas persona – a hard drinking, fierce-cussing, fun-loving 'broad' with an outsize Texas drawl. The drawl was so exaggerated that it called attention to her Texas persona. She called me and almost everyone else 'Sweetpea' – a handy nickname in a state where men of power teased each other with nicknames. Governor and later President George Bush called Vladimir Putin 'Pooty-Poot,' Tony Blair 'Landslide,' Dick Cheney 'Vice,' and his political advisor Karl Rove 'Turd Blossom.' Ivins called Bush 'Shrub.'

Ivins was known for making outrageous generalizations – "As they say around the Texas Legislature, if you can't drink their whiskey, screw their women, take their money, and vote against 'em anyway, you don't belong in office" (1991, p.1) Outrageousness became such a significant aspect of her persona that it inspired the title of one of her best-selling books *Molly Ivins Can't Say That, Can She?* (Ivins, 1991). Obvious exaggeration is so much a part of the Texas style that Ivins got away with trenchant criticism by simply stepping into the role of a good-ol'-boy Texas storyteller.

Like Queen Elizabeth and Joan of Arc, Ivins, too, built a three-layered persona. The exaggerated, outrageous macho Texan persona would not have worked had she not signaled her awareness that she was, in fact, a woman. But unlike Elizabeth, she didn't acknowledge acceptance of a female stereotype – 'I know I have the body of a weak and feeble woman' – but rather presented herself as a *failed* stereotype. She had wanted to be a 'participant in Texas Womanhood' – the 'spirit was willing' – but she had simply failed at it: "I spent my girlhood as a Clydesdale among thoroughbreds." Her story was that she was simply too tall. "You can't be six feet tall and cute, both" (Ivins, 2003, pp.698–699).

This aspect of her persona was crafted under a keen awareness of the Texas macho myth. In an op-ed for the *New York Times*, she wrote that the "Lone Star State Culture is a marriage of several strains of male chauvinism" and went on to describe them as "the machismo of our Latino tradition," the "Southern belle concept of our Confederate heritage; the pervasive good ol' boyism; the jock idolatry (football is not a game here; it is a matter of blood and death) and, most important, the legacy of the frontier, as it was when John Wayne lived on it" (*New York Times* article from 1971, quoted in Minutaglio & Smith, 2009, p.148).

The third level of persona – what I've called the 'Self,' capitalized to point to a dimension beyond the opposites of male and female – was a fierce devotion to justice and the exposure of hypocrisy. Underneath the outrageousness was outrage – as if she expected government to work and legislators to act on behalf of the people they represented. She was not funny just to entertain. She wanted things to change. The poet Maya Angelou's appreciation of her in the *Washington Post* began with the lines:

Up to the walls of Jericho
She marched with a spear in her hand
Go blow them ram horns she cried
For the battle is in my hand

(Angelou, 2007)

At her memorial service in the First Methodist Church in Austin, after prayers to the God she sometimes referred to as 'Fred,' we all stood and clapped and sang Jerry Lee Lewis's 'Great Balls of Fire.'

Women, power, and the Texas myth: Ann Richards

In 1988, I was at a women's lunch hosted by Liz Carpenter – former press secretary to Lady Bird Johnson and a Texas myth in her own right – when State Treasurer Ann Richards dropped by to tell us she had been asked to be the keynote speaker for the Democratic party convention. She was only the second woman to have been asked, the first having been another Texan, Barbara Jordan. We brainstormed not only about what Ann might say – but also what she might wear.

Characteristic of the way she handled the creation of her political persona, Richards was careful in her dress, make-up, and hair. She looked the part of a

Dallas socialite – and indeed, although she grew up in Waco, she had started her career in Dallas. But as the wife of a progressive labor lawyer and the only child of a father from Bugtussle, Texas, and a mother from Hogjaw, she was certainly not of social register stock.

Unlike Ivins, whose three-layered persona was topped by a rather masculine, good-ol'-boy exterior, Richards wore the uniform of an unthreatening Dallas matron and often spoke of her children and grandchildren. The only visual indication of armor in Richards' female costume was her big upswept silver bouffant helmet of hair.

But under the non-threatening female women's club exterior, there lurked a sly mischief-maker who could unexpectedly deliver a string of cuss words from her perfectly lipsticked mouth or strike out with devastating one-liners delivered in a slow Texas drawl. She used wit as a weapon, knowing very well that many of the men she had to deal with in politics feared being laughed at. ("I get a lot of cracks about my hair, mainly from men who don't have any.") But she delivered her sometimes devastating put-downs with a 'nice' bright smile. Her mockery seemed funny, not cruel – an almost parody performance of the Texas myth. Fittingly, perhaps, she kept a parrot in the upstairs private quarters of the governor's mansion.

In her Democratic convention speech, she called attention to herself as an authentic Texan, saying that "after listening to George Bush all these years, I figured you needed to know what a real Texas accent is like." Whatever power she had, the persona seemed to say, came from her authenticity as a Texan. Her cussing, she said, she learned from her Daddy.

Texans are friendly. When Clayton Williams, her Republican opponent in the race for governor, refused to shake her outstretched hand at a televised luncheon in Dallas, it was perceived not just as lack of gallantry, but pointedly un-Texan. Even as the *Washington Post* noted at the time, the race for governor was seen as a performance of gender and power:

> When it was all over, when the melodrama known as 'Claytie and the Lady' finally ended, the only figure still riding high in the macho world of Lone Star politics was the Lady, Democrat Ann Richards, a resilient 57-year-old grandmother who awoke this morning as governor-elect of Texas and the most visible, if not the most powerful, female elected official in the nation.
>
> (Maraniss, 1990)

The most iconic image of Richards as governor appeared on the cover of *Texas Monthly*. She was pictured in white fringed jacket and white boots, with a red bandanna around her neck, and riding on a white Harley motorcycle. But her teased and sprayed helmet of white hair was perfectly in place, and her abundant make-up was perfect. The performance of macho Texan under the perfectly presented lady was captured explicitly in this photoshopped image.

Richards delighted in exploiting the gap between the lady stereotype and the embodiment of Texas macho, the proper and the outrageous, exploiting her identification with Texas every time she spoke. But unlike Ivins and Jordan, she was elected to a position of executive power – and so the evocation of the third, deepest level of persona, the level beyond male and female, whether God or the inheritance of English kingship or justice, was not entirely within the control of her storytelling.

From Richards' perspective, she was fighting for justice, like her friend Ivins. But she fought with deeds, not words, putting women and minorities in positions of power throughout Texas government and attempting to reform the way government worked, as she had done as State Treasurer where her managerial reforms saved Texas millions of dollars.

But when Richards ran for re-election as governor, she was defeated by George W. Bush, who, unlike his Yankee father, spoke with a Texas drawl and was associated with Texas sports and Texas oil. Bush treated his rival like a lady while not discouraging stories that Texas was being run by undeserving minorities and Richards's lesbian cronies. The Texas myth was a far more powerful aid to Bush than to Richards in that fight, especially because Bush presented himself as a former businessman aligned with the upsurging of Republican sentiment that was overtaking Texas politics. During the next twenty-five years (and beyond), no Democrat won a statewide office in Texas.

Women, power, and the Texas myth: Barbara Jordan

Barbara Jordan faced two disempowering obstacles when it came to electoral politics: her race and her gender. But unlike any other woman before or since in Texas politics, she consciously built a public persona around a physical feature that was beyond male or female – her distinctive voice. Jordan's voice was powerful, rich, and resonant, and she emphasized it by pronouncing every syllable with almost exaggerated precision. Many called it 'the voice of God':

> The voice was god-like not just in its all -commanding tone but also in the sense that it seemed to have no beginning. The girl and then woman who deployed it was a black Texan from segregated Houston's Fourth Ward, but there was no accent, nowhere in particular to place it. It was the voice of someone determined to create herself and announce herself to the world.
>
> (Harrigan, 2019, p.715)

Jordan, like other powerful women, built a three-layered persona – but in a significantly different way. Ivins, Richards, Joan of Arc, Elizabeth I – all rode out in the hero's armor (first level), but acknowledged the reality of being a woman (second level); the third level of the three-layer persona consists of a source of authority beyond male or female. For Elizabeth, it was the line of English kings, chosen by God; for Joan of Arc, it was God Himself; for Ivins, it was the principle of justice; for Richards, it was justice, too, but the authority that would usually come from an abstract principle was diluted by the gendered image of justice emerging from all the women who suddenly appeared in positions of power in Texas government. In the short term, correcting gender or racial equality can look like a sudden, unjust upsurge of one side.

Jordan turned the layers inside out by overtly performing a non-gendered, direct authority through her voice. Joan of Arc's Voice of God was now a public experience, not a private one. And under that top layer, rather than an acknowledgment of being a female, Jordan swerved to an acknowledgment of being African American. Under the Voice, and in part empowered by the Voice, was a persona layer constructed on the model of a black preacher as community leader.

In a world of black disempowerment in the South, including Texas, the educated and articulate leader of the community was the black preacher. What the Texas hero was to the white community, the black preacher was to the black community, culminating in the towering figure of Dr. Martin Luther King, Jr. King was a hero not through violence, but through non-violence. Like Jesus, he did not have the *power* of the soldier but the *authority* of the martyr.

As community leaders, black preachers spoke with gravity, precision, and authority. Performing the role of a religious leader was the only (relatively) safe way for a black man to be strong and powerful without eliciting racist fear. When Jordan evoked her blackness rather than her femaleness, her voice and way of speaking called up the authority of the black leader over the identity of a black woman.

Another reason Jordan was able to avoid the gendered female dynamic was that the history of black women in the United States was very unlike the image of protected southern womanhood or the lady of the manor protected by her lord. The conditions and history of slavery precluded the male protector-weak female dynamic.

In place of the three-layered *hero-female-genderless authority* persona of Elizabeth I, or Joan of Arc, or Molly Ivins, Jordan constructed a persona of *genderless authority* (the 'Voice of God') – *racial male authority* (black preacher as community leader) – *genderless authority* (the Constitution).

All three levels of this powerful persona can be seen in her performance during the Senate Judiciary Committee hearings on Watergate. When she rose to speak, she immediately established her power with 'The Voice,' even though she was merely thanking the committee chairman. Then, after the formal opening of her speech, she called attention to her race by pointing out that when the Constitution was written, she had not been included in its Preamble, which began "We, the people." "I felt somehow for many years that George Washington and Alexander Hamilton just left me out by mistake." But that had changed – and she ended this initial performance of her persona by standing firmly on the third, genderless authority level of her persona, memorably proclaiming, "My faith in the Constitution is whole; it is complete; it is total" (Jordan, 1974).

Jordan always carried a copy of the Constitution with her. So identified was her persona with the gravity of the Constitution that the life-size statue depicting her in the Barbara Jordan Terminal of the Austin Airport subtly echoes the seated statue of Lincoln in the Lincoln Memorial.

Another reason for the seated pose might also have been that for the last decades of her life, she suffered from multiple sclerosis and was confined to a wheel chair. She never talked about the pain she endured, keeping the nature of her illness a secret for years. And the contrast between the wheelchair and her voice made The Voice seem even more powerful. At a private party, I once heard her sing the Bessie Smith favorite, 'Nobody knows you when you're down and out.' The performance was strong and exuberant and created joy.

When she died, "hundreds of ordinary people stood in front of feed stores, service, stations, and tractor dealerships with their hands, or their cowboy hats, over their hearts as the small motorcade carrying her body made its way from Houston to her burial site in Austin 150 miles away" (Rogers, 1998, p.xiv). And as if to underscore her many 'firsts' in death, as in life, she was the first black person to be buried in the State Cemetery in Austin.

Empowered by myth

The hero myth is an enduring one. On the final exam of a sophomore philosophy course I took under the only professor I had who was a native Texan, a quotation appeared for discussion: "We shall not have civilization until the last brave man is dead." I thought that was an interesting proposition to support since civilizations from the Greeks onward appear to come and go as a result of war. Without heroes and political leaders who wanted to be seen as heroes, maybe we could have a lasting civilization that would just evolve rather than be violently overthrown. Apparently, that was the wrong response to a proposition I was expected to dispute.

But there are other ways to be a hero. I wonder what life as a schoolgirl in Texas would have been like had we studied the myth of the goddess Inanna along with Greek myths and the stories of heroes like Davy Crockett (see Wolkstein & Kramer, 1983). After all, Inanna did everything a male hero did, even if not backward and in high heels. She assumed equality by drinking the god of wisdom under the table and then taking what she needed to build a city. Molly Ivins did the same thing, drinking with the power brokers in bars around the Texas capital to gather what she needed to expose the shenanigans in the legislature. She became good friends with Bob Bullock, Lt. Governor of Texas when George Bush was governor.

What many people outside Texas don't understand is how powerful the Lt. Governor position is. During Reconstruction, after ex-Confederate soldiers were given the right to vote again, Texans rewrote the Constitution to prevent the governor from having too much power. Within that power vacuum, the Lt. Governor not only controls the Senate, but also the Legislative Budget Board, which controls state programs, state policy, and the budget. (It's perhaps not surprising that the Texas State History Museum is named after Bullock, not Bush, with whom he served. And observers might wonder if Bush assumed the same working relationship with his vice-president, Dick Cheney, when he became president.)

Inanna knew where the power was and how to get it. And even though the god of wisdom sent fighting men after her when he discovered what she'd taken from him, in her time of deepest need, it was this same god who fashioned little creatures from the dirt under his fingernails that brought about her return from the dead. The bond was close – perhaps one of mutual respect.

Ivins knew where the power was and how to get what she needed. The bond with Bullock was close – one of mutual respect. On his deathbed, Bullock "kept muttering Ivins's name. He'd sit up, say her name, and then fall back down" (Minutaglio & Smith, 2009, p.276).

The myth of Inanna is a compelling mash-up of the hero myth and the myth of the dying and resurrected god. In addition to her heroic exploits, Inanna descends to the underworld, is killed, and then is resurrected.

But there are other lessons in the myth that are missing from most hero myths. Inanna takes what she needs to build her civilization. But she also honors her own desire, insisting on marrying a shepherd rather than a farmer against the wishes of the other gods. And she listens to an inner voice that compels her to undertake an adventure into the depths – a journey that requires her to give up all the symbols of her queenship, all her power, and even her life.

The tale of both her heroic journey to establish her city and her resurrection involve the crucial loyalty of her best friend, Ninshubar. And she does not hesitate either to ask for help, or to express appreciation for the things her sons do for her. She shares her power with her husband, who is sitting on the throne when she returns from the underworld – but she also insists that he share in her suffering. Imagine a civilization based on these attributes of heroic power…

The myth of Innana has many lessons to teach young girls interested in the exercise of power and leadership, whether in politics, business, or other areas. It has all the archetypal heroic qualities and more, including an important one that is almost impossible for women leaders to express – the celebration of their own female embodiment. When Odysseus returns to Ithaka in disguise, he succeeds in stringing the bow when the attempt of every other man has failed. Arthur pulls the sword out of the stone. The celebration of male physical strength is a powerful aspect of the hero myth.

But the myth of Inanna has an equivalent celebration of female embodiment. At the very beginning of her journey, Inanna leans back against an apple tree and celebrates her vulva. "Rejoicing at her wondrous vulva, the young woman Inanna applauded herself" (Wolkstein & Kramer, 1983, p.12). She admires the beauty and the power of the source of life in herself. No public school textbook I know of has that story in it. Will that day ever come, I wonder?

If so, it will be brought about through artists. In the 2018 Grammy-nominated video of her song 'Pynk,' Janelle Monae is actually dressed as a vulva. She embodies female power, not as a way of being attractive to men but as self-expression. This is not a power *over* but the evocation of a power *within* – "cause boy, it's cool if you got blue / we got the pynk" (Monáe, 2018).

The performance of persona – or maybe Self – that female artists, including comedians, are bringing forth these days might eventually widen the pathway for political and other women leaders. We shall not have civilization until the last brave man … is also a woman.

References

Albright, M., 2009, *Read My Pins: Stories from a Diplomat's Jewel Box*, New York: Melcher Media.

Angelou, M., 2007, 'Molly Ivins Shook the Walls with Her Clarion Call', *The Washington Post*. https://www.washingtonpost.com/wp-dyn/content/article/2007/02/01/AR200 7020101909.html (Accessed 15 January 2020).

Arendt, H., 1958, *The Human Condition*, Chicago: University of Chicago Press.

British Library, n.d., 'Elizabeth's Tilbury Speech', http://www.bl.uk/learning/timeline/ item102878.html (Accessed 15 January 2020).

Clarke, K., n.d., 'Women and Domestic Service in Victorian Society', *The History Press*. https://www.thehistorypress.co.uk/articles/women-and-domestic-service-in-victori an-society/ (Accessed 15 January 2020).

Flowers, B., 2003, 'Why Texas Is the Way It Is'. In: Graham, D. (ed), *Lone Star Literature: A Texas Anthology*, New York: W. W. Norton & Company, pp. 692–697.

Flowers, B., 2011, 'The Shield of Athena: Archetypal Images and Women as Political Leaders'. In: Rutter, V. & Singer, T. (eds), *Ancient Myth, Modern Psyche: Archetypes in the Making*, New Orleans: Spring Journal Books, pp. 205–217.

Flowers, B., 2016, 'Politics, Character, and the Socially Mediated Candidate', *ARAS*. https://aras.org/newsletters/aras-connections-special-edition-2016-presidency-papers (Accessed 15 January 2020).

Harrigan, S., 2019, *Big Wonderful Thing: A History of Texas*, Austin: University of Texas Press.

Huddleston, J., n.d., 'Governors of Texas: Miriam A. Ferguson', *The Texas Politics Project*. https://texaspolitics.utexas.edu/archive/html/exec/governors/15.html (Accessed 15 January 2020).

Ivins, M., 1991, *Molly Ivins Can't Say That, Can She?* New York: Random House.

Ivins, M., 2003, 'Texas Women: True Grit and All the Rest'. In: Graham, D. (ed), *Lone Star Literature: A Texas Anthology*, New York: W. W. Norton & Company, pp. 698–699.

Jones, A., 1967, 'Robert Browning and the Dramatic Monologue: The Impersonal Art', *Critical Quarterly* 9(4), pp. 301–330.

Jordan, B.C., 1974, 'Statement on the Articles of Impeachment Delivered 25 July 1974, House Judiciary Committee', https://americanrhetoric.com/speeches/barbarajordanjudi ciarystatement.htm (Accessed 15 January 2020).

Jung, C.G., 1966, *Two Essays on Analytical Psychology*, trans. Hull, R.F.C., London: Routledge & Kegan Paul Ltd.

Maraniss, D., 1990, '"Claytie and the Lady": Only the Lady Is Left Standing in Texas', *The Washington Post*. https://www.washingtonpost.com/archive/politics/1990/11/08/clayti e-and-the-lady-only-the-lady-is-left-standing-in-texas/fd91af86-1e83-4219-90e0-9 49190f9a306/ (Accessed 15 January 2020).

Minutaglio, B., Smith, W.M., 2009, *Molly Ivins: A Rebel Life*, New York: Public Affairs.

Monáe, J., 2018, 'PYNK [Official Music Video]', 10 April. https://www.youtube.com/w atch?v=PaYvlVR_BEc (Accessed 15 January 2020).

Rogers, M.B., 1998, *Barbara Jordan: American Hero*, New York: Bantam.

Sedgwick Davis, S., 2019, *To Stop a Warlord: My Story of Justice, Grace, and the Fight for Peace*, New York: Spiegel & Grau.

Wolkstein, D., Kramer, S.N., 1983, *Inanna: Queen of Heaven and Earth: Her Stories and Hymns from Sumer*, New York: Harper & Row.

Chapter 2

The jouissance of 'nasty women'

Daring to re-possess dynamic feminine desire

Laura Camille Tuley

'Such a nasty woman …'
— Donald J. Trump, referring to Hillary Rodham Clinton
during the final televised US presidential debate,
19 October 2016.

Like many Americans, I found the 2016 US presidential election to be a profoundly painful experience. This was not merely because of the unprecedented character of the winning nominee, but also because of the level of vitriol directed at his female opponent by so many individuals of both sexes and all ages, from both sides of the political spectrum, throughout the campaign. At the point, during the Republican national convention, at which the audience was aroused to a mob-like frenzy, chanting 'lock her up!' en masse, my despair and confusion at the long and desperate campaign to discredit this woman deepened into a feeling of dread. The seemingly unstoppable drive within the collective to obliterate She whose level of competence and political legacy were, arguably, entirely sound, not to mention effectively bi-partisan (if too conservative for some and too liberal for others), was and is nonsensical to me—literally beyond reason—driven more by a collective fear and distrust of the feminine sex as it was embodied by this woman in this particular culture and moment in time than by any real 'crimes' she may have perpetrated or missteps she may have taken. Was she too ambitious? Too old? Too calculating, stoic and cold? Not feeling or soft enough? *Too masculine???* These questions had percolated for years around the figure of an individual who—even prior to her presidential campaign—seemed to evoke disproportionate levels of ire and scathing criticism from the moment she stepped into the political arena. Now I wondered if Hillary Clinton had triggered an unconscious and ancient fear of the wily, deceitful, trickster feminine archetype and energy. A witch and crone whose 'black magic' threatened to usurp the supremacy of the phallic order (consider the NRA's effective campaign to convince American gun owners that a Clinton administration would not only restrict gun purchases but would actually seize their weapons).

My sense is that 'yes', would be a valid response to any of my questions which, taken together, highlight the reality of how, despite dramatic social and economic progress over the past few decades, women are still profoundly restricted by the narrowly conceived notions of 'femininity' which continue to constrain and preclude their participation in leadership roles. The scholar and activist analyst Andrew Samuels observes of the historically negative reaction to Clinton that, "collective responses over the years to Hillary Clinton show how hard it is for a female leader to fulfill compellingly the role of a heroic leader" (Samuels, 2015, p. 21). Samuels rightly associates 'heroic' with 'masculine' and 'father' and goes on to note that our infatuation with those leaders we cast as uber masculine heroes often leads us, as a society, to enter into abusive relationships with sadistic men (Trump is an apt illustration of this). Samuels' analysis can be reasonably paired with my sense of the threat embodied by a powerful (read: 'masculine') woman who attempts to 'usurp' a role that is designated in our collective imagination for the father. The sooner we are able, psychologically, to detach the functions of 'feminine' and 'masculine' or 'mothering' and 'fathering' from anatomy, the better women will fare in both public and private life.

The #MeToo Movement which has erupted in part, I would argue, as a backlash to the election of our current president and the re-installation of phallic power in its crudest form, is both heartening and long overdue. Yet, I wonder about the extent to which the movement also reifies limited perceptions of what it means to be 'feminine': namely, casting women as victims, and thereby unavoidably reinforcing a gendered binary between masculine predator and feminine prey. However concretely true and collectively resonant within the context of a patriarchal society, such a view is missing vital aspects of women's power and experience. In this chapter, I hope to frame C. G. Jung's use of the feminine and women along similar lines—as ultimately reifying a limited and limiting binary—and, in contrast, to highlight clinical material and corresponding mythological imagery that disrupts and, ideally, makes space for something Other; something reflected in and by She who captures the gaze and engages the desire of other women for their own unimagined potential.

The observation that Jung was 'a man of his time' is often proposed as a means to excuse and essentially side-step a discussion of Jung's at best ambivalent and at worse misogynist view of the female sex. Yes, Jung was at once a 'man of his time' *and* forward-thinking in his critique of the West as an overly rational and one-sided culture. Where he evokes the 'otherness' of the unconscious shadow as a persistent disruption and rebalancing of the conscious personality, Jung was progressive. Where he attempted to delineate the content of masculine and feminine archetypes, Jung fell prey to cultural and social norms, as well as to his own complexes. The question that continues to plague Jung's legacy is the extent to which his theory and the practice of analytical psychology are contaminated by the negatively skewed projections and temporally bound values of its founder. Certainly, as the analyst and scholar Claire Douglas demonstrates in her book *The Woman in the Mirror*, Jung's bias is evident in more classical approaches to his theory of Anima and Animus, and in the culturally arcane way in which the psychological functions of thinking and feeling are often extended to masculine and feminine principles and, concretely, to men and women, both reflecting and reinforcing the social repression of women in his time and after (Douglas, 1990). For example, in reference to a woman's inferior thinking capacity as that is manifest in relationship to her animus, Jung writes:

> If the woman happens to be pretty, these animus opinions have for the man something rather touching and childlike about them which makes him adopt a benevolent, fatherly, professorial manner. But if the woman does not stir his sentimental side, and competence is expected of her rather than appealing helplessness and stupidity, then her animus opinions irritate the man to death.
>
> (Jung, 1953, p. 206)

Jung's bias is also reflected, and perhaps deeply embedded, in the gendering of Logos and Eros, still prevalent in Jungian circles today. As Susan Rowland observes in *Jung: A Feminist Revision*, "[L]inking the anima to Eros characteristics (the way he describes his own anima) is the only theoretical way he [Jung] has of defining masculine consciousness as primarily Logos dominated" (Rowland, 2002, p. 42). I would argue that in subscribing to both Jung's idea of the contrasexual distribution of Anima and Animus and to his gendered characterization of those terms, we contemporary Jungians unconsciously and, at times consciously, maintain the rigid and decapitating binary that Jung and his cohort—of women and men—assumed, regardless of subsequent revolutions in our understanding of the relation between sex and gender and the instability of both terms.

That Jung cites a need to cultivate the 'inferior' or subordinated aspects of psyche and culture remains useful conceptually, particularly within the context of the current political climate. In his *Visions Seminars*, Jung emphasizes the value (in theory) of recognizing those aspects of 'feminine' (and human) nature that society's requirements for feminine 'niceness' by definition preclude: "[W]omen often pick up tremendously when they are allowed to think all the disagreeable things which they denied themselves before" (Jung, 1976, cited in Douglas, 1990, p. 77). That Jung appears just as often to essentialize anatomy, and to confuse his personal psychology or myth with metaphysical 'truth', was and is not useful for 'real-life' women and men who do not exist as opposites but rather within a complex and fluctuating network of differences that can never be fully pinned down as such and are experienced only as traces of an essentially mysterious and fluid dynamic. I would like to explore possible avenues to create space for women (and men) to be in the world differently—psychologically and physically—if only as points of rupture in the dominant symbolic, but ecstatic spaces nonetheless that, at times, gain mass and flower, like algae blooms, on those lakes of knowledge that 'Men' have attempted to preserve for themselves.

An image from myth: Demeter, goddess of the harvest, archetypal symbol of motherhood, stands in the hall of Eleusis, inconsolable. She has appeared there disguised as an old nurse, after a long and futile search for her daughter, Persephone, who was abducted and raped by Hades, the god of the underworld. Upon her arrival, Metaneira, queen of Eleusis, offers the stranger a seat on her couch, but Demeter remains standing, paralyzed by her sorrow. It is only Iambe—or Baubo as she is more commonly known—the old crone and servant of the Eleusinian household, who is able to break the spell of Demeter's grief, long enough for the goddess to smile, laugh and remember herself as more than Persephone's mother:

> She [Demeter] stayed silent, with her beautiful eyes downcast,
> Until devoted Iambe, set out for her
> a well-pieced seat and threw over it a silver-white fleece.
> Then sitting down she held her veil before her with her hands.
> For a long time she sat on the chair speechless in her grief,
> nor did she greet anyone by word or gesture,
> but unsmiling, tasting no food or drink,
> she sat wasting away with longing for her deep-girded daughter,
> until devoted Iambe, intervening with jokes,
> and many jests, moved the holy lady,
> to smile and laugh and have a propitious heart [*thûmos*].
>
> (Shelmerdine, 1995, p. 44)

In this version of the myth, we see how Baubo deploys humor and irreverence to restore the breath of life or *thûmos* (spiritedness) to the goddess, Demeter. In other versions of the myth, she is said to have lifted her skirts, while joking, in order to flash her vulva in a ribald, impious and self-affirming gesture. Together with her bawdy jokes, the bold provocation of Baubo's skirt-lifting, or *ana-suromai*, represents a vital and healing aspect of women's sexuality: their capacity to play self-referentially, to use irreverence to enjoy themselves and, moreover, to display that enjoyment to each other—embodied, earthy and liberated from the more rigid and limiting images that have circumscribed the feminine historically.

Beyond her cursory role in Homer's *Hymn to Demeter*, Baubo is also at times conceived as a deity who may have played a role in the sacred rituals associated with Demeter and performed at the Attic festivals of Thesmophoria and in the Eleusinian Mysteries. Intended to honor the goddess of the harvest and her loss of her daughter, as well as to symbolically initiate the transformation of women, each of these festivals contained segments designated for joking, bawdiness and buffoonery that followed more solemn expressions of communal mourning (among other things), very much in the spirit of Baubo's strategy with the deeply depressed goddess of the Homeric *Hymn*. Such buffoonery was seen as having a marked restorative function—the substitution of anger and grief for the detachment and freedom afforded by laughter (Lubell, 1994, pp. 39–40). The existence of sanctioned spaces for women to express themselves freely was not, in fact, evidence of the progressiveness of the dominant culture. Rather, within the context of Attic society, in which the sexes were rigidly polarized and policed, these festivals offered what the historian Eva Keuls refers to as 'an escape valve', providing "the intoxication of temporarily limited freedom from social restraint, so that that the participants will be more pliable the remainder of the time" (Keuls, 1985, p. 350). In other words, these festivals functioned as a kind of 'contagion control', in which women were permitted a structured outlet in which to express feelings and engage in behaviors that might otherwise disrupt the social hierarchy. During the colonial era in America, slave owners often organized a similar ritual during holidays, in which slaves were granted a brief 'respite' from the restrictions to which they were normally bound in order, theoretically, to reinforce their compliance throughout the rest of the year. Similarly, Mardi Gras in America, like the celebration of carnival across Latin America and the Caribbean (i.e., within the context of communities built on the legacy of colonialism) echoes in its traditions, if only to a limited degree, the socially sanctioned transgression of boundaries during the space of a holiday season, in which inhibitions around gender, race and class are routinely, if only symbolically, crossed in order to exceed but not erase the strictures of one's culturally constructed identities (Berry, 2018; Mitchell, 1995). Nevertheless, despite the ultimately conservative underpinning of such traditions, in the case of the Attic festivals, women in the ancient world were seemingly able to honor a range of psychological and emotional experience and enjoy a sense of renewal not as readily available in the post-pagan world.

Baubo's figure assumed more monstrous proportions in later centuries within the context of Judeo-Christianity, wherein she was "replaced, muted, or transformed into the shapes of demons, grotesqueries, and witches" as the religious and culturally patriarchal order attempted to solidify its power and influence. According to the author Winifred Milius Lubell, in her text *The Metamorphosis of Baubo: Myths of Woman's Sexual Energy*, Baubo's spirit can be identified in the forms of Medusa, mermaid images and the stark sculptures of Sheilah-Na Gigs, which are found in medieval churches across Ireland, Wales, and England (Lubell, 1994, p. xvi). Just as Medusa came to be equated with the 'the evil eye', Baubo as vulva was increasingly interpreted as 'evil', although some semblance of protective power was still attributed to her (one theory for why her figure inscribed on the walls of so many churches). Disconnected from an earlier association with fertility and nurturance, Baubo's image as a symbol of woman's 'lust', about which the custodians of patriarchy were obsessively concerned, was accentuated in the centuries following the rise of the church: "This prurient concern gave birth not only to a suppression of imagery but to an intolerance of female sexuality that eventually grew into the monstrous slaughter of women as witches and whores of the devil" (Lubell, 1994, p. 129). In contrast, Lubell highlights the association of Baubo's flippant antics and passionate affirmation of the female anatomy as the hidden side of women's sexuality, one that insists on pleasure over reproduction and provides a needed antitoxin for a woman's psyche, however threatening she appeared and appears to patriarchal and Christian institutions.

While Jung seems to recognize the vital and autonomous character of the Demeter-Kore (or Persephone) dyad as a dynamic for and between women, reflecting that "Demeter-Kore exists on the plane of mother-daughter experience, which is alien to man and shuts him out" (Jung, 1959, p. 203), he misses or denies the nutritive, if not essential role of Baubo within women's psychological development, reducing her, instead, to a kind of primitive and unconscious aspect of the maternal embodied by certain individuals, observing:

> For many such women, Baubo rather than Demeter would be the appropriate symbol. The mind is not cultivated for its own sake but usually remains in its original condition, altogether primitive, unrelated and ruthless, but also true, and sometimes profound as Nature herself.
>
> (Jung, 1959, p. 88)

Thus, the unrelated and un-feeling feminine, while acknowledged as powerful , like 'Nature herself', is deemed both undeveloped and 'ruthless'. Douglas suggests that in missing the full significance of Baubo, and insisting on 'feeling' and the capacity for relationship as the signature feature and pinnacle of women's development, Jung is missing a potentially vital balancing ingredient in his ambivalent relationship to his own inner 'feminine' or Anima figure, Salome. She writes:

> The prejudices of the time, the lack of opportunities for women's own development, Jung's personal experiences, especially of his mother, led to the absence of the one figure who could have helped Salome and balanced her in Jung's inner and outer psychology. This was the figure of a vigorously assertive, vital, wise and passionate adult woman – Baucis/Baubo. This potent feminine appeared archaically and monstrously in Jung's (and his era's) unconscious in the form of the black serpent. ... Neither the time nor Jung were ready for her human form.
>
> (Lubell, 1994, p. 51)

The collective's complex laden reaction to Hillary Clinton, as a female political candidate, who also happened to be an older woman/crone figure and might be seen as 'vigorously assertive' and 'vital', if not 'wise', begs the question of whether the collective of our time, as least as it is manifest in America, is ready to accept a more complex iteration of the feminine in human form.

An image from my consulting room: for the past few years I have worked with three women in their mid-30s to whom I will refer as patients A, B and C. Patient A, a university professor, came to see me first. She later referred patient B, a colleague from another department, and patient C, a business owner. This was a complex clinical arrangement for me, as the three are close friends, but I live in a college town in which dual relationships can be hard to avoid. Moreover, I genuinely liked each of the three women, who were strikingly different in personality structure and background. After a period of working with each of them individually, I began to develop an impression of how they related to one another. In addition to referring the other two, patient A was clearly the 'dominant' of the trio, the lubricant, you might say, of their collective social lives and a kind of mirror to both B and C, who leaned heavily on A for emotional support. From one angle, A exhibited the 'feminine psychology' Jung ascribes to women who, he contends, use 'Eros' as 'the great binder and loosener' of relationship (Jung, 1964, p. 123). In contrast, A also appeared to me, at times, as a kind of predator, in her large sexual appetite for both men and women. While she maintained a steady relationship with a younger man who lived in another part of the country, Patient A participated actively in the 'hook-up' culture of millennials, using Tinder to indulge her desire whenever she traveled to conferences, as well as locally. In mining A's relationship to sex in a session, A would observe that for her sex was both 'light' and often full of humor, in her sense of the body's capacity to surprise and play.

Initially, I worried, like a mother, about the possibility of A falling prey to sexual assault, but she assured me, when we explored this possibility, that she had a sixth sense for threatening individuals and knew how to extricate herself from dangerous situations. Moreover, as I was to learn after about a year and a half of seeing A, she had, in fact, been raped in college, but had chosen, according to her narrative-framing of the experience, not to allow the incident to paralyze her emotionally or spoil her enjoyment of sexuality, observing that 'avoiding harm is not what motivates me' (a position I found both unusual and somewhat refreshing in a woman). While I might have read what I have called A's 'predatory' approach to sex as a reaction formation to her violation which, combined with factors from her childhood, suggested an underlying ambivalence around intimacy – considerations that, I would not, in fact, discount in a comprehensive clinical portrait – what struck me most powerfully was A's frank and defiant insistence on her own pleasure. This, I felt, was an inherently valuable, albeit risky, dimension of her life force. A described her femininity to me as 'a real power source'. Here A seemed to locate 'femininity' – at least *her* femininity – not solely in her capacity for relatedness or nurturing (i.e., as per cultural stereotypes) but in her desire to revel, play and consume, as well as to be consumed by others.

I could see the effect of A's libido on B and C in many ways, but perhaps most clearly in the context of a ritual retreat during the summer months. As it was recounted to me, the three were invited, with several other women, for weekend visits to a lake house, owned by a former student of A's and her 41-year-old boyfriend. The outings invariably culminated in a kind of bacchanal, in which many of the women undressed and, lubricated by tequila, began to dance and engage in sexual activity, 'making out' with each other and their single male host. B and C tended only to dance or stand on the sidelines and watch, while A participated, as per her character, with abandon and enthusiasm. Initially, my response (inwardly) was one of alarm and judgement.

First of all, I thought, these were three women professionals, two of them colleagues, within the context of a relatively small community, and in my experience and observation, sex and work do not intermingle to good effect for women, who are already vulnerable to objectification and/or harassment that often undermines their historically hard-won credibility. Moreover, the fact that the one member of the couple was a former student of A's suggested an ethical dilemma or boundary issue to me. But underlying these more surface and pragmatic concerns was, I think, my own discomfort with and, perhaps, anger at the notion of this Dionysian older man, voyeuristically observing the sexual interplay of young women (and, I would learn, propositioning each of them in turn), like a king in his harem.

Over time in working with each of the three women, however, a very different picture emerged in my imagination. None of the women seemed, in actuality, to care much about the man or his advances (which, with the exception of A, they routinely rebuked). Rather, the erotic focal point, so to speak, for B and C, was without a doubt patient A, her engagement with others and, more importantly, her relationship to herself. Their gaze was trained on the woman whose confident, bawdy and exhibitionist performance was an energy source for them all, inspiring and enlivening, despite their own, more timid and reserved participation in the weekend bacchanals. While both B and C would tell me in session that they would never choose to live A's life in reality (i.e., to engage in frequent and random 'hook-ups' or open relationships), they desired A's lightness, freedom and agency in her own body as in the world. In short, *they desired A's desire* which, while it existed within a 'masculine economy', was also in a sense autonomous in its dynamic expression of self-possession. A's behavior and influence in this context reminded me of the figure of Baubo as a subversive version of the feminine and of women's sexuality not generally welcome by or intended for men but, rather, one that evokes an Anima or 'soul-figure' and salve for other women. In this way Baubo's and, to an extent, A's energy escapes or steals past the culture's regulation of her sexuality ('lust') and life drive. As Lubell observes of Baubo in the ancient world:

> She survived as a comic link, understood primarily by women who valued her laughter and her ability to 'steal through'. They remembered her and understood her ability to reveal the sexual and emotional power of woman. They also understood her use of obscene humor (*aischorologia*) when confronting Demeter. She represented the mystic link between earth's fertility and human Fecundity. The paradox is that in the Attic world – where men so carefully controlled and denigrated female sexual power – any trace of Baubo remained.
>
> (Lubell, 1994, p. 40)

Douglas suggests the idea of a Dynamic Feminine as an image of what might develop psychologically, socially and physically as women become more fully attuned to themselves, allowing the object that is one's self to inspire delight and gratification rather than the shame, self-loathing and abjection that have been conditioned in, carried by, and trafficked among women historically. She muses thoughtfully, and with a spirit of common sense, that "if a girl's first sensuous object other than herself is a feminine body, how deep that connection must lie in our psyches and how natural for adult men and women both to be aroused by a woman's body. For a heterosexual woman, the object doesn't just change gender, it also remains female: it is herself" (Douglas, 1990, p. 87). Although she was not a crone like the figure of Baubo, patient A performed Baubo-like gestures of bawdiness and affirmation. Her 'display' was observed by both women and men, but its self-referential, playful and irreverent nature was digested by B and C in the manner imagined by Douglas. This relation or dynamic does not necessarily imply a form of 'homo-sexuality' (although homoeroticism is certainly a component). Rather, it is an invitation to the Other woman to re-view herself—as in a mirror—through a lens of desire as opposed to the critical lens of judgement and censorship so central in the conditioning of women. As Douglas says:

> When she has regained this embodied reality, she serves the erotic by being turned on by her own body and its responses. Out in the world, she serves her libido by being kindled by the spark she creates in herself, in her work, and in relationships.
>
> (Douglas, 1990, p. 87)

In her vision of femininity as both self-sufficient (i.e., unencumbered by the need for validation or articulation by the male—lover, philosopher or analyst) and more or other than its sanctioned associations within analytic psychology and Western thought, Douglas's image evokes a connotation of the term *jouissance* as that which, according to the psychoanalyst Jacques Lacan, exceeds comprehension by the dominant symbolic order against which the woman is defined (Lacan, 1982).

The myth of Baubo suggests something further about women's jouissance; in her 'nasty' misbehavior, Baubo elicits a pleasure that resides in the sheer fact of transgression; that is, in 'stealing through' or past the masculine gaze and dominant cultural codes. In this sense, Baubo's act of subversion is, in itself, a source of arousal, so to speak. Or, to put it otherwise, her transgression embodies both the form and content of feminine desire. As the analyst Sue Austin writes, "[E]ncountering the kinds of limitations and taboos structured into gender and cultural fantasies about sexuality immediately invites the transgression of those limitations" (Austin, 2005, p. 116). This is not to suggest that the disruption Baubo creates is *merely* pleasant. Rather, the experience of jouissance, according to both Lacan and Austin, both attracts and repels (or implies the simultaneity of pleasure and pain). Likewise, while Baubo performs a subversion that contains a corrective opening up to a shadow or otherness normally forbidden to women (bawdiness, joking, desire etc.), it also "discomforts, unsettles assumptions and leaves nothing the same" (Austin, 2005, p. 113). Not only does transgressive behavior expose women to what is potentially alien and disruptive to their sense of selves, as subjects constructed, in part, via the exclusion of what does not adhere to traditional notions of 'femininity' (for example, expressions of self-assertion or aggression by women), it is likely to incite defensive, if not volatile reactions from others (both men and women) who are invested in a binary and hierarchical positioning of masculine and feminine subjects as archetypal and essential.

Douglas's vision of the Dynamic Feminine potential in women is, in this light, perhaps slightly utopian in tone and does not take into account the dissonance and violence that can result when women act as autonomous agents (or simply as a result of their embodiment as girls and women), and the implicit threat to a patriarchal culture that is failing and desperate,as evidenced, I would argue, in the 2016 election. Nevertheless, it appears that Jung's black serpent is indeed emergent among us in human form, persistent in her psychic and somatic energy, regardless of the 'readiness' of our time psychologically – whether her energy be expressed via a much reviled female presidential candidate or the unapologetic expression of women's sexuality as aggressive, desirous and impious. For this, I take comfort and find pleasure, even as I mourn the far-ranging and ongoing effects of violence against the feminine sex.

References

Austin, S., 2005, *Women's Aggressive Fantasies: A Post-Jungian Exploration of Self-Hatred, Love and Agency*, London: Routledge.

Berry, J., 2018, *City of a Million Dreams: A History of New Orleans at 300*, Chapel Hill: University of North Carolina Press.

Douglas, C., 1990, *The Woman in the Mirror: Analytical Psychology and the Feminine*, Boston: Sigo Press.

Jung, C.G., 1953, *Two Essays on Analytical Psychology*, Princeton: Princeton University Press.

Jung, C.G., 1959, *The Archetypes and the Collective Unconscious*, Princeton: Princeton University Press.

Jung, C.G., 1964, *Civilization in Transition*, Princeton: Princeton University Press.

Jung, C.G., 1976a, *The Visons Seminars: Book One*, Zurich: Spring Publications.

Jung, C.G., 1976b, *The Visons Seminars: Book Two*, Zurich: Spring Publications.

Keuls, E., 1985, *The Reign of the Phallus: Sexual Politics in Ancient Athens*, New York: Harper and Row.

Lacan, J., 1982, *Feminine Sexuality: Jacques Lacan and the école freudienne*, New York: Norton.

Lubell, W.M., 1994, *The Metamorphosis of Baubo: Myths of Woman's Sexual Energy*, Nashville: Vanderbilt University Press.

Mitchell, R., 1995, *All on a Mardi Gras Day: Episodes in the History of New Orleans Carnival*, Cambridge, MA: Harvard University Press.

Rowland, S., 2002, *Jung: A Feminist Revision*, Cambridge: Polity Press.

Samuels, A., 2015, *A New Therapy for Politics?* London: Karnac.

Shelmerdine, S., 1995, *The Homeric Hymns*, Newburyport, MA: Focus Publishing.

Chapter 3

The concept of 'therapeutic space' as maternal space in depth psychology – a critique

Martyna Chrzescijanska

Space is one of the key categories in depth psychology but is rarely a subject of critical analysis. Psychoanalytic thinking about space stems from a long-standing Western idea of *res extensa* and *res cogitans*, a space of external world in opposition to the inner space, identified with psyche or soul. In this view, our psychic world is the 'inner space' that interacts with the outside world. The key terms of psychoanalysis, such as transference, projection, interiorization, or internal objects, demonstrate that psychoanalytic thinking is embedded in thinking about space in terms of inside/outside. The space in depth psychology is also understood as the 'setting', the physical space where the therapy takes place. It is related to 'framework' and 'boundaries' referring to the regularity of time and space, but also to confidentiality and the ethical standards of therapeutic work (Cox, 1976; Temperley, 1984; Zur, 2007). These various ways of understanding space in depth psychology can be confusing as they are intertwined: the physical space mirrors the inner space and, on the other hand, the inner space is affected by the physical space.

This chapter focuses on the idea of 'therapeutic space' as described in different theories of psychotherapy (for instance, for Jung it is the *temenos* and *vas bene clausum*; Winnicott calls it the 'holding space'; and Bion conceptualizes therapeutic space as a 'container/containing space'). What is meant by therapeutic space here is a space that aids a healing or developmental process. It refers to the setting but also includes the analysand-analyst relationship. Importantly, all of these concepts of therapeutic space highlight its feminine or maternal nature. It focuses on the most popular and well-known ideas and images of the therapeutic space that 'survived' in the social imagination and psychotherapy, such as containing space or holding space. It must be noted here that it does not mean that depth psychology has not produced other ideas about therapeutic space. From an academic perspective that is focused on discourse analysis, it is interesting to track ideas that survive and constitute the dominant narratives.

To discuss the image of 'therapeutic space' in depth psychology, it is important to contextualize it. Therefore, this chapter will investigate the patriarchal discourse and historical contexts of depth psychology. Discourse analysis is concerned with the way texts/theories are constructed and inquiries into how relations of social power, dominance, and inequality are expressed in different forms of discourse, such as texts and theories (van Dijk, 2008). Therefore, this chapter will discuss the binary oppositions and their associations (feminine/masculine; nature/culture; Eros/Logos) in depth psychology as shared assumptions in late nineteenth and early-twentieth-century Europe.

Depth psychology and patriarchal discourse

Psychoanalysis was born and for a long time remained a discipline created from a male perspective despite its reliance on predominantly female patients and their role in shaping psychoanalysis as a discipline. The key ideas of Freudian psychoanalysis were the male-centric categories, such as Oedipus complex, castration complex, penis envy, or even later the Jungian ideas of anima and animus, which maintained the predominantly patriarchal *status quo* of the superior status of masculinity. It was not until Melanie Klein, Karen Horney, Anna Freud, and many other female psychoanalysts began to shed light on female psychology that psychoanalysis started thinking more about the importance of psychology of and for women (Sayers, 1991). The slow 'feminisation' of psychoanalysis did not change the fact, however, that psychoanalysis as a discipline remained the invention of nineteenth- and early-twentieth-century patriarchal discourse. It can also be claimed that the appearance of female psychoanalysts did not change the masculine character of psychoanalysis overnight.

As many authors point out, the beginnings of psychoanalysis are embedded in the predominantly patriarchal society of nineteenth- and twentieth-century Europe, and it can therefore be argued that psychoanalysis has been a part of the patriarchal discourse (Millet, 1970; Gallop, 1987; Freeman, 2008). The patriarchal discourse is grounded in the differences between men and women in a way that determines an unprivileged position for women in society. Patriarchy is also grounded in the conviction of the power of masculinity and the superior position of the father, yet it diminishes the parental role of the father as caregiver As Freeman (2008) demonstrated, the same tension between the symbolic power of the masculine and the actual absence of the father can be observed in psychoanalytic theory, and as such it can be seen as part of patriarchal discourse. This absence of the 'paternal' at the pre-Oedipal stage of infancy in the concept of safe space will be discussed in this chapter.

Discourse theory investigates how words and images are used and in which contexts they appear. The patriarchal discourse can be 'tracked' in a language that is used and associations related to both feminine/masculine: for instance, in associations between femininity and nature, and, on the other hand, identification between masculinity and what is cultural, public, or political. In the twentieth century, the early anthropology supported these beliefs, arguing a universal division between nature and culture, in which nature was identified with femininity and culture with masculinity. This idea of a universal binary division between masculine/feminine and culture/nature, which was widely accepted by anthropologists and popularized by, for instance, Claude Lévi-Strauss (1963), only came under criticism in the 1970s (Ortner, 1974) and is currently regarded as a devaluation of women.

A similar opposition can be found in depth psychology. Anthropology pro-moted the binary oppositions, such as light/dark, civilized/savage, cooked/raw, that were also reflected in psychoanalysis in the form of oppositions between conscious/unconscious and Logos/Eros. Femininity was associated with weak-ness, emotions, nature, and unconscious, while masculinity was identified with reasoning, conscious, and logical thinking.

For instance, in Carl Gustav Jung's theory of anima and animus, the femi-nine part was associated with the irrational, emotional aspect (Eros), while the masculine part was associated with rational Logos. Attributing certain traits as essentially feminine or masculine is problematic in itself (gender essentialism), but additionally Jung used the traits socially regarded as inferior to describe femi-ninity. Anima is described in terms of emotionality, vanity, and sexuality, while animus is associated with intellectual abilities, such as science and logical think-ing. As Jung described:

> The animus likes to project itself upon 'intellectuals' and all kinds of 'heroes' (including tenors, artists, and sporting celebrities). The anima had a predi-lection for everything that is unconscious, dark, equivocal and unrelated in woman, and also for her vanity, frigidity, helplessness and so forth.
>
> (Jung, 1954, p. 303)

As Goldenberg (1976) observed, while it is true that Jung valued women for their Eros, understood as an ability to connect, he also confined them to the traits asso-ciated with Eros. It is also true that Jung claimed that both men and women have inner archetypal representations of both anima and animus, which is often praised as a liberating concept in terms of non-fixed or androgynous/non-binary gender. Nevertheless, he identified womanhood and femininity with certain traits and as he assumed "A woman possessed by the animus is always in danger of losing her femininity" (Jung, 1966, p. 208). Although anima and animus may seem to be abstract and intuitive concepts, for Jung they had very practical consequences in one's life. For instance, being too close to Logos can be dangerous for a woman: "No one can get around the fact that by taking up a masculine profession, studying and working like a man, woman is doing something not wholly in accord with, if not directly injurious to, her feminine nature" (Jung, 1964, p. 117). In other words, women have their domain, which is the caring, emotional, and loving envi-ronment and any other role can be potentially dangerous for this fixed identity. As I will discuss later in this chapter, this was possibly one of the elements underpin-ning the concept of therapeutic space in depth psychology.

Safe space in depth psychology

The concept of therapeutic space became popular in depth psychology mostly due to Carl Gustav Jung, Donald Winnicott, and Wilfred Bion, and the modern ideas of the setting, frame, and boundaries in psychotherapy (Corey, 2017; Temperley, 1984).

The idea of space as feminine/maternal space seems to be a recurrent motif in psychoanalytic/psychotherapeutic thinking. Different models of psychotherapeutic thinking about space share certain features when it comes to describing therapeutic space.

For instance, Jung used the image of the *temenos* to represent a perfectly safe space where the (psychological) transformation can take place. *Temenos* is a Greek word and refers to a sacred enclosure or precinct. Interestingly, it stems from *temnein* meaning 'cut off' (Oxford English Dictionary, n.d.). *Temenos* was a protected piece of land, dedicated to the gods. Jung used this term to describe the therapeutic, safe space. Other images that he used to represent the safe space were the well-sealed vessel, *vas bene clausum,* taken from alchemy, and the mandala, the circle representing the universe in Buddhism. The purpose of the *vas bene clausum* was to "protect what is within from the intrusion and admixture of what is without, as well as to prevent it from escaping" (Jung, 1953, p. 167).

In many places, Jung drew an analogy between both the *temenos* or vessel and the uterus. "It is a kind of matrix or uterus from which the *filius philosophorum,* the miraculous stone, is to be born" (Jung, 1953, p. 237). He also refers to the *temenos* as a feminine space: "feminine nature of the *temenos,* just as the *hortus conclusus* (enclosed garden) is often used as an image of the Virgin Mary in medieval hymns, and the *rosa mystica* is one of her attributes in the Litany of Loreto" (Jung, 1953, p. 186). Although he draws this analogy in his alchemical writings, he also puts it in the context of Freudian theory: "We can easily translate these ideas into the concretism of Freudian theory: the *temenos* would then be the womb of the mother and the rite a regression to incest" (Jung, 1953, p. 131).

Jung identifies the safe space with feminine space in an uncritical way, without reflecting on social meanings that such an identification could have. This is not surprising as Jung as a thinker was interested in universal symbols and meanings and not the social and political contexts of these symbols and meanings. Therefore, it is a task of contemporary researchers and analysts to look into some analogies and images produced by depth psychology.

The image of therapeutic space as a maternal space is maintained as a dominant in post-Jungian therapies. For instance, the Jungian idea of the *temenos* as a maternal space survived in post-Jungian therapies and techniques, such as sandplay: "The aim [in sandplay] is to provide a maternal space or psychological womb, an emotional metaphor for the uroboric mother-child unit. In this safe 'space' healing of the inner child re-discovered, with all of its potentiality for creativity and renewal" (Weinrib, 1983, p. 28). The feminine space is also associated with the pre-verbal and safe, hence, containing space, as opposed to the masculine 'talking cure': "Sandplay provides a way of 'dropping' into the pre-verbal, matriarchal areas of psyche. Verbalization with its demand for conscious articulation, may interfere with this" (Weinrib, 1983, p. 29). This might demonstrate thinking in terms of the nature/culture division in which femininity is identified with nature and masculinity with culture. The maternal is pre-verbal, safe, and less developed, while the masculine is identified with more complex forms, such as speech and culture.

The idea of therapeutic space as maternal space also became popular in psychotherapy due to developing child psychotherapy and the object-relation school. Although Donald Winnicott, Wilfred Bion, and Melanie Klein are usually regarded as post-Freudian psychoanalysts, their work inspired the Developmental School in post-Jungian psychology. Most of these schools agreed that the mother and what is maternal play a pivotal role in the development of the child, and consequently, of the adult. The relationship with the mother is regarded as primal and is a prototype of the therapeutic setting (which usually offers a 'reparation' of the primal relationship).

For instance, we can find such ideas in Winnicott's (1971) formulation of holding space that stems from literal understanding of the physical holding of the infant by the mother. This maternal holding became the metaphor of therapeutic holding and the holding space in therapy. Similarly, the transitional space with the transitional objects is a symbolic representative of the mother (Winnicott, 1971). As such, the transitional space is, in fact, also 'maternal'. It differs from the holding space or Jungian *temenos* in many ways: Winnicott describes it as a space of possibilities and exploration. Nevertheless, it is a safe space, within limits, where exploration is possible only because separation (from the mother) can be negotiated by transitional objects 'replacing' the primal object (the mother).

The idea of different spaces as 'reconstruction' of maternal space became popular outside of psychoanalysis. Adrien Stokes, a twentieth-century art historian, drew on the Kleinian idea of reparation, claiming that architecture can be regarded as 'reconstruction' of the mother that was lost due to separation. In other words, art, particularly architecture, alleviates the experience of loss by providing the experience of an intact maternal body. Architecture is then "the return of the mourned mother" (Stokes, 2014, p. 83).

Probably the most popular and well-known idea of therapeutic space is the concept of containment and containing space. The idea of containment (Bion, 1962) was inspired by the Kleinian concept of projective identification. By containment or the containing process, Bion meant the mother's capacity to take in the infant's undigested states of mind, process them, and convey them back in a modified form. The same function is provided within the therapeutic space. The containing space is a space of integration of the patients' undigested feelings and it enables the creation of meaning.

The concept of containment demonstrates the tendency in psychoanalysis to create a parallel between the infant-mother dyad and patient-therapist dyad, in which the therapist takes over the maternal function of providing care. Consequently, the therapeutic space, which is a safe and bounded space (the setting), becomes the maternal space. This parallel that creates a framework for psychoanalytic therapy is already problematic due to the involvement of power relations (the therapist as a 'parental figure'), but in this chapter we will focus on analysis of the maternal metaphor as part of psychoanalytic involvement in a masculine-oriented discourse.

The idea of the therapeutic container has been criticized, often for its idealized character. For instance, Cartwright claims that the process of containing is idealized and that a container is presented as "a three-dimensional object, a near-physical repository" (2010, p. 6). The idea of containing became very popular in psychotherapy and was treated as almost a magical cure. Psychotherapists, however, rarely question whether a therapeutic space is always containing and whether it must be identified as maternal.

The idea of the containing space and container is often interpreted in a literal sense. Suzanne Maiello (2012) claims that the mental abstraction of containment may come from the physical reality of the proto-containing experience of the union of uterus and fetus. In that sense, the aim of the container/containing space in therapy would be to create a new 'uterus' for the experience of the patients.

The question that we aim to pose is why the therapeutic space is described as maternal or feminine space and why this idea became and remains such a popular concept in psychotherapy.

Therapeutic space as maternal space

One of the key strategies of patriarchal discourse is to control female sexuality and reproduction. The untamed feminine sexuality becomes a 'safe land' when it becomes maternal. As Chodorow writes, "Women's mothering is a central and defining feature of the social organization of gender and is implicated in the construction and reproduction of male dominance itself" (Chodorow, 1999, p. 9). We may assume that this might be a reason for thinking about a therapeutic space not only as a feminine space but as a maternal space.

Depth psychology's fantasy about maternal space and identifying the containing space with a uterine space can be interpreted in terms of the objectivization of the feminine body. The feminine body imagined as the container/vessel becomes tamed, well-known, and protective. It is represented as an abstract and idealized form, neglecting nuances of both the therapeutic process and motherhood/femininity. We can say that in the concept of maternal therapeutic space, far more complex phenomena were replaced with a representation that simplifies them. On the one hand, the therapeutic process cannot be simply described in terms of containment or the safe space; on the other hand, femininity and motherhood is more complex than being containing and 'holding'.

Importantly, by imagining the maternal/feminine space as enclosed, safe, well-sealed, and well-contained, the psychotherapeutic imagination takes part in a much broader discourse on femininity. In this discourse, femininity is reduced to the idea of the womb and a safe, nurturing space.

Why is the fact of describing safe space as maternal space in depth psychology problematic, however?

First, if psychotherapists imagine the containing space as a maternal and feminine space, they implicitly define femininity and maternity in certain categories, such as: passivity, receptiveness, and bounding. These are not socially and politically neutral images. They reproduce the pattern of thinking about gender in terms of oppositions, reinforcing the stereotype of females as more receptive, patient, or passive. It also imposes some (sometimes unrealistic) standards on mothers, dismissing the complexity related to motherhood (such as post-natal depression, struggling with breastfeeding, or accepting the change related to becoming the mother; the role of father in taking care of the child). It does not sufficiently include mismatches, lack of continuity, and problematic aspects of motherhood. The by-product of idealization is guilt, and as Diane Eyer (1992) argues, presumably scientific research into the mother-infant bond was largely based on social assumptions about the role of the woman as the mother and the instinctual nature of motherhood and bonding. Her key idea is that science and social beliefs are entangled and very often science is used to reify conservative social views. In this case, bonding theory affirms the woman's place at home after the infant's birth, or even, in general, the domestic nature of womanhood.

The idea of associating femininity with 'safe space' or 'enclosed space' is not neutral either. For centuries, the feminine space was associated with the private space of the household in opposition to the external space of politics that belonged to men (McDowell, 1999; Massey, 1994). It can be asked if this is the reason why the safe, enclosed space of psychotherapy is identified with the feminine space. There might be a link between depicting the psyche as a house (Jung, 1964, p. 31), psychotherapeutic thinking about psyche as the 'inner world', the safe space of the setting, and the traditional association of the private space with femininity. It comes from a traditional social practice and a societal discourse on feminine space as the private space of the household.

The traditional idea of associating the public space with men and the household space with women drew on the division between nature/culture. Due to 'domestication', nature becomes 'processed', just as food is processed and becomes a safe space, while the male domain is situated in public and is related in particular to politics. Feminist studies demonstrated that gender oppositions (nature/culture; public/private; reproduction/production; nurturing/creating) were used to legitimate hegemonic masculinity. The model of the Victorian, middle class family kept this binary opposition alive, associating women with 'inside' spaces, while men were identified with the outside and the public. Women in outside spaces were identified with prostitution (Gorman-Murray, 2008). In other words, the image of women in 'outside space' was sexualized, while the image of womanhood in 'inside spaces' was related to the social and family role (as daughter, wife, mother).

It is likely that psychoanalytic thinking about space stems from this binary division that was also discussed above in the context of maintaining nature/culture, Eros/Logos oppositions. The idea of the therapeutic space as a safe space followed the patriarchal discourse that turned potentially dangerous femininity into the tamed, domesticated, and safe space of motherhood. In this perspective, Eros is perceived as a space of safety and nurturing; and nature becomes 'mother nature'.

However, the social use of space has changed over the centuries and femininity can no longer be associated with interiority. As such, the idea of safe space as feminine space in psychotherapy is a remnant of traditional, patriarchal thinking about womanhood. Depth psychology should become more aware of its own position in relation to this change and take responsibility for it.

Can we re-imagine therapeutic space? Can we re-imagine feminine space(s)?

Depth psychology has been taking a social and political turn for a while now (Samuels, 1993, 2001; Tweedy, 2016). It is important for psychotherapy to become more and more aware of its own position and embedment in social norms and discourses. Only this recognition can enable psychotherapy to take an active role in changing potentially harmful narratives and practices. It is particularly important for psychotherapy to look at its own 'childhood', as many of its habits and categories stem from social discourse. The socio-political and cultural context in which psychoanalysis was created affected it to a large extent and its task now is to reflect on this. Psychotherapy has well-developed tools of critical reflection and can become its own patient. It can also use other tools developed by other disciplines, such as discourse analysis and critical analysis.

Some elements of psychoanalytic thinking that are seemingly innocent turn out to be a reservoir of old-fashioned beliefs that reinforce the patriarchal discourse. One necessity is to notice them, as they are often disguised as key and seemingly neutral concepts. Another necessity is not to be afraid of change and experimentation within the psychoanalytic field. One way to do this is to re-think and re-imagine the idea of therapeutic space. We can ask ourselves whether therapeutic space must be exclusively an enclosed, containing, bounded space? We can think of therapeutic spaces that are spaces of exploration, discontinuity, and transgression. There are many possible uses of space that can be therapeutic: dance, movement, walking, exploration, and contact with nature.

Secondly, we can ask ourselves whether we need to think about therapeutic space in terms of gender. There are several problems with thinking about therapeutic space as gendered space. The therapeutic space can be a paternal or masculine space just as it can be a feminine/maternal one. It can also be gender-neutral, or it can be a space of gender ambivalence and transition. Many of the recent studies emphasizing the need to 'do and undo gender' focus on gendered spaces and interconnections between gender, identity, and spaces (Rezeanu, 2015). Psychotherapy has not yet reflected on how these ideas can support therapeutic thinking.

Psychotherapy should also re-think the connection that is made between the mother-infant relationship and the therapist-patient relationship. It potentially puts the psychotherapist in the superior role of a care giver, a person who knows more and has a higher status. It also involves both the client and psychotherapist in a power relations dynamic.

Another aspect to be taken into consideration is deconstructing the binary divisions between femininity and masculinity and the features attributed to them. For instance, femininity does not have to be associated with passivity, nurturing, or bounding. As Yuval-Davis and Stoetzler (2002) suggest, femininity can be thought rather in terms of crossing and transcending than bounded spaces. This change in thinking could transform political and social narratives. For instance, in the new feminine spaces, "transversal politics is so central to women's political work" (2002, p. 342). Femininity can also be re-defined as dynamic femininity and represent "undirected movement toward the new, the nonrational, the playful. It is the flow of experience, vital, spontaneous, open to the unexpected, yielding and responsive to being acted from the experience of transformed awareness" (Gomes & Kanner, 1995, p. 119). The feminine space does not have to be understood as maternal, passive, and protective. In fact, as it is a socio-cultural construct it can be understood and re-defined in many possible ways. Depth psychology, instead of reproducing the socio-political patterns, needs to take an active role in transforming them.

This chapter has discussed the concept of therapeutic space as maternal space in depth psychology. It suggested that we need to investigate how the concepts are used and what are the possible social meanings related to associating safe space with femininity/maternity.

There are some limitations to the critical analysis presented in this chapter. As it mostly discusses and analyzes the discursive and narrative aspects of psychoanalytic theory, it does not take the psychoanalytic practice into consideration. This can be more deconstructive and sensitive toward thinking about space and gender than the theory demonstrates. As we are limited when it comes to researching how psychoanalysis is practiced by individual psychotherapists/psychoanalysts, we are inclined to focus on its theoretical aspects that are easier to analyze. However, saying that, theory affects practice and vice versa, therefore, active engagement with and changing of theory is one of the important tasks that depth psychology should take up as part of its reflexive practice.

This chapter has demonstrated some possible strands of critical analysis of the concept of maternal space in depth psychology. It is a matter of further research to discover how this concept can be transformed and what the practical implications for therapeutic practice would be.

References

Bion, W.R., 1962, *Learning from Experience*, London: Karnac.

Cartwright, D., 2010, *Containing States of Mind: Exploring Bion's 'Container Model' in Psychoanalytic Psychotherapy*, London: Routledge.

Chodorow, N.J., 1999, *The Reproduction of Mothering: Psychoanalysis and the Sociology of Gender*, Berkeley, CA: University of California Press.

Corey, G., 2017, *Theory and Practice of Counselling and Psychotherapy*, Boston, MA: Cengage Learning.

Cox, M., 1976, 'Group psychotherapy in a secure setting', *Proceedings from the Royal Society of Medicine*, 69(3), pp. 215–220.

Eyer, E.D., 1992, *Mother-Infant Bonding: A Scientific Fiction*, New Haven, CT: Yale University Press.

Freeman, T., 2008, 'Psychoanalytic concepts of fatherhood: Patriarchal paradoxes and the presence of an absent authority', *Studies in Gender and Sexuality*, 9(2), pp. 113–139.

Gallop, J., 1987, 'Reading the mother tongue: Psychoanalytic feminist criticism', *Critical Inquiry*, 13(2), pp. 314–329.

Goldenberg, N.R., 1976, 'A feminist critique of Jung', *Signs: Journal of Women in Culture and Society*, 2(2), pp. 443–449.

Gomes, M.E., & Kanner, A.D., 1995, 'The rape of the well-maidens. Feminist psychology and the environmental crisis'. In: T. Roszak, M.E. Gomes, A.D. Kanner (eds.), *Ecopsychology: Restoring the Earth, Healing the Mind*, San Francisco, CA: Sierra Club, pp. 111–121.

Gorman-Murray, A., 2008, 'Masculinity and the home: A critical review and conceptual framework', *Australian Geographer*, 39(3), pp. 367–379.

Jung, C.G., 1953, *Psychology and Alchemy*, Hove: Routledge & Kegan Paul Ltd.

Jung, C.G., 1954, *The Practice of Psychotherapy*, Hove: Routledge and Kegan Paul Ltd.

Jung, C.G., 1964, *Civilisation in Transition*, London: Routledge and Kegan Paul Ltd.

Jung, C.G., 1966, *Two Essays on Analytical Psychology*, Hove: Routledge & Kegan Paul Ltd.

Lévi-Strauss, C., 1963, *Structural Anthropology*, New York: Basic Books.

Maiello, S., 2012, 'Prenatal experiences of containment in the light of Bion's model of container/contained', *Journal of Child Psychotherapy*, 38(3), pp. 250–267.

Massey, D., 1994, *Space, Place and Gender*, Minneapolis: University of Minnesota Press.

McDowell, L., 1999, *Gender, Identity and Place: Understanding Feminist Geographies*, Minneapolis: University of Minnesota Press.

Millet, K., 1970, *Sexual Politics*, Garden City, NY: Doubleday.

Ortner, S.B., 1974. 'Is female to male as nature is to culture?' In: M.Z. Rosaldo and L. Lamphere (eds.), *Woman, Culture, and Society*, Stanford, CA: Stanford University Press, pp. 68–87.

Oxford English Dictionary, n.d. Available at: https://en.oxforddictionaries.com/definition/temenos (Accessed 13 July 2019).

Rezeanu, C.I., 2015, 'The relationship between domestic space and gender identity: Some signs of emergence of alternative domestic femininity and masculinity', *Journal of Comparative Research in Anthropology and Sociology*, 6(2), pp. 9–29.

Samuels, A., 1993, *The Political Psyche*, London: Routledge.

Samuels, A., 2001, *Politics on the Couch: Citizenship and the Internal Life*, London: Karnac Books.

Sayers, J., 1991, *Mothering Psychoanalysis: Helene Deutsch, Karen Horney, Anna Freud and Melanie Klein*, London: Hamish Hamilton.

Stokes, A., 2014, *Art and Analysis: An Adrian Stokes Reade*, H. Williams (ed.), London: Karnac Books.

Temperley, J., 1984, 'Settings for psychotherapy', *British Journal of Psychotherapy*, 1(2), pp. 101–111.

Tweedy, R., (ed.), 2016, *The Political Self: Understanding the Social Context for Mental Illness*, London: Karnac Books.

Van Dijk, T.A., 2008, *Discourse and Context: A Sociocognitive Approach*, Cambridge: Cambridge University Press.

Weinrib, E., 1983, *Images of the Self: The Sandplay Therapy Process*, Boston, MA: Sigo Press.

Winnicott, D.W., 1971, *Playing and Reality*, London: Tavistock.

Yuval-Davis, N., & Stoetzler, M., 2002, 'Imagined boundaries and borders: A gendered gaze', *European Journal of Women's Studies*, 9(3), pp. 329–344.

Zur, O., 2007, *Boundaries in Psychotherapy: Ethical and Clinical Explorations*, Washington, DC: American Psychological Association.

Chapter 4

Sexual counter-revolution

Sexism, homophobia and the new right

Lene Auestad

These reflections start from the political events of the summer of 2017, when a neo-Nazi group which calls itself the Nordic Resistance Movement declared their intention to march in the coastal town of Fredrikstad in the South of Norway. Most of this Nazi group were Swedish, with some Norwegians, and eighteen of them were stopped when crossing the border between Sweden and Norway. The weapons confiscated by the police included pepper spray, fighting gloves and knives. Efforts were made to stop the Nazis from marching, and the local police banned both the Nazi march and the counter-protestors, stating that the anti-racist protestors may present a threat of violence. The Nazis then decided, on the morning of the 29th July, to drive to the small southern town of Kristiansand instead. Although the police were aware of their changed plans from the morning onward, they did not call in reinforcements to stop the march, but instead allowed their march through the main street of the small town to proceed, walking alongside them, in effect protecting the Nazis. One man stood up against them. The actor and author Ole Tellefsen stood calmly in the middle of the street facing the marching Nazis, who yelled at him and broke one of his ribs. The police, in response, handcuffed the protestor, and forced him away from the scene. The Nazis handed out flyers showing pictures of gallows with the text "reserved for traitors to the people" (Auestad, 2017).

"Fight the gay lobby"

The banner the group marched under was that of "Fight the gay lobby". Their protest is directed mainly against gay men, and they formulated their ideology as a reaction against the increased sexual and cultural freedoms of the last century. These are men who march in the streets carrying flags with what looks like a phallic symbol, and who appear to have chosen gay men as their main enemies.

Their symbol, a black arrow pointing upwards, has clear phallic connotations. A search for what meaning they themselves assign to this symbol, gives the following result. It is a letter in the Runic, or Futhark, alphabet. There are at least three main varieties of runic script: Early, or Common, Germanic (Teutonic); Anglo-Saxon, or Anglian; and Nordic, or Scandinavian; the latter was used from the 8th to about the 12th or 13th century A.D. in Scandinavia and Iceland. Its letter forms were angular, and it was written from right to left. The sounds of the first six letters were f, u, th, a, r, and k, respectively, giving the alphabet its name: Futhark (*Encyclopædia Britannica,* n.d., 'Runic Alphabet'). The letter is called the Tyr rune, which:

> To us symbolizes the fight and inheritance. Tyr was the god of war according to our forefathers' beliefs; he stood for courage, honour and not least the willingness to sacrifice. Tyr expressed the willingness to make sacrifices when he sacrifices his own hand to the jaws of the Fenris wolf, to the betterment of gods and mankind. The Tyr rune makes us look backwards to our forefathers, but also, and perhaps first and foremost makes us look ahead to the battles we face. The rune signifies the race's will to life, and the preparedness to secure life itself, whatever it may demand from those of us who follow its path. The rune is black. To us the black colour represents structure, order and discipline – important qualities to an organisation which is faced with a mission as important as ours.
> (Nordfront's editors, 2015, my translation;
> see also Expo, 2017)

The symbol is thereby linked to Tyr, the Norse god of war, who is said to represent traditional virtues such as courage and a striving for honour. The main story associated with this figure features the god losing his hand in order tie up the Fenris wolf, who had freed itself and was on the loose (*Encyclopædia Britannica,* n.d., 'Tyr'). The Fenris wolf is a large beast, one of the children of Loki. Loki is a god, of the type that Jung would term a trickster, sometimes acting for good, sometimes for evil; he was also sexually ambiguous, being the father of some mythological creatures and the mother of others. To control the Fenris wolf the gods had the dwarfs make a magical rope out of bird's spit, women's beards, mountain roots, bear's ligaments, fishes' breath and the sound of cat's paws – and this is why these things don't exist anymore. Tyr held his hand in the wolf's jaws as the rope was put round its neck, and on feeling the rope tighten, the wolf snapped its jaws shut in surprise, and Tyr lost his hand.

Nordfront interprets this element as signalling a willingness to sacrifice, although it is striking that it also introduces a theme of castration which returns in their presentation of homosexuality, the supposed reason for their march in 2017. In that context it has become something threatening and frightening rather than a positive, heroic element. As they say:

> In the background lurk even more ill people who with 100% certainty will move forward as the gay lobby is allowed to advance. These can be paedophiles, necrophiliacs, zoophiles, or why not apotemnophiles (a wish for and sexual excitement at the idea of being an amputee) which is actually not much stranger than a will to cut off one's own sex.
> (Nordfront, 2016, my translation)

The latter formulation is probably aimed at transsexuals, where the focus is the male-to-female transsexual, and where the frightening aspect of this figure is the idea of castration. The duality of this theme recurs in the far-right terrorist Anders Behring Breivik's fantasy world, as described by Aage Borchgrevink (2013). Worried about what he calls "the feminization of society", the terrorist declared that "not only are women unstable, they also contribute to regression in terms of reproduction. They open the door for homosexuality. They seem to be susceptible to treason, or at least 'total surrender' to the hostile, sexually aggressive and masculine Islam" (2013, p.176). In Breivik's vision of the future the state will take control of procreation, and women are to return to the home and leave working life and academia. Not only that, he fantasises about removing women altogether, by using surrogate mothers in third world countries and by artificial wombs. The end result would be a society where women are practically non-existent, and where sex is strictly regulated by a cultural conservative guardian council (Borchgrevink, 2013, p.177). He felt that his mother had infected him with femininity; if it were not for that, he would be perfect, in the same way as she gave him throat infections which sometimes made him wear a face mask at home. Female influence had, in the same way, he thought, brought Europe to its knees at the feet of the Muslim invader (Borchgrevink, 2013, p.178). In his compendium, Breivik exacts revenge upon his mother, puts his father back on the throne, overcomes depression and defeat, and is thus liberated, free to live out his sadistic fantasies (Borchgrevink, 2013, p.179).

In Elisabeth Young-Bruehl's terms, sexists are usually men who cannot tolerate the idea that there are people in existence who are not like them. These are prejudices of boundary establishment – "On the other side of the narcissists' boundaries there is not a 'them,' a 'not-us' but blank, a lack – or at the most, a profound mystery" (Young-Bruehl, 1996, p.35). She continues, "The Other is so different as to be, in effect, nothing. [...] Women are, in these cultural terms, mindless. What these creeds mean, fundamentally, is 'no one here but us'" (Young-Bruehl, 1996, p.234). According to Breivik's fantasies above, what he wants from women is just one body part, in order to reproduce, essentially, himself.

To Breivik, white Western men, are the victims of the 'Eurabian conspiracy', as non-white men enjoy greater respect, and white women prefer the non-white men. The Eurabian conspiracy theory states that Europe will be Islamized in the near future, and that this is being deliberately planned by European elites, and the European Union in particular. A twist is added to this theme of sexual and civilizational warfare as Breivik declared his willingness to castrate himself to collaborate with al-Qaeda, for 'the greater good of our cause':

> The difference between the 'system protectors' of democracies and nationalist freedom fighters is that the latter are willing to make sacrifices, including gladly sacrificing their own lives. As a result '[t]he entity should demand that the alleged Justiciar Knight in question surgically remove his penis

and testicles and/or execute a fixed number of civilian children. While this requirement seems morbid, absurd or unreasonable, it is perhaps the most effective method of confirming the intentions of an individual.

(Breivik cited by Borchgrevink, 2013, p.165)

Thus castration occurs both as a fear and a wish – as what he sees as having already happened and what is happening in the family and in civilization – and as a wish for a sexual union with the imagined Islamist, where Breivik is the passive part in the relationship (Auestad, 2014, p.52). In this fantasy, being a gay man is equated with being castrated, which in its turn is equated with being a woman. In reality, he made no such 'sacrifices', and martyrdom remained an idea. Borchgrevink also reveals that Breivik's sexualized racism was inspired by Hans Rustad, who wrote in an article, 'Sex as a weapon' in December 2009 that Muslim men rape Western women, that this is a war, and that Western men are slowly being castrated (2013, pp.177–178). In Rustad's imagery, sex is described as a 'currency' in a market where Western men are losing out. 'Muslims' are imagined as a monolithic unit, and as the opposite of the 'Western', and a sexual war is imagined as taking place on a group level. "Incredibly well written, Hans," wrote Breivik as a comment on Rustad's article on Document.no. In this account, the imagined encounter between Islam and the West is violent while also being erotic. In Borchgrevink's account, it is being hinted that Breivik made up relations to women which never existed, so as to support an idea of his own masculinity. At the same time, he had some affairs with men which he refused to admit to (Borchgrevink, 2013, pp.190–191). This would support the idea that the narrative of a battle between men over women as objects is a cover story, and that the real desired object is the figure of the 'sexy Islamist', whom he sees as being more masculine than he himself is. Although in Breivik's case, the confusion, you might say, is about who he actually wants to get into bed with which comes on top of a deeper identity confusion, about who he is, thus I do not argue that this is the deepest layer.

Bisexuality in psychoanalysis

"It is popularly believed that a human being is either a man or a woman", wrote Freud in 1905 in *Three Essays on the Theory of Sexuality*, and continued:

> Science, however, knows of cases in which the sexual characters are obscured, and in which it is consequently difficult to determine the sex. [...] The impor- tance of these abnormalities lies in the unexpected fact that they facilitate our understanding of normal development. For it appears that a certain degree of anatomical hermaphroditism occurs normally. In every normal male or female individual, traces are found of the apparatus of the opposite sex. These either persist without function as rudimentary organs or become modified and take on other functions.

(Freud, 1905, p.141)

Although Freud never doubted the psychological importance of bisexuality, Freud's thinking about the problem includes some reservations. The concept of bisexuality presupposes a clear grasp of the antithesis between masculinity and femininity. However, these notions have different meanings for biology, psychology and sociology – meanings which are often confused. The biological meaning is the clearest, and refers to people's genitals. The most serviceable in psychoanalysis, states Freud, is the distinction between activity and passivity, and the sociological meaning is based on observations of existing people's behaviours. But such observation shows that "pure masculinity or femininity is not to be found either in a psychological or biological sense. Every individual on the contrary displays a mixture of the character-traits belonging to his own or the opposite sex" (Freud, 1905, p.220).

Homosexuality, as Freud describes it, may be *absolute*, when sexual objects are exclusively of one's own sex, *amphigenic*, when sexual objects may equally well be of either sex, or *contingent*, that is, variable according to external conditions (Freud, 1905, pp.136–137). A person may alternate between these dispositions, and may also change throughout his or her lifespan, from one disposition to another.

He wrote, in 1915, that:

> Psycho-analytic research is most decidedly opposed to any attempt at separating off homosexuals from the rest of mankind as a group of special character. By studying sexual excitations other than those that are manifestly displayed, it has found that all human beings are capable of making a homosexual object-choice and have in fact made one in their unconscious.
>
> (Freud, 1905, p.145)

In the last part of that statement he is referring to people having loved both their parents as children. He went on state that:

> libidinal attachments to persons of the same sex play no less a part as factors in normal mental life, and a greater part as a motive for illness, than do similar attachments to the opposite sex. On the contrary, psycho-analysis considers that a choice of an object independently of its sex – freedom to range equally over male and female objects – as it is found in childhood, in primitive states of society and early periods of history, is the original basis from which, as a result of restriction in one direction or the other, both the normal and the inverted types develop. Thus from the point of view of psycho-analysis the exclusive sexual interest felt by men for women is also a problem that needs elucidating and is not a self-evident fact based upon an attraction that is ultimately of a chemical nature.
>
> (Freud, 1905, pp.145–146, footnote added 1915)

So, according to this view, love is at first freely directed towards a range of different objects, or people, and then afterwards, social restrictions and taboos enter in, banning some objects, sometimes inflicting punishments – and to a greater or lesser extent changing the direction of the desire. So that sometimes you desire not to desire what you desire.

The homosocial

The word 'homosocial' denotes social bonds between people of the same sex; the word is formed in analogy with the word 'homosexual' but is intended as separate from it. It is used in connection with 'male bonding', which may be characterized by intense homophobia in our society. Eve Kosovsky Sedgwick argues that it is a continuum; the homosocial is linked with desire, it is potentially erotic, although for men in our society, far less so for women, there is a radical break in the visibility of this continuity. She wrote that:

> much of the most useful recent writing about patriarchal structures suggests that 'obligatory heterosexuality' is built into male-dominated kinship systems, or that homophobia is a necessary consequence of such patriarchal institutions as heterosexual marriage. […] From the vantage point of our own society, at any rate, it has apparently been impossible to imagine a form of patriarchy that was not homophobic.
>
> (Sedgwick, 1985/2016, p.3)

Daniel Paul Schreber's *Memoirs* were published in 1903; they later attracted Freud's attention, leading to his case study on paranoia from 1911. Homosexual desire and homophobia play a central part in Schreber's nervous illness. Judge Schreber woke up one morning with the thought that it would be pleasant to 'succumb' to sexual intercourse as a woman. He was alarmed and felt that this thought had come from somewhere else, from a doctor who had experimented with hypnosis on him, and had telepathically invaded his mind. He believed his primary psychiatrist, Professor Paul Flechsig, had contact with him using a 'nerve-language' of which humans are unaware. The case story forms the basis for Freud's formulations on paranoia as contradictions of a proposition, "I, Schreber, a man, love him, Flechsig, a man". This is turned into, "I do not love him, I hate him – because he persecutes me" (Freud, 1911, p.63). Adding the part about persecution is necessary because the mode of symptom-formation in paranoia requires that internal perceptions – feelings – be replaced by external perceptions.

Expanding upon Freud's thesis, Sedgwick argued that in nineteenth-century bourgeois society the normal patterns and procedures of male entitlement demand a high degree of homosocial desire from men that can only be distinguished from homosexuality by means of arbitrary and inconsistent cultural mappings. Thus the powerful homosocial elite Judge Schreber was part of would also have exposed him to the permanent threat of homosexual panic. As Eric L. Santner points out in his exploration of the case:

If such compulsory relationships as male friendship, mentorship, admiring identification, bureaucratic subordination, and heterosexual rivalry all involve forms of investment that force men into the arbitrarily mapped, self-contradictory [...] quicksands of male homosocial desire, then it appears that men enter into adult masculine entitlement only through acceding to the permanent threat that the small space they have cleared for themselves [...] be foreclosed.

(Santner, 1996, p.55).

War, battle, killing

In the first quote from Nordfront I referred to, it is hinted that the authors see themselves as descendants of Tyr. This idea is again linked with the theme of battle and an idea of 'race'. Life, it is claimed, depends on battle; it is under threat and needs to be secured, while the colour black is assigned a symbolic value as hardness, 'structure, order and discipline', or stiffness and rigidity. These qualities appear to be necessary for tackling the task at hand, probably to do with survival, a survival which is experienced as being threatened. It also echoes the idea from Nazi Germany of the soldier as the representative of true masculinity. To the Nazi regime, male bonding was considered to be the foundation of the state, and the idea of the *Männerbund* (male collective) was heavily promoted (Oosterhuis, 1991).

In Klaus Theweleit's study of the fantasies of the *Freikorps* soldiers through their own writings, the author argues that these men emerged incompletely individuated from the militarized institutions of late-nineteenth-century imperial Germany. Thus they approached what they perceived as threats to the integrity of both their nation and their bodies with a thoroughly disciplined annihilating violence. The Freikorps units were paramilitary groups composed of World War I veterans who fought against the newly formed Weimar Republic between 1918 and 1923. They managed to survive the relatively warless years between 1923 and 1933, becoming the core of Hitler's Sturmabteilung (SA) and, in several cases, going on to become key functionaries in the Third Reich. Their letters and writings express their love for horses, guns, hunting, shooting, their native villages, homeland soil, the German people and other men – especially other soldiers (Theweleit, 1987, pp.60–62).

These soldiers were afraid of and deeply hostile to women, and split them into two categories, 'red' and 'white'. The White woman was the nurse, the mother, the sister, virtuous, distantly supportive, asexual, physically unavailable and non-threatening. The Red woman, on the other hand, was a whore and a Communist, threatening, erotic, sexually promiscuous and potentially castrating. She threatened to engulf the male in a whirlpool of bodily and emotional ecstasy. This was the woman that the Freikorps soldier wished to kill, because she endangered his identity, his sense of self as a fixed and bounded being. Theweleit examines two distinctive elements in the fascist imagination, liquidity and dirt, and argues that aquatic and other liquid metaphors were associated in the minds of these soldiers with the loss of a firm sense of identity. Their literature speaks of Communism as a flood, a stream, or a kind of boiling or exploding of the earth – images associated with sexuality. Similarly, he argues that the idea of dirt terrified the Freikorps soldiers because it also was linked in their minds to the loss of self and to bodily pleasure. The connection is clearest when the metaphors of liquidity and filth are combined, as in such notions as mire, morass, slime and excrement. Theweleit shows how the anti-Communist rhetoric of the Freikorps soldiers was systematically informed by such metaphors, and he makes a plausible case for linking this political sentiment to their fear of sexuality.

Recent empirical studies support the psychoanalytic assumption that homophobia is more marked in people who have a suppressed attraction to people of the same sex and who grew up with authoritarian parents who banned such desire. These people would have identified as heterosexual, though psychological tests showed that they were strongly attracted to people of their own sex. They feel threatened by lesbian and gay people because they remind them of similar tendencies within themselves.

"In many cases these people are at war with themselves, and they turn this war outwards", states one of the researchers, Richard Ryan (ScienceDaily, 2012, Weinstein et al., 2012). In connection with the documentary *Licenced to Kill* (an episode of the PBS series *Point of View*, 1998) containing interviews of men who have killed gay men, Donald Moss describes how each of these men refer to an experience of rage before the killings. Without exception the rage is explained as a reaction to someone's assumption that the killer may be open to homosexual activity (Moss, 2002, p.31).

The Nordic Resistance Movement is explicit in its threats to kill homosexuals. They compare homosexuals (probably in so far as they are in the closet) with drug addicts, and what they call the gay sex lobby (presumably everyone who is out of the closet) with drug dealers (someone who sells something that is tempting and hard to resist), and they threaten to kill the latter. An article on their homepage presents their view. It is worth presenting a close reading of these particular passages:

> The fact that the gay lobby's propaganda leads to an increase in the number of people who confess to deviant sexual norms is as given as the fact that more people who carry genes for substance abuse will succumb to abuse if they are exposed to considerable influence to start using drugs.
>
> Whether it is a matter of brainwashing or food poisoning, it is of course a pity for these people who cannot live a life in their natural inborn gender roles. In our future national socialist state, we plan to take care even of the weak and at risk in society. Thus we do not direct any hatred or resentment against gays, just like we don't direct our hatred towards a person who is stuck in substance abuse.

To the contrary, a drug dealer who has supplied the abuser with the addictive poison from the beginning shall of course be punished harshly, in severe cases by death. This is where the gay sex lobby comes into the picture, since just like the drug dealer, they destroy people's lives through spreading their poison.

(Nordfront, 2016, my translation).

The 'structure, order and discipline' evoked by the use of the symbol of the Tyr rune is needed as a barrier against the frivolous desire which is repressed, and which is re-encountered in women or femininity, in gay people and in representatives of other 'races'. As against these forces, there is an appeal to a sense of community, a homogenous community of those who represent the same:

In the Resistance movement, we gather the people to fight against the insanity, and among us you will be welcomed rather than branded when you react against the fact that the town priest, police officer or local politician demonstrate against you and your family together with naked sexual minorities, or when you protest against your daughter being taught in pre-school that it is good that she strokes herself or that you son is encouraged to play with Barbie dolls.

(Nordfront, 2016, my translation)

The so-called gay lobby is then linked to an antisemitic conspiracy theory:

After 1945, the Jews have been the system's holy and unassailable 'cow'. More Jews have been very quick, as opposed to other minority groups, to scream very loudly at the least sign of attack in their direction. […] Perhaps that is why it is not so surprising that the gay lobby was founded by a Jew and has been pushed forward by Zionist organisations ever since, as a conscious part of a fight to neglect the Nordic people?!

(Nordfront, 2016, my translation)

Sander Gilman's historical writings offer a source for the links that are made here between Jews, crime, insanity and hyper-sexuality: the medical literature of the *fin de siècle*. Here, Jewish men were stereotyped as feminine, and parallels were drawn between the body of the woman and the body of the Jewish man. The fantasy of male circumcision as castration links the ideas of women and Jews as both being castrated, and the clitoris was known in Viennese slang at the time as 'the Jew'. The Aryan male represented the healthy, normal baseline, compared to which both the Jewish male and the woman were linked with disease, both physical and mental (Gilman, 1993a, pp.38–40). The idea of feminization as degeneration formed a fantasy about the entire body, including the voice. Both Jewish men and homosexual men were stereotyped as speaking in a high-pitched voice, which reflected their essence as being ill or degenerate (Gilman, 1993a, pp.163–165).

The image of the hypersexual male Jew seducing young Christian women was the central theme of one of the best-selling antisemitic novels of the early twentieth century, Artur Dinter's *Sin Against the Blood* (1918), where the main character is out to seduce blond Aryan women in order to corrupt the Aryan race (1993b, p.191). One of the most successful Nazi propaganda films, *Jüd Süss*, was based on the same theme. The black man has often been cast in this same part, and in contemporary far-right propaganda the Muslim man is assigned with this stereotype.

In emphasizing these connections between prejudices, I do not wish to argue that one of them is deeper than the other, or that one of them causes the other. The fact that this chapter focuses mostly on homophobia, and to some extent sexism, should not be taken to mean that these are somehow more original than or prior to racism, antisemitism or islamophobia. Rather, my point is to examine how they are both structurally similar and interconnected (see also Auestad, 2015). And, as I have implied, there is something more going on in the more violent and extreme cases.

Masculinity and desire

Theweleit reflects, after having described the things the Freikorps-men do love, such as guns, horses and the fatherland:

> The only human objects appearing here are men and male organizations. It would be possible to draw the conclusion that something like homosexual libido must be in play here. If however I do not draw that conclusion, then this is because it seems to me that the general difficulty of establishing any object relations is such a dominant theme in the material dealt with so far, that the whole matter first requires closer inspection.
>
> (Theweleit, 1987, p.61)

To my mind, what clearly goes beyond desire and the blocking of desire in such violent cases is the sense that one's identity is threated – that the other, who can be a range of different others, represents a threat to being who one is. A social unit which is seen as being the same as oneself, is then needed to support one's identity, which is very fragile.

Here, one's own desire, which has become something alien, is placed in a series of 'strangers' where it can be fought in a violent way, and the community serves as a protection against these others. Donald Moss describes a male homosocial desire that must be shielded from, protected against open homosexual desire in order to function. As Moss illustrates by means of an account from the first year of analysis of Mr. A, a heterosexual man:

> Masculinity felt like an attribute he was missing. It therefore had to be found in other men, then cultivated, and finally internalized. Mr. A thus yearned to be with the kind of men who could provide him with the masculinity he

craved. Joined with them, feeling himself at one with them, he could almost identify with them, thus partaking in a masculinity that he sensed was originally theirs.

(Moss, 2002, p.48)

A hallmark of the masculinity sought by Mr. A was a complete absence of any sign of homoerotic desire. The man Mr. A wanted to be in fantasy was a man who desired only to be with women. For Mr. A, any sign of a desire for what a man already had was a sign that one was not already a man, and therefore an indication of potential femininity. The intense desire to become a man through being with men, even when satisfied, thus invalidated the very masculinity that it might achieve. Mr. A could not tolerate being a man because this experience was inevitably infiltrated with a simultaneous experience of wanting to be a man. In the first person singular voice, such wanting was too close to wanting to be with a man. That voice was transformed, then, into its plural form: "Men like us, who desire nothing from each other, hate men like them, who desire everything from each other" (Moss, 2002, p.48).

In Moss' words:

The force of internalized homophobia's first person plural voice stems from its promise of safety and power. The normatively freighted plurality *we* identifies the individual as a member of a strong, masculine collective. The first person plural voice in men thus simultaneously satisfies homoerotic yearning and protects against it; it forbids union between men while promising solidarity amongst men.

(Moss, 2002, p.49)

The imagined homogenous 'we' protects against the 'I's fluctuating desire. The doubt and multiplicity of the subjective viewpoint is replaced with the quasi-objective conviction of the 'we'. The collective ban keeps the singular person's desire in check and identifies it as belonging to 'others', whose presence upsets the fragile balance. The promise of power and security is linked with a constellation which kills.

There are few accurate records of anti-gay violence in Norway and Sweden. According to the historian of ideas Magnus Eriksson in a report published by the charity The Norwegian Centre Against Racism (2018, p.46), these hate crimes were not registered as such in Norway until 2006, although at least ten people have been murdered since the 1990s. Swedish LGBT papers criticize the police for their unwillingness to protect gay people from Nazi violence. In the same report, Helene Lööw stated that the reports were characterized by a lack of willingness to handle homophobia as part of the Nazi and racist ideology (Eriksson, 2018, p.48). More than twenty gay people have been murdered by Nazis, and many more brutally tortured in Sweden between 1983 and 2000. In connection with such a brutal attack and near-murder, Kim Fredriksson described how the neo-Nazi use of violence is a consciously chosen political strategy, designed to frighten their opponents (Eriksson, 2018, pp.96–97). This violence carries over into arguments to the effect that 'If we don't get to speak, we will be violent', a reasoning which is echoed by the mainstream, and which increases their influence. The freedom that is claimed is the freedom of the 'I' made 'we', for a view according to which no others exist, or if they do, they must be eliminated. Thus, I close on pointing to the dangers of the social support for this violent stance, of symbolic followed by physical elimination of the 'other'. As we saw in the beginning of this chapter, the Nazis were allowed to march through the small town of Kristiansand and spread their hateful and threatening message. The continued spread of far-right hate speech has led to a normalization of racist, sexist and homophobic views, which has created a more threatening climate for many of our fellow citizens, and has, arguably, led to further episodes of violence. Rather than expressing just another political view, their stance aims at making life fundamentally unsafe for a range of people defined as 'others'. Thus we need to work to ensure a public space which is safe for all.

References

Auestad, L., 2014, 'Idealised sameness and orchestrated hatred: Extreme and mainstream nationalism in Norway'. In: L. Auestad (ed.) *Nationalism and the Body Politic: Psychoanalysis and the Rise of Ethnocentrism and Xenophobia*, London: Karnac Books Ltd.

Auestad, L., 2015, *Respect, Plurality, and Prejudice. A Psychoanalytical and Philosophical Enquiry into the Dynamics of Social Exclusion and Discrimination*, London: Karnac Books Ltd.

Auestad, L., 2017, 'Nazister beskyttet, motstanden forhindret – hva står politiet for?' *Radikal Portal*. https://radikalportal.no/2017/07/30/nazister-beskyttet-motstanden-forh indret-hva-star-politiet-for/ (Accessed 22 September 2019).

Borchgrevink, A. S., 2013, *A Norwegian Tragedy. Anders Behring Brevik and the Road to Utoya*, Malden, MA: Polity Press.

Encyclopædia Britannica, n.d., 'Runic alphabet'. https://www.britannica.com/topic/ru nic-alphabet (Accessed 12 February 2020).

Encyclopædia Britannica, n.d., 'Tyr'. https://www.britannica.com/topic/Tyr (Accessed 17th October 2019).

Eriksson, J. M., 2018, 'Nordiske motstandsbevegelsen – forestillingen om en homolobby'. *Antirasistisk Senter*. http://antirasistisk.no/wp-content/uploads/2019/02/Forestillingen -om-en-homolobby.pdf (Accessed 24 September 2019).

'Expo symbollexikon, entry: Tyrrunan, updated November 17th 2017'. https://expo.se/fakt a/symbollexikon/tyrrunan (Accessed 23 September 2019).

Freud, S., 1905, 'Three essays on the Theory of Sexuality'. In: J. Strachey (ed.) *The Standard Edition of the Complete Psychological Works of Sigmund Freud*, Volume 7, London: Vintage Books, pp. 123–245.

Freud, S., 1911, 'Psycho-Analytic Notes on an Autobiographical Account of a Case of Paranoia (Dementia Paranoides)'. In: J. Strachey (ed.) *The Standard Edition of the*

Complete Psychological Works of Sigmund Freud, Volume 7, Volume 12, London: Vintage Books, pp. 1–82.

Gilman, S., 1993a, *Freud, Race, and Gender*, Princeton, NJ: Princeton University Press.

Gilman, S., 1993b, *The Case of Sigmund Freud. Medicine and Identity at the Fin de Siècle*, London and Baltimore, MD: Johns Hopkins University Press.

Nordfront, 2016, 'Nordiska motståndsrörelsen – den sista utposten i kampen mot homolobbyn'. *Nordfront*, https://web.archive.org/save/https://www.nordfront.se/nor diska-motstandsrorelsen-den-sista-utposten-kampen-mot-homolobbyn.smr (Accessed 13 November 2019).

Moss, D., 2002, 'Internalized homophobia in men: Wanting in the first person singular, hating in the first person plural'. *Psychoanalytic Quarterly*, LXXI(1), pp. 21–60.

Nordfront, 2015, 'Motståndsrörelsen lanserar symbolen för den parlamentariska grenen'. https://web.archive.org/save/https://www.nordfront.se/symbolen-for-den-parlamentar iska-grenen.smr (Accessed 13 November 2019).

Oosterhuis, H., 1991, 'Male bonding and the persecution of homosexual men in Nazi Germany'. *Amsterdams Sociologish Tijdschrift*, 17(4). https://ugp.rug.nl/ast/article/ view/23494 (Accessed 17 October 2019).

Santner, E. L., 1996, *My Own Private Germany. Daniel Paul Schreber's Secret History of Modernity*, Princeton, NJ: Princeton University Press.

ScienceDaily, 2012, 'Is some homophobia self-phobia?' https://www.sciencedaily.com/r eleases/2012/04/120406234458.htm (Accessed 23 September 2019).

Sedgwick, E. K., 1985/2016, *Between Men. English Literature and Male Homosocial Desire*, New York: Columbia University Press.

Theweleit, K., 1987, *Male Fantasies: Women, Floods, Bodies, History*, Cambridge: Polity Press.

Weinstein, N.; Ryan, W. S.; DeHaan, C. R.; Przybylski, A. K.; Legate, N.; Ryan, R. M., 2012, 'Parental autonomy support and discrepancies between implicit and explicit sexual identities: Dynamics of self-acceptance and defense'. *Journal of Personality and Social Psychology*, 102(4), pp. 815–832.

Young-Bruehl, E., 1996, *The Anatomy of Prejudices*, Cambridge, MA: Harvard University Press.

Chapter 5

Gender difference

Real or fake news?

Phil Goss

Is the idea of gender difference fake news? Or might the word 'news', with its implication of 'being new' or of contemporary relevance, not quite capture it? Rather, is the premise of gender difference an obsolete story, a fantasy thoroughly sustained by the smoke and mirrors of patriarchy – still casting its spell on us, in order to sustain structures, which protect male power and maintain unhelpful role expectations and patterns of relating between men and women?

At times, and not least within the context of the escalating momentum surrounding the increasing fluidity of gendered being, where transgendered and non-binary and gender fluid self-identification becomes more and more a common feature of the personal and social landscape, it can feel as if the idea of gender difference barely belongs, and instead represents a mind-set which is clinging to it as a way of reaching out for certainty and order in a world where all in regard to gender and sexuality is loosened, and up for grabs. There are many strong arguments for concluding that debates about whether women and men are really different merely sustain unhelpful illusions (e.g. Butler, 1990, Connel, 2002, Rippon, 2019); repeating patterns of socially constructed splits, based around patriarchal tropes about male and female roles and ways of being.

However, I want to argue that gender difference is still with us – not just as a social construction (which for sure it is and in highly influential ways). I am interested in the proposal there are deeper unconscious processes at work which mean gender differences retain a legitimate if rather inscrutable influence. Recognising this influence, I believe, is fundamental to enabling us to work towards a kind of settlement in this contentious area of human being and relating. I will also argue in this chapter, that we need to look closer, in support of arriving at such a working settlement around gender and power, at what the investment in either downplaying the significance of gender difference on the one hand, or advocating for it on the other, may be about. Why does it matter to us, and are there ways in which aspects of the Feminist project, as well as post-modern forays into gender politics and narratives, over-rely to some degree on the idea of gender difference as being irrelevant and unhelpful? If there is any mileage in this observation, then there may be something of real value in the debates about gender relations which is being overlooked. I will consider the phenomenology of gendered experiencing and its importance for identity formation. This includes self-identity as a forma-tive aspect of a person's self-concept (what 'I' identify myself as gender-wise), as well as 'self-to-other' identity (i.e. what 'your' gendered identity might mean to 'me' and vice versa). This is posited as fundamentally significant whether situated in conventional/fixed gender identities or more fluid ones, with a focus on early developmental and psychosexual dynamics which can play out in many forms. These, I argue, can invert the undoubted social, political and, in some forms, familial domination by patriarchal codes of male – female relational/social trans-actions (to stick with a heteronormative frame of reference at this stage).

Here, certain conscious and unconscious modes of thinking and emotional transaction lend a different kind of tone and possibly power dynamic to aspects of female/male relations where women may have more power than men. I am aware of the polemical risk in suggesting this point as possibly a perspective which does not sit well with some Feminist orthodoxies, however, there is no reason why this idea has to be precluded and I will revisit this point in querying our investments in positions in gender politics, which may not always promote receptivity to dif-fering ideas about male – female relations.

This exploration is contextualised within the contemporary influence of the identification, and appropriation, of a multiplicity of sexualities and gendered identities in the Westernised world. Here a long continuum of possible identities stretches between the weathered book ends of 'male' and 'female' at either end of the contemporary 'gender shelf'. Could this burgeoning purely reinforce the point-lessness of holding to fixed 'distinctions' between women and men? Or, could this freeing up of self-identified ways of gendered-sexual being help us get closer to what is distinctive about being female or male (and 'being heterosexual')?

The politics of gender is another key influence, especially considering what groups within society may have an investment in maintaining clear demarcations around fixed gender difference, as against those for whom more fluid and neu-tral versions of gender portrayals may support their agenda or position. This has relevance to the development of Feminism and its various forms (Walter, 2005) which are unarguably vital for the full establishment of gender equality, espe-cially in terms of the de-objectification of women, the dismantling of stereotypes (and their consequent injustices) and reviving of human potential in all arenas – work and home, public and private.

On the other hand – as with any body of thought or social movement – Feminism will carry its own *shadow* side, as *shadow* is an archetypal psychic phenomenon which extends back and forth between the personal and the collec-tive and seeps into all human thought and activity (Jung, 1968a). So how might Feminism's shadow inadvertently impact on gender relations and debate? This is a difficult question to confidently address, particularly by a man (and one who is middle-aged, white and middle class at that). Nevertheless, taking my courage in my hands I see this as something worth bringing some criticality to, if only to offer a useful counterpoint through which to see some positions on the gender sameness vs. difference debate.

Both influences help us closer to a clearer ('truer'?) picture about whether gender difference exists beyond being a hackneyed (possibly oppressive) social construct and what the ongoing debates about this tell us about why this question can seem to matter so much. But before situating the 'real' or 'fake' question within these contexts, I want to revisit the schemas and developmental model on gendered development I proposed in earlier writings (see Goss, 2010), in order to update my arguments on why gender difference may have at least *some* importantly real dimensions (where 'real' refers to consistently evident in lived experience). I previously argued possible differences in such areas have their roots in developmental and psychosexual aspects of 'gendered maturation'. Here, my thinking was and remains influenced by some clinically informed writers (e.g. Benjamin, Kristeva), and developments beyond Jung's awkward thinking on contra-sexual influences, to imply a subtle but profound set of distinctions between patterns of female and male development as they unfold across the lifespan. This as I have argued may show itself in areas of human experiencing, and even behaviours, where maleness and femaleness may carry broadly different patterns around *identification, continuity in time and space, the erotic* and, *felt expression.* This chapter picks up on my argument that there remains much we do not understand about gender identity formation, and yet many public (and private) debates get charged with an unhelpful certitude not conducive to fuller understanding, or happy patterns of gendered relating. In this light, the question of whether Feminism needs, or sees itself as needing, to rely on 'debunking gender difference' to make further inroads into gender inequality will be queried.

The psychosexual aspects of 'gendered development' and maturation

The key arguments within psychoanalytic/object relations/Jungian thinking about the significance or otherwise of key developmental and psychological differences between females and males are, like all lines of thought in this area, fraught with the risk of over-generalisation and the foisting of conscious and unconscious agendas on assertions about gender. Freud's theorising (2011) about the primacy of the phallus implies a degree of lack in the female experience (while the phallus takes a more general and symbolic form for Lacan, 1977). Fundamental differences between male and female infantile development for Freud, as focused on the desired 'other' of the opposite sex parent, set a tone which was root and branch in its influence on theory and practice in an era where gender difference was barely questioned as a key familial and social influence. Jung meanwhile held firmly to this 'given' while asserting that gendered influence should also be seen in terms of internal archetypal influences which represented the 'gendered other' within us (*anima* as contra-sexual 'other' in every man and *animus* as contra-sexual 'other' in all women (Jung, 1968b, p.13ff)). He notoriously conflated male/female with *anima/animus*, with his unpalatable descriptions of features of *animus.* Nevertheless, his creative deployment of the importance of the *feminine-masculine* dyad offers valuable tools for 'playing with gender' which I will come back to in this discussion.

Developments post-Jung (e.g. Emma Jung, 1985 and Sanford, 1980) included considered, if at times uneasy, attempts to accommodate the problem of whether sexed gender difference between men and women can be equated with generalised personality traits as originally posited. Examples include where the male *anima* took a negative form which was characterised as 'overly sentimental', and more controversially where a woman's *animus* supposedly generated an overly rigid and opinionated line of thinking (Jung, 1968b, p.16).

However, thinking developed beyond these approaches (e.g. Samuels, 1993, and Hauke, 2000) which re-situated the notion of gender and gender difference in terms of the importance of recognising the plurality and individuality of human beings and how it may be mistaken to ascribe distinctive characteristics between men and women. Rather, the psychological significance of 'otherness' in identity formation and social discourse has been emphasised, not least in how 'the feminine' comes to parallel and even represent the unconscious 'other' in conventional patriarchal frameworks. The latter are seen as socially constructed in their overt influence on gender relations and reflect a tendency for unconscious splitting.

In my own theorising about gender, my interest has mainly lain in the traditional bifurcation between male and female and what may have influenced and sustained this foundational feature of the ordering of societies around the world (although not in all of course). Behind this pervasive male–female, heterosexual, settlement lies the question of whether sexed difference between boys/men and girls/women has a *developmental* as well as bodily based, genetic root. In other words, is the way males and females turn out (usually) to seem different, more than a social construction? Is there something at work which goes much deeper and evinces the identity of 'female' or 'male' from sources within the building blocks of who we are which are more visceral and unconscious? Could these be authentically aligned to the nature and evolutionary purpose of the organism in the context of the primary object relationship, as distinct from only being introjected and projected (although it goes without saying the two aspects overlap)?

My position remains that within the obfuscation of social construction of gender which corals us into 'being a boy or girl' (as we move through the supremely influential early phases of socialisation and identity formation) there are some very important areas of influence which go deep and root us in gendered being. I write this with the equally important caveat that gender can be fluid as well as fixed; we can be born into a male body and feel overwhelmingly female (or vice versa), or we can notice over time our felt and sensed identity being shaped by both male and female influences. There are further factors such as the intersex presence of discrepancy between internal and external genitalia, and other biopsychological influences which lend a proper uncertainty to the quest for the supposed 'certainty' of gender difference.

However, it is important, in true Jungian style, to value how *the opposite is always present*. Where there is uncertainty, 'certainties' may well be present, in the same way certainty easily turns into uncertainty once one interrogates a particular standpoint, or 'fact' proclaiming itself too loudly. The value of applying Jung's adoption of Heraclitus's concept of *enantodromia* (Kahn, 1979) to the area of gender is that it asks us to consider, and regularly monitor, whether the position we take on it is a living one or whether it has become fixed within traditional, *or,* contemporary social norms or ideological priorities.

Holding open the possibilities here, I want to briefly itemise the arguments for a fundamental root beneath distinctions between male and female, as based in psychodynamic thinking on models of early development (and it may be worth mentioning most of the theorists I draw on are female, rather than a fundamentally male lens being applied). The approach I take tries to reconcile the influence of identificatory processes in childhood (from same or opposite parent identification via oedipal dynamics, through to societal installation and reinforcement of gender stereotypes), with bodily based psychosexual tendencies which usually differ between infant boys and girls, and intersects with an erotic–relational continuum for establishing sexed gender identity.

So usually, for infant girls, a powerful identification with mother (which plays into the development of a mothering capacity (Chodorow, 1978)) works alongside unconscious oedipal solidarity with mother to hold the taboo intact in relation to father (Falzeder, 2002), deeply underpinned by a pre-verbal relational and erotic 'bi-'connection established with mother (Kristeva, 2004) which deeply embeds the identity of the girl in her 'femaleness' and gives her sexed gender identity a body – mind installation which is in a sense 'hard-wired' and can be emmeshed with mother where the erotic and relational intersect.

It is important to qualify these observations by recognising variation: in perception of self and relation to others as the child emerges in their environment over time. To use Michael Fordham's concept (Astor, 1995), the infant unconsciously de-integrates (reaches out/unfolds, makes themselves available) towards the mother and then re-integrates (takes back in) a new or evolving version of self which is stamped unconsciously by a gendered identity. This of course comes – in a child's life experience anyway – some time before socialisation reinforces gendered identity, often in unhelpful ways. Although mother would be unconsciously transmitting some of this, it is not the foundation for what is a psychosexual and instinctual, not socially constructed, process.

To mirror this, but as distinct to it, maleness in infant boys is awakened via a dis-identification from mother (Benjamin, 1988), where the instinctual driver between son and mother is for the latter to love and nurture the boy but to psychologically push him out so that he can live out his bodily based difference to her and identify with father. As Kristeva argues (2004), for the infant boy the splitting of the relational from the erotic (Kristeva, 2004) in maternal connection is fundamental to identity formation, as is the oedipal taboo, conjoined with tendencies in mother to reinforce differentiation (Chodorow, 1978).

The implications of the above assertions, if valid, may be very significant in terms of formulating possible distinctions between female and male development, but I am nervous of over generalising or reifying causal arguments for gender difference. So, to say that, for example, because of this psychosexual framework, a girl may feel a deeper draw to 'being mother' later in life, as more than a socialising message, or a boy may have a tendency to be less naturally au fait with intimacy and will feel motivated to adopt a persona which is 'hard', can become sweeping generalisation. Nevertheless, I suggest it unwise within a post-modern, diversity inspired, contemporary context to throw out bifurcated models of gendered development with the pre-modern and modern bathwater just because they seem to reinforce old stereotypes or role assignations. These patterns I propose go clearly deeper than a purely plastic set of styles of living and behaving, imposed upon women and men by society/patriarchy etc which they have gone on to unconsciously reinforce and replicate to render their relationships layered by caricature.

In my own play with this problematic I have previously proposed Jung's initial (1968b) contra-sexual frame of reference for understanding inner influences on women and men has something helpful (and acceptable) to offer if we see *anima* and *animus* as energic influences of 'otherness', combining this idea with Freud's (1990) emphasis on *Eros* and *Thanatos* as life giving or deathly unconscious influences on the human psyche. Thus, *Eros with animus* (*Erosimus*) comes to describe a woman's masculine aspects charged with erotic, relational energy, and *Thanatos* combined with *anima* reflects where a man's feminine aspects have been infused with deathly (depressed?) or destructive energies. This model allows a fluidity and flexibility around gendered development, while positing there is a generally pervasive (but certainly not ubiquitous) fork in the road which unconsciously generates these subtly differing ways of being between female and male as these aspects interplay with the early developmental influences described above.

In this regard, I posit that although there is fundamental commonality and overlap between how women and men think, feel and intuit there are also ways in which there may be variation – nuanced, subtle, but still having an effect of lived experience and relationships. For boys and then men I have suggested before a generally greater vulnerability to a sense of discontinuity in time and space (interruptions or deadening of being in a stable sense of self, and relation to a significant other) may be one such subtle influence due to the unconscious influence of the early break in identification with mother. For girls and then women the *Thanatos* influence could take the form of a depressing feeling of insignificance in relation to others, something which may reflect the early immersion in mother. These observations are speculative but do speak to clinical experience of working with clients who I have experienced as deadened in affect and/or struggling to locate themselves in relationship and to their 'sequential' place in life, whatever age they may be. I do sense a nuanced difference in quality/tone of these difficulties between men and women, though this may be influenced by my projections and must be open to critical challenge.

The idea that mothers may consciously or unconsciously reinforce identity differentiation in their relationship with sons is also open to challenge as a

generalisation which covers too many different individual nuances of early relational dynamics to be ubiquitous. However, the idea there might be a tendency
for mothers to psychologically 'push out' their sons into the world, is one worth
holding onto in helping to make sense of what can happen in male – female relationships later in life. This idea, based on clinical theory and insights, carries the
connotation that this tendency is instigated as a paradoxical part of the holding
dynamic of mother-son relations in the face of the incest taboo, and because of
mother's instinctively based intuition her male child may need to experience his
biological and relational 'otherness' to her, to healthily form his sense of (gendered?) identity.

Relating this idea to patterns of social operation, leads to thoughts about the
world of work where historically in some respects at least, men have been pushed
into roles in life which are 'out there' in the world rather than 'in here' (i.e. at, or
close to, home). Of course, one could read what has happened as something about
patriarchal entitlement, even greed, and that men have taken roles which carry
financial reward and status. This view is often posited within Feminist literature
(see Hawkesworth, 2019), and I for one am not going to disagree with the truth
in this. However, I also want to argue that alongside the 'man-grab' of status,
money and power, there is also a 'man-pushed' dynamic in how aspects of social/
employment and other role assignment take place; roles which can carry privilege
but also demands, risks and constraint to self-expression.

Perhaps the most historically prevalent example of this – though it is starting to
change, with more women coming to serve in more frontline roles – can be found
in the theatres of war where men have been regarded as the ones who fight (and
sometimes die) 'there' on the battlefield in order to protect the women and children in the 'here' of the home). In this way warfare in many parts of the world has
historically been hallmarked not just as male, and a masculine proving and killing
ground, but also by a female/feminine 'pushing out' into that theatre. This comes
with a deep fear of what might happen to their loved ones, but also an expectation
of heroism in defence of national and familial security, as well as the values associated with them. This aspect is captured in the lyrics of a song *The Women were
Watching* (Phillips and Scott, 1983) which describes the dynamics in a scene from
a news video of the British Royal Naval fleet setting off from Portsmouth harbour
on the south coast of England for the Falkland Islands in June 1982, to do battle
with the Argentine fleet in the South Atlantic:

> And though it was no-one's fault
> That men went off to war I saw a thousand faces all along the shore …
> The women were watching
> So no-one thought of turning back.

In striving to avoid both over-simplification and an exclusive emphasis on tra-
ditional/heteronormative ideas about gender identity formation it is important to
situate this example and other possible portrayals of gendered dynamics within

the context of contemporary psycho-social developments. The powerful influence of Feminism, alongside other social developments and emerging ways of thinking about gender and sexuality demand that we broaden and deepen the scope of this discussion. The burgeoning range of gendered identities (including transgender, non-binary and gender fluid) and sexual assignations and preferences (within and beyond the LGBTQ continuum to include, for example, polyamory) clearly shifts the ground around heteronormativity. In sexual and gender relations, nuanced expression of individual identity is emerging as a 'new norm' rather than the collective lumping together of male and female as an exclusive dyad which describes who we can be.

The power and the glory – the question of authority in gender relations

In Chaucer's fourteenth-century comedy *The Canterbury Tales* (2007), the Wife of Bath tells a tale which illuminates medieval ideas about female-male relations: a knight is given the challenge, on pain of death, of discovering, and reporting back to the royal court, on what women desire most. This is because he has been found guilty of raping a woman – a ghastly backdrop to the story which has disturbing currency. After being given a confusing range of female opinions on this, from 'pleasure' to 'money' to 'a good name', he stumbles upon an old crone who agrees to tell him the true answer if he agrees to marry her. The answer she whispers to him is 'authority over men'.

When he reports this, he is spared execution as the queen confirms it is the right answer. So, relieved but having no choice but to go along with marriage against his wishes, the old woman asks him whether he could choose between accepting having an old unattractive wife offering fidelity to him as against an unfaithful, beautiful, young woman who will she says be pursued by all the men in the kingdom. The reluctant new husband pauses and asks his wife if she would make this decision for him. At this crucial handing over of authority to the woman she tells him because of this she will transform into a beautiful young woman who will be thoroughly loyal to him. This happens and they live happily to the end of their days.

So, what does this old tale tell us about perceptions and location of authority in male–female relations? Applying a classical contra-sexual approach, we can play with the juxtaposition of *anima* and *animus* as projections of authority between men and women, via of course the *anima* of the male author, Geoffrey Chaucer. In the story, the figure of the old woman or 'crone' can be seen as a shadowy but positive anima figure in the knight's psyche – challenging him to find a relationship to his *anima* which accepts the value of stability in relationships and the healthy channelling of *eros* (or *erosima*) within this frame of reference, rather than the objectification (and abuse) of women, where his *anima* is also used as an object to get gratification for himself. On the other hand, where the knight is seen as the *animus* of the old woman, he becomes a route for her to fulfil a guiding power over a man.

Here, it gets more controversial, as her disclosure that it is 'authority over men' which women most desire could be seen as a projection of the author's (Chaucer) male wish to dominate women or an expression of a kind of fear of women's power *or* as suggesting this really *is* what medieval women wanted in their domestic relations.

It is likely the real picture is a mix of all these. Strikingly, we do seem to see in this tale the presence of a medieval view of women which some men at least still have in the twenty-first century (and which *may* have a subtle influence in it from the relational power dynamic with mother in infancy). Here women are both feared as wanting power and authority over them, especially in close hetero-sexual relationships, but as in the story, there is also a search for the man to find the right relation to women's power. This struggle is also reflected in a comedic portrayal of women attaining totalitarian political power in the United Kingdom in a series of sketches in the popular show *The Two Ronnies* (BBC, 1971–1987), titled *The Worm that Turned*, which aired in 1980 (see nymphofwater, 2011, for *YouTube* availability), and where male fear of women mistreating *them* as they have mistreated women for centuries is the central theme. It is also notable that the two male originators of the series may also reveal a common male projection of a fear of *anima's* power. There is also a sexualised warping of this power issue seen in how some men sexually and dangerously objectify women, reflecting the awful sexual crime committed by the knight at the outset of the Chaucer story. This could not be more outrageously portrayed – even if for comedic effect – than in the faux-military garb the women police are dressed up in by the male writers, complete with leather shorts and high heeled boots.

In turn, the combination of influences on male development reflects the pres-ence of a problematic erotic impetus in men which can get split off from a more holistic, relational, love in terms of a purely sexualised 'craving' which at times is acted out inappropriately, as if by a transgressive, dangerous sub-personality. This also gets conflated with unresolved hetero power relations to women. One can see traces or more of this in the sinister, un-boundaried and often illegal behaviours of men exposed by the 'MeToo' campaign (Beard, 2018).

It is possible to think of this developmentally in terms of a male split in their *anima* which emerges at the stage where mother and son part ways erotically/psychologically in the move from pre-oedipal to oedipal, so the boy then can find there are two ways to feel/sense about mother/girls/women – either as erotic objects where love/feeling is side-lined and deadened/killed off (*Thanatos* gener-ating *thanima*), or, as reliable love objects where *Eros* is primarily relational and meaningful (*Eros* generating *erosima*). It is also possible to see this problematic process in the familiar and helpful language of Klein (1946), that is the task of the male psyche, in response to the problematic separation from mother in early life is to move from a split *anima* position, where sexual *Eros* is separated from rela-tional *Eros* (cf. Klein's 'paranoid schizoid' position), to an acceptance that they cannot 'have' mother in both the sexually erotic as well as relationally intimate way – and more than this they have to accept how they are different from their mother, not just in terms of (usually) genitalia which looks different, but also in terms of a felt sense of needing to carve out a way of being themselves as 'not the same as mother' (cf. Klein's 'depressive' position) – a perhaps simplistic but clear way of defining what being male 'is'.

In this regard there may be a grain of truth in Chaucer's projection onto the old woman around authority: that is, boys/men may carry an imprint of this sense that women want authority over them from these crucial early developments in the relationship with mother, which may lead to problematic dynamics the other way around. I would also argue there may be something in the mother-daughter transmission of this dynamic that can sometimes get unconsciously acted out in domestic relations between women and men, where a woman may take certain types of power over a man in the home (I will come back to this in my conclusion).

Fluidity and diversity as the norm

The proposal that male and female really are different in some subtle forms, also recognises this can be more overt, especially around the conception and gestation, birth and early post-natal care of children, where differing biological impetuses in each come to the fore. It can be said fundamental instincts to be mother or father in heterosexual relationships are pretty much carved out by nature. However, there have been long-standing challenges to standard notions of motherhood from Feminist writers (see Delphy, 1992). Also, there are many ways individuals and couples can put their original stamp on the processes and experiences which surround it (in heterosexual and same sex relationships). Parental roles do not represent fixed instincts and behaviours. As Samuels rightly points out 'Maternity and Paternity have evolving histories' (2015, p.128).

In this respect, mentioning childbirth and 'roles' may be unhelpful – perhaps because it plays into the hands of traditional, conservative thinkers and denies the possibility of new and different ways of describing what gender identity and relations can 'look like' or 'be allowed to be'. However, I argue we need to be able to do *something* with this reality of bodily (and psychosexual) distinction between women and men, because it is real, and what are we saying if we marginalise its significance?

Such points all require continual reflection and revision as the world of gender identity extends – or rather the diversity which was always there but suppressed by social norms and the threat of stigma and punishment by the law, has lost its prohibitions and can now be made conscious and acceptable within twenty-first century cultural and social narratives. Furthermore, there is an established body of highly credible theorising about the fluid nature of sexuality and its embodiment (Hawksworth, ibid.). The notion of gender and gender difference in relation to bodily sex is more free-floating (or a matter of 'soft assembly' as Harris, 2004, puts it) and less binary in its provenance, not least because it is clear how problematic the effort to maintain a fixed view of gender and gender difference can be (see Butler, 1990).

So where might this leave the question of so-called 'gender difference' when sat alongside, or in some ways, in opposition to theories and research which purport to demonstrate differences between men and women as 'hard-wired' (see Baron-Cohen, 2004, Brizendine, 2007, Moir, 2009)? This body of research has been strongly critiqued as 'neuro-sexism' (Rippon, 2019, p.72) and undoubtedly has flaws. However, it is not in my view to be lightly dismissed because of unconscious bias in some places and nor because it does not accord with agendas which advocate a 'no-difference' stance. Instead, my approach to the validity of neuro-scientific 'evidence' and what it purports to demonstrate is to park it, as the jury will be out on it until we have more cast-iron and independent means to assess this properly.

If it is possible to think in terms of a continuum of gendered being, as contemporary developments would strongly propose, then does this not further water down the legitimacy and value of sticking with the idea of subtle but significant distinctions between femaleness and maleness? This is a complex question to do justice to within this chapter's confines so I will restrict myself to making a couple of points. Firstly, the recognition of patterns of being in boys/men as sometimes different to patterns of being in girls/women (in a generalised sense) does not preclude the possibility and reality of the presence of a whole range of gendered ways of being which straddles both traditional binary and non-traditional trans, fluid, queer or non-binary ways of gendered being, as routinely represented in communities of people, including in the consulting room (see Withers, 2015). Instead, an understanding of the shift from pre-oedipal states to oedipal ones allows for the recognition of the foundational reality of bisexuality in the human condition. The term operates in the context of early development as described by Benjamin, who said "By recapturing the bisexual identifications of the pre-oedipal position, we counterbalance the oedipal position of mutual exclusivity, in which we can only be like the one or the other" (1998, p.xvii).

'Bisexuality' is of course a term which also links to Jung's idea of the *syzygy* (1968b) as describing the idealised state of union, as well as continuum, between feminine and masculine, encompassing all possibilities. In this respect other terms such as 'pansexuality' and 'pangender' or 'gender fluid' may be more relevant here. In applying a psychoanalytic reading to gendered development and to cover all possibilities of gendered and sexual expression as emerging from a very early, pre-oedipal state, this speaks to the multiple possibilities of gender and sexual development. With the blending in of a contra-sexual component (*anima/animus* and charged with *Eros* energy) it becomes possible to imagine how the interplay of gendered 'otherness' within the infant can configure into a 'fit' with a binary position – either cisgender (feeling like one is the same gender as the physical body one is born with) or transgender; *or* how it may proliferate and manifest in non-binary, fluid ways. So, in loosely applying Jung's model for archetypal manifestation, gender can operate in a polarised way where it operates in terms of complementarity or opposition to the gendered 'other' (i.e. female or male) or it can be 'both' (non-binary), or at any point on a continuum of expression of identity, desire and relational mutuality or conflict. The point I am making in terms of whether gender difference exists or not is there is no reason why the possibility or reality of differences between women and men cannot exist, within this belatedly recognised plurality and diversity of gendered and sexual identity expression.

The second point arises from the above and acts as a bridge to the concluding discussion on the politics of gender difference. To take the archetypal theme further, I am interested in whether the proliferation of genders and sexualities we are currently witnessing in parts of the West at least speaks to the wish for not just freedom of self-expression but also the wish for transformation (Goss, 2020). This is in no way to query or play down the reality and importance (and courage involved) of finding and expressing a non-heteronormative gendered or sexual identity. I rather make this point to suggest a contrast with the business of 'staying male or female' (or 'staying straight/heterosexual') in identity formation and its continuity, where the wish for freedom of expression or even transformation needs to be expressed within more conventional tram lines.

Neither is better or worse but the principle of a dynamic between explicit expression of different versus same or even 'old normal' versus 'new normal' is a concomitant of social change but I suggest may make it harder to get to the truth of what is worth preserving of the 'old normal' alongside the 'new'.

From early fork in the road to two-way gendered street: 'psyche' and 'world'

To summarise, before I interrogate the question of why the discussion about gender difference (or lack of) seems to be so important in contemporary debate about gender and power I want to tightly summarise the argument this far in this chapter. First, we do not know enough about the neuro-biological and genetic influences on human development to be clear to what degree males and females are constitutionally different or not (apart from the pivotal factor of the capacity for bearing children). Second, psychoanalytic clinical practice and theory does afford some insight into ways in which male and female development bifurcate crucially in early life, subtly underpinning, and impinging on, male – female relations across the life span. Third, the recognition of contra-, bi- and pan-sexual influences from early life speak to the presence of a panoply of gendered and sexualised possibilities in feeling, behaviour and identity. Contra-sexual energies, alongside the (Feminist) deconstruction of gender stereotypes, help to free up capacities in men and women to more fully 'become', relate and contribute to a fuller range and acceptance of sexualities and gendered identities. However, there are ways in which the developmental conventions of male–female bifurcation retain their highly significant influence in this broader context. Gender/sexual diversity does not rule out differences between female and male which we would do well to take into account.

So how does all this play into the question of gender difference and truth/lies and the place of 'gendered subjectivity': individual and collective positions taken, depending on whether the commentator is male or female; with an acute recognition on my part that I formulate my ideas in the biographical context of my own maleness? It is clear there are deeply pervasive patterns at work in the world which are patriarchal and as Criado-Perez (2019, p.1) describes it, 'default male' with respect to how one sided the design of the economic, cultural and social world can be. This includes (Beard, 2018) who historically has been given a public voice – men – as against who have not – women (who as Beard shows have tended to be publicly listened to, at least up to the late twentieth century, only when they emulate a male style of being and expression).

The default male position can also link to the dangerous and unacceptable territory around sexual predation exposed by the #MeToo movement (Beard, ibid) and horrific patterns of male abuse and violence against women (for example Bindel, 2018) where there may sometimes be a flavour of entitlement to be abusive and/or violent towards women. Without downplaying the unacceptable horrors committed against women, there is more to understand about this as well as wider male patterns of behaviour and social, economic and political privilege and power.

It is striking that writers like Beard, Gomez and Rippon on gender, society and neuro-research do not factor in the possible influences of crucial early relations between infants and their primary carers (usually mother) in the forming of gendered being and identity. As conveyed, my argument is the deep patterns established in the pre-oedipal and oedipal psychosexual journey through early childhood – although often reified unhelpfully into stereotyped assumptions by social influences – can generate adult patterns of gendered relations between women and men. These are all open to individual difference and change but can be grouped around themes of *identification*: women more identified with parenting, family and home, men less so; *time and space*: men more attached to a linear fulfilment of their own 'story' over time/women more attached to a shared space for the fulfilment of shared 'story'; *the erotic*: men more prone to split this erotic into sexual and relational/women less so; *felt expression:* men more prone to struggle in ownership and expression of relational needs than women; and finally *authority:* men more holding historical authority 'out there' in the world/women more holding it 'in here' in the home.

It is this last point I want to focus on in relation to gendered subjectivity and agendas as I try to tie the strands of this inevitab.ly broad ranging discussion together. I have argued (Goss, 2010) that domestic space can be something women feel more ownership of, and responsibility for than men – who have often (from clinical and personal experience) needed to be 'woken up' in various regards to take that responsibility. Although this may well be changing in some ways, as tropes about who belongs 'where' in the male/female role-play loosen their grip, the preponderance of thinking about the 'home' does seem to have been about male *lack* (see ONS, 2016, on men and housework) rather than the power women may have in heteronormative domestic spaces. Here transmission of mother to daughter authority to determine how space is organised and utilised, and the benevolent, matriarchal, exercise of power, is usually strong. The patterns inherent to this exercise of power can get reflected in the wider world where conventions around child care and education dominate as I have previously described in the context of special educational needs schooling. Here, the significant preponderance of female teachers and teaching assistants lends its own flavour to the learning and relational experience of the children and young people they serve (Goss, 2003). In this vein, Beard writes of how her mother was a headteacher of a primary school and: "I am sure she was the very embodiment of *power* to the generations of boys and girls in her charge" (2018, p.vii). Such settings I suggest are ones well established in promoting women's power 'in the world'.

So, do notions of gender difference lack currency? This question seems to me to be tied up with the indisputable importance of addressing the 'outer' manifestations of gender inequality ('gender in the world') and its imposition, and the fear that once we start to bring possible differences in gendered 'being and experiencing' this somehow provides 'excuses/reasons' for, for example, unacceptable pay discrepancies and intolerable sexual behaviours, and open the door to take us backwards in time to a society governed by glaring and oppressive stereotypes about men and women, boys and girls.

As with all individual and collective fears the principle that the more we sideline the challenge represented by what we fear, the more hamstrung and even endangered we can become by it. This I propose may be what is happening with the challenge to acknowledge the possibility of gender difference. Also, thinking about 'gendered subjectivity', the possibility that sometimes men and women may think differently about this question needs to be considered. It is possible men may feel they have more to lose than women by arriving at a position where gender differences 'do not exist', not just because they may think their outdated patriarchal privileges are threatened and they have to give the moral high ground to women, but their sense of identity, not uncommonly wrapped up in being male, is also under question. It is also possible some women prize a sense of distinctiveness from men. Overall, though one could argue that women – and the Feminist project – have more to gain from this position as it enables disempowerment of patriarchal biases and further space for women to claim their power.

However, I think a crucial distinction is being missed: the distinction between 'gender in the world' (where deep injustices and problems remain), and 'the gendered psyche' – that is: what within us makes us different as a woman and man. Somehow, I propose, in the Feminist project the two have become conflated so that it is very hard to explore the possibility of 'difference' without shaking the foundations of the mental solidarity needed to successfully continue to expedite the opportunities for both women and men to remove unhelpful and oppressive structural obstacles to equality in many contexts.

This is a thoroughly embedded conflation and creates a kind of stasis around the task of fully understanding the psychology as well as the politics of gender, both of which have got stuck in structures, processes and behavioural patterns from medieval to modern to post-modern societies. Rippon seems to be thinking within the tradition which needs to 'prove' there are no differences (neuro-scientifically in this case) so that we can raise "dauntless daughters … (and) … sympathetic sons" (2019, p.346), as if 'proving' anything on either side of this debate can transform gender relations.

Identifying differences between male and female human beings is a slippery fish. As Kristeva (1980) indicates, gender is a metaphysical term. In this respect, gender difference is liminal, it operates in between mind and body, collective and individual, person to person. But it is not fake news.

In this spirit, I pose three questions to conclude:

- Does Feminism need to rely on 'debunking gender difference' to make further inroads into the unhelpful rigidity of key structures of thought which help sustain inequality, and unhappy gender relations?
- Has the relevance of gender difference been relegated to Feminism's *shadow* because of a fear that an openness to its possibility will undermine this project?
- If 'knowledge is power' (or 'gnosis brings insight') then do we not all gain by exploring possible gender differences, even in an 'as if' way, to try and better understand how and why women and men get stuck or conflicted in their ways of relating, and how they take power in the world as well as at home?

References

Astor, J., 1995, *Innovations in Analytical Psychology*, London: Routledge.

Baren-Cohen, S., 2004, *The Essential Difference*, London: Penguin.

Beard, M., 2018, *Women and Power*, London: Profile Books.

Benjamin, J., 1998, *Shadow of the Other: Intersubjectivity & Gender in Psychoanalysis*, New York: Routledge.

Benjamin, J., 1988, *The Bonds of Love*, New York: Pantheon.

Bindel, J., 2018, 'A War on Women Is Raging in the UK – The Femicide Statistics Prove It'. *The Guardian*. https://www.theguardian.com/commentisfree/2018/dec/18/women-uk-femicide-statistics-died-male-violence (Accessed 30 September 2019).

Brizendine, L., 2007, *The Female Brain*, London: Bantam.

Butler, J., 1990, *Gender Trouble*, London: Routledge.

Chaucer, G., 2007, 'The Tale of the Wife of Bath'. In: Croft, S., ed., *The Canterbury Tales*, Oxford: Oxford University Press.

Chodorow, N., 1978, *The Reproduction of Mothering*, London: University of California Press.

Connell, R., 2002, *Gender*, Cambridge: Polity.

Criado-Perez, C., 2019, *Invisible Women: Exposing Data Bias in a World Designed for Men*, London: Vintage.

Delphy, C., 1992, 'Mothers' Union?' *Trouble and Strife, the Radical Feminist Magazine*, Issue 24, Summer 1992, pp. 12–19. https://www.troubleandstrife.org/issues/Issue24_FullScan.pdf (Accessed 1 October 2019).

Falzeder, E., ed., 2002, *The Complete Correspondence of Sigmund Freud and Karl Abraham 1907 – 1925 Completed Edition*, London: Karnac.

Freud, S., 1990, *Beyond the Pleasure, Principle*, New York: W.W. Norton.

Freud, S., 2011, *Three Essays on the Theory of Sexuality*, Eastford, CT: Martino Fine Books.

Goss, P., 2003, 'The Gender Mix among Staff in Schools for Pupils Who Have Severe and Profound and Multiple Learning Difficulties'. *British Journal of Special Education*, 30(2), pp. 87–92.

Goss, P., 2010, *Men, Women and Relationships, A Post-Jungian Approach; Gender Electrics and Magic Beans*, London: Routledge.

Goss, P., 2020, 'Selfies, Self-Definition, Therapy and the Transrelational Quest for Meaningful Connection'. In: West W. and Nolan G., eds., *Extending Horizons in Helping and Caring Therapies: Beyond the Liminal in the Healing Encounter*, London: Routledge.

Harris, A., 2004, *Gender as Soft Assembly*, New York: Routledge.

Hauke, C., 2000, *Jung and the Postmodern: The Interpretation of Realities*, London: Routledge.

Hawksworth, M., 2019, *Gender and Political Theory*, Cambridge: Polity Press.

Jung, C.G., 1968a, 'The Shadow'. In: Read H., Fordham M., Adler G., eds., Hull R.F.C., trans., *Aion: Researches into the Phenomenology of the Self*, Hove: Routledge & Kegan Paul Ltd, pp. 8–10.

Jung, C.G., 1968b, 'The Syzygy: Anima and Animus'. In: Read H., Fordham M., Adler G., eds., Hull R.F.C., trans., *Aion: Researches into the Phenomenology of the Self*, Hove: Routledge & Kegan Paul Ltd, pp. 11–22.

Jung, E., 1985, *Animus and Anima*, Ashland, OH: Spring.

Kahn, C., 1979, *The Art and Thought of Heraclitus*, Cambridge: Cambridge University Press.

Klein, M., 1946, 'Notes on some schizoid mechanisms'. In: *The Writings of Melanie Klein, Volume 3*, New York, NY: Free Press, pp. 1–24.

Kristeva, J., 1980, *Desire in Language*, New York: Columbia University Press.

Kristeva, J., 2004, 'Some Observations on Female Sexuality'. In: Matthis I., ed., *Dialogues on Sexuality, Gender and Psychoanalysis*, London: Karnac, pp. 41–52.

Lacan, J., 1977, 'The Signification of the Phallus'. In: Fink B., ed., *Ecrits: A Selection*, New York: W.W. Norton & Co, pp. 575–584.

Moir, A., 2009, *Male and Female: Equal but Different*, Unpublished course notes, MindFields College, East Sussex.

Nymphofwater, 2011, 'The Two Ronnies – The Worm That Turned'. 11 September. https://www.youtube.com/watch?v=GcMd1F1acSo (Accessed 2 December 2019).

Office for National Statistics, 2016, 'Women Shoulder the Responsibility of 'Unpaid Work'. https://www.ons.gov.uk/employmentandlabourmarket/peopleinwork/earningsandworkinghours/articles/womenshouldertheresponsibilityofunpaidwork/2016-11-10 (Accessed 2 October 2019).

Phillips, A. and Scott, R., 1983, *The Women Were Watching*, London: Universal Music Publishing.

Rippon, G., 2019, *The Gendered Brain: The New Neuroscience That Shatters the Myth of the Female Brain*, London: Bodley Head.

Samuels, A., 1993, *The Political Psyche*, London: Routledge.

Samuels, A., 2015, *A New Therapy for Politics?* London: Karnac.

Sandford, J., 1980, *The Invisible Partners; How the Male and Female in Each of Us Affects Our Relationships*, Mahwah, NJ: Paulist Press.

Walters, M., 2005, *Feminism: A Very Short Introduction*, Oxford: Oxford University Press.

Withers, R., 2015, 'The Seventh Penis: Towards Effective Psychoanalytic Work with Pre-Surgical Transsexuals'. *Journal of Analytical Psychology*, 60(3), pp. 390–412.

Part 2

Stories: ancient and contemporary

Chapter 6

Becoming queen

Inanna and Claire Underwood

Catriona Miller

In the ancient Sumerian story called *Inanna and Ebih*, Inanna is appalled to find the mountain Ebih is not prepared to offer her the respect she is due as a goddess. She appeals to her grandfather, An, whose name means 'heaven', but he is unwilling to help. Then, in a vivid turn of phrase, 'fury overturns her heart' (de Shong Meador, 2000, p.99) and Inanna takes care of the mountain herself. The story concludes with the building of a temple for the worship of Inanna.

The Netflix Originals drama series *House of Cards* (Netflix, 2013–2019) portrays the rise of power-couple Frank and Claire Underwood to the top of the US political system. Claire (Robin Wright) has always been shown to be as ambitious as her husband (played by Kevin Spacey), but in Season 3, a brutal exchange between the two makes it clear that Frank, now president, will not help Claire rise further than First Lady, a ceremonial role with no real power. Like Inanna, however, Claire does not accept that this is the end of the matter and, by the end of the final season, Frank is dead and Claire is president.

These stories were created at least four and a half millennia apart and yet they contain points of contact, for although different in a great many respects, both tell the rare story of a female protagonist who stakes a claim to agency and power, then backs up that claim through acts of violence. This is an accepted route to power for many male protagonists, but women who exhibit such forms of aggression are often considered aberrant, or even pathological. In many ways, the two stories are shocking and surprising because their central protagonists are female and as Jungian clinician Austin has pointed out, in contemporary culture "women's aggressive energies remain somehow contrary to an assumed natural order" (Austin, 2005, p.4).

Using a specifically Jungian understanding of the purpose of myth, this chapter will explore the psychological territory of the two stories, examining their similarities and what they might tell us about a woman's path to autonomy and leadership.

Jung and myth

Comparing two stories whose origins lie so far apart in time is a difficult analytical task which perhaps threatens to trample over the specific cultural and historical contexts of both stories. However, I take a specifically Jungian view of mythology as a starting point, a view which sits in contrast to other approaches to myth which, for example, have viewed it as a kind of primitive science, such as Edward Tylor's influential *Primitive Culture* from 1871 or as a form of disguised wish fulfilment as in the psychoanalytic view. For Jung, however, myth was always symbolic, not literal, and its subject matter was really the psyche, where the function of myth is to elucidate the unconscious for the purposes of achieving a better psychic balance, since the psyche in Jung's view is a homeostatic system. As he put it, "Myths are original revelations of the preconscious psyche, involuntary statements about unconscious psychic happenings" (Jung, 1968, p.154). Elsewhere he noted his view that myths are projections onto the external world, "in fact, the whole of mythology," he said "could be taken as a sort of projection of the collective unconscious. ... Just as the constellations were projected onto the heavens, similar figures were projected into legends and fairy tales or upon historical persons" (Jung, 1960, pp.152–153).

This approach to myth then sees such stories as an expression of a psyche always seeking balance, through the mechanism of the transcendent function. The transcendent function "mediates opposites. Expressing itself by way of the symbol, it facilitates a transition from one psychological attitude or condition to another" (Samuels, Shorter and Plaut, 1991, p.150). In fact, the transcendent function is the key mechanism of the self-regulating psyche, a way of facilitating a shift in consciousness. Jung called it 'transcendent' – not in any spiritual sense, but in the sense of transcending two opposites, usually conscious and unconscious, through symbolic images which contain both. In the Jungian model of psyche, the unconscious is an active participant in the psychic ecosystem, rather than a repository of repressed contents. As Samuels explains, the transcendent function allows dialogue. "The ego is holding the tension of the opposites to let a mediatory symbol come through – a facilitation of the process of the self which permits the unconscious-conscious transcendence" (Samuels, 1994, p.59).

The shift in consciousness that both these particular stories call to mind can be related to another Jungian concept, that of individuation, which is the process of becoming oneself, that is "whole, indivisible and distinct from other people or collective psychology (though also in relation to these)" (Samuels, Shorter and Plaut, 1991, p.76). Jung thought that the first part of individuation was a necessary separation from the unconscious, where "Consciousness," he said, "grows out of an unconscious psyche which is older than it, and which goes on functioning together with it or even in spite of it" (Jung, 1968, p.281). So the development of the ego and the persona (outward social adaptation) are the goals of the first part of that process. However, in the Jungian model, "Adaptation is never achieved once and for all" (Jung, 1960, p.73), and the second, life-long part of individuation is work to listen once more to the 'other voice' of the unconscious (Jung, 1960, p.88). Stein has described these two 'great movements' of individuation as analytic and synthetic where the first part focuses on separation and the second part on (re)synthesis (see Stein, 2006, p.xviff). Hero narratives have been explored extensively as examples of the first part of individuation with Strauss (1962) and Covington (1989), for example, seeing the hero as a symbol of separation and differentiation. There are, however, particular issues with this model for women who live within a patriarchal culture, where the route to becoming an autonomous adult entity still contains paradoxes and contradictions, which will be discussed more fully below.

I extend this Jungian view of myth to audio-visual narratives (film and television drama) so prevalent in contemporary life. Following Jung's lead on myth, I suggest that contemporary audio-visual narratives act to elucidate aspects of the unconscious psyche, through the transcendent function. Whilst of course, much media is consumed without great thought or attention, sometimes audiences develop very intense relationships with stories that deliver 'psychological savour': images, characters and emotional dynamics that can speak to them very deeply, sparking an engagement that goes beyond mere entertainment. So the approach adopted here is a kind of comparative mythology, which sees both stories offering similar psychological dynamics to a modern audience. It is not an examination of what the story of *Inanna and Ebih* may have meant to the Sumerians themselves, or indeed what it may have meant to the priestess Enheduanna who wrote the story down in around 2300 BCE. Rather it is a closer look at the common psychological threads that run through both.

Inanna and Ebih

The story of *Inanna and Ebih* is one of several major works relating to the goddess Inanna, which have survived to the present day. Inanna is not a goddess of the domestic sphere – she is the 'lady of blazing dominion' and 'foe smasher' in *Inanna and Ebih* (de Shong Meador, 2000, p.91), and 'keen for battle queen' in *Lady of Largest Heart* (de Shong Meador, 2000, p.117) also known as *Hymn to Inanna C*. She is also an erotic figure, featuring in songs of courtship and consummation such as *The Courtship of Inanna and Dumuzi*. Indeed, one poem begins with Inanna's delight in her own sexual self. As she takes a rest:

> She leaned back against the apple tree.
> When she leaned against the apple tree, her vulva was wonderous to behold.
> Rejoicing at her wonderous vulva, the young woman Inanna applauded herself.
>
> (Wolkstein and Kramer, 1983, p.12)

She is an important figure in the Sumerian pantheon which did not have a fixed hierarchy. There were around 5,000 minor Sumerian deities (Hallo, 1996, p.233) and about a dozen major ones, and it is interesting that the assembled gods were often referred to collectively as the *Anuna* which means 'princely offspring' (Black and Green, 1992, p.34), leading one writer to describe them as a committee, with an executive branch, often, though not always, led by the god Enlil (Vanstiphout, 1984, p.226).

Inanna was certainly a member of the executive committee, but their relationship was not always cordial. Some hymns describe the *Anuna* bowing to Inanna or even crawling before her (*see Hymn to Inanna C*, ETCSL, 2016b), or fluttering away from her like bats from a ruin (see *Exultation of Inanna*, or *Hymn to Inanna B*, 2015). One hymn has Inanna proclaim that "The gods are small birds, but I am the falcon" (see *Hymn to Inanna F*, ETCSL, 2016c) and at one time or another, Inanna seems to have come into conflict with many of the major male gods. Nevertheless, Inanna is indisputably one of the major gods of the Sumerian pantheon, and her name probably means 'Lady of Heaven'.

Relatively complete texts of Inanna's major exploits, including *Inanna and Ebih*, have survived thanks to their inclusion in what has been called the Decad – a group of ten compositions which were used extensively to train scribes. It is even suggested that *Inanna and Ebih* was "intended to introduce apprentice scribes to more complex grammar and longer, continuous texts" (Delnero, 2011, p.141). When renowned Sumeriologist Samuel Noah Kramer first summarised the work in 1944, only eight sources were known, but the number of preserved duplicates has since grown to eighty sources (Delnero, 2011, p.124).

The story is a relatively straightforward one, at least in terms of its action. Inanna is outraged when the mountain Ebih will not bow down to her and offer her the respect that she is due. She threatens it to no avail and so Inanna prepares herself, putting on her best jewellery and make up – in a 'queen's robe'; paints fire beams on her face; fastens red carnelians around her throat, takes her seven headed mace and goes to visit An who as the head of the pantheon "gives [her] word weight over all others" (de Shong Meador, 2000, p.95). However, although he is pleased with her and her offering, when she explains the disrespect of the mountain, he addresses her, "Little One, my Little One" and goes on "you ask for the mountain, you want the heart of it" but when he looks down and sees the beauty of the mountain, he grows in awe of it and says "I will not set my head with yours against the fiery radiance of the mountain" (de Shong Meador, 2000, pp.98–99), concluding "Maiden Inanna, you cannot oppose it" (*Inanna and Ebih*, ETCSL, 2016a).

Inanna, however, does not like this answer:

Fury overturns her heart!

with screech of hinge
she flings wide the gate
of the house of battle
…
bedlam unleashed
she sends down a raging battle
hurls a storm from her wide arms
to the ground below.

(de Shong Meador, 2000, p.99)

Inanna is victorious and has no compunction about celebrating this in the final section of the composition. Inanna 'wrestles the mountain to its knees' (de Shong Meador, 2000, p.100) and then builds a temple to herself.

Inanna's roots go back to the 'old, old gods', as de Shong Meador puts it (2000, p.92), though the gods are actually named in the Sumerian text, however as Attinger (2015, p.40, fn.123) points out, we know nothing else about them except that they came 'before'. But now Inanna must stake her own claim, not relying on An to back her up. The mountain itself, though a beautiful paradise, seems to represent a pull back towards an undifferentiated state, which must be resisted and more, it must be made to respect the goddess (de Shong Meador, 2000, p.90). This is a point reiterated in Attinger (2015, p.38) where he mentions this Jungian interpretation alongside the more standard historical explanation of the work which relates it to a campaign of conquest of the mountainous region Jebel Hamrin (in modern-day Iraq). To re-state this moment in psychological terms, the ego must separate itself from the unconscious and stake a claim to autonomy, but in fact, Inanna must undertake two separations here. She must separate herself both from the pull of Mount Ebih's paradise, *and* from the previously doting patronage of An, representing social acceptance, or at least the collective identity of the Anuna with An at its head, from whom at least some of her power and authority derives.

The parallels in this story with the very modern television drama *House of Cards* are perhaps not immediately apparent, but Claire Underwood too has her moment of 'asking for power' that is turned down and thus must undertake two separations in order to achieve autonomy.

House of Cards (Netflix, 2013–2018)

House of Cards was a flagship original drama for the streaming service Netflix, being their first directly commissioned big budget drama designed to encourage audiences to subscribe. It was based on a 1990 series for the BBC, adapted by Andrew Davies, from a novel of the same name by Michael Dobbs, published in 1989. Dobbs had worked in the Conservative party in the 1970s and 1980s as a speech writer and government special adviser. He said, "Most of the stuff I put into *House of Cards* was material from events I'd either seen, or participated in, or done, or watched other people do" (Chakelian, 2015), although one hopes it did not also include the murders! Dobbs is now a Conservative life peer in the House of Lords. Both Davies and Dobbs became executive producers for the Netflix show, but the American adaptation was created by Beau Willimon, with David Fincher and Kevin Spacey also on board as executive producers. The story tells of the rise to power of Francis (Frank) Underwood through fair means or foul, but mostly foul, in a series of manipulations of a personal and political nature alongside outright skulduggery, all accompanied by sly asides and self-justifications to the camera (a Shakespearean technique drawn from *Richard III*). It all combined to make the character of Francis a favourite anti-hero with audiences.

House of Cards was an important series for Netflix in 2013, designed to position the streaming service as a rival to the more established HBO as a source of 'quality' drama. *House of Cards* was key to this, with Jenner pointing out that the combination of "authorship, Hollywood stars with an emphasis on dramatic roles, complex narrative structures, 'serious' subject matter, accomplished aesthetics" (Jenner, 2018, p.172) were important elements working to establish the Netflix Originals brand. Finn (2017), however, makes clear the critical importance of Netflix's knowledge of its audience base in the decision to commission original drama in general and this drama in particular. "Netflix commissioned its hit series *House of Cards* ..." he explained "based in large part on its algorithmic calculus: it had significant statistical evidence to suggest that its users would embrace a reboot of a BBC political drama starring Kevin Spacey, with director David Fincher at the helm" (Finn, 2017, p.98). The company bid $100 million against HBO for the rights to the show, and moved straight to a two series order, eschewing any need for a pilot proof of concept. Finn goes on to point out that what looked like a huge gamble to traditional broadcasters was simply a careful calculation by Netflix, which was confident about the formula components (as articulated by Jenner above) and because of its "immense power to capture the attention and interest of its customers" (Finn, 2017, p.99).

The series ran for six seasons, although the final series was shortened to eight episodes rather than the more usual thirteen, after a scandal hit the actor Kevin Spacey, in the form of a series of accusations of sexual misconduct in the United States and United Kingdom (see Jang, 2017). In December 2017 Netflix announced that the final series would be produced without Spacey, with the focus fully on Frank's wife, Robin Wright's character Claire. It is interesting that Netflix did not just cancel the show as they might have done, given that their 'star' and a major element of their algorithmic calculation, not to mention the central protagonist of the drama, was being removed from the story. Presumably the popularity of Claire's character must have grown sufficiently to justify the resolution of the show's narrative. Robin Wright's role had been growing, shaping the direction of the show and the storylines for her character. From Season 2 onwards, she had directing credits, and from 2016 (Season 4) an executive production role, along with parity of pay with her co-star. Spacey had been executive producer since the first episode but was dropped at the end of Season 5. He had no directing credits. Wright's creative influence on the series mirrors Claire's rise to political power.

The Netflix version of *House of Cards* diverged significantly from its forebears in many ways, but one of the most obvious changes was that it developed the role of the wife, Claire Underwood, very substantially. In the BBC version, Francis's wife is an almost invisible supporter with no obvious agenda other than loyalty to her husband. In the American version, however, Claire becomes a highly visible and an explicit partner to Frank, with some definite ideas and agenda of her own which gradually becomes clearer as the series progresses. Claire appears at first as if she is playing the role of the "partner, or partner-to-be of the hero", that is "women who play a waiting role, resisting the flow of time, and whose aim is to be united with the hero" (Covington, 1989, pp.243–244), but her agency means she begins to evolve away from her position as a simple supporter of her husband.

Other than narrative placement, of course, part of what makes Frank the central protagonist is that he is permitted to directly address the camera, to explain his thinking, his goals, and his feelings to a complicit audience, thus drawing them into his world. This 'breaking of the fourth wall' which acknowledges that there is audience viewing events is still relatively rare in television drama as it tends to jolt an audience out of its willing suspension of disbelief. It was a major stylistic decision by the show's original adaptor, Andrew Davies, and a change to the novel which was delivered entirely in the third person. Davies used the direct address to camera to give the audience entry to the "thoughts and feelings of an unsympathetic character, compelling us to engage with him. The programme grants us access to [Frank's] subjectivity and voice" (Cardwell, 2005, p.94). This special kind of dramatic voice is one Doane calls a "privileged mark of interiority" (Doane, 1980, p.41) manifesting the inner lining of the body and displaying the inner life of the character, but in this case it is even more than that. In *House of Cards*, the audience is also treated to the direct *gaze* of the character, and Frank's point of view becomes the inescapable core of the drama. This is worth mentioning because one of the ways that Claire's shift to a more central role is marked is through her own relationship to that direct address.

At first, Claire's character is opaque. There is no insight into her thinking as with the monologues of her husband, and instead the audience must read her character through speech and action, and from the external cues on offer through the *mise en scène*. The show's *mise en scène* is austere, minimalist, deliberate, where the lighting is largely naturalistic, making much use of motivated lighting (such as windows, lamps and so on), even though this often leaves faces in shadow. The colour palette is ruthlessly restrained, nothing flashy or attention grabbing, neutrals abound and control is all, which is, in fact, a fair description of Claire's character. Her self-possession is extraordinary, with every expression and gesture carefully controlled to the extent that her body language is almost silent, often said to be a marker of leaders who have no need of self-calming gestures or movements to attract attention. Far from being a trivial matter, Claire's personal style is an important clue to her character. Like the production design more generally, Claire's fashion style is also almost brutally simple and equally controlled: clear lines, neutral shades, short hair carefully cropped to retain its femininity, figure strong and slim, the height of her high heels impressive.

In fact, the physical composure and perfect grooming demonstrate to the audience once again a level of control (physical and mental) that are a clue to her own abilities and desires. Kemal Harris, stylist on the final season, explained that Claire is under a "lot of pressure, she's female, she has a lot of battles with people who were working closely with her husband. It feels like Claire against the world this final season, and she doesn't really have that many close friends. She's in battle this final season" (Fratti, 2018). Her clothes function as her armour. As Andò puts it, her "style is an integral part of her personality and behaviour. Her style seems to be able to enhance an unconventional femininity and an unusual capacity for power management in a very familiar way for the audience" (2015, p.216). It is familiar because Claire's costume is reminiscent of 'power dressing', a style developed in the 1980s to allow women in top business positions to mimic masculine norms (suit, white shirt and tie) whilst retaining their femininity through pencil skirts, high heels and red lipstick. Claire's costume, for example, often incorporates an Oxford shirt, a staple of smart upper class men's fashion, but in her case it is tailored to be very close fitting to the female form. It is also perhaps an unconventional femininity because it is designed to display strength rather than prettiness. The closer to power she gets, the darker Claire's colour palette becomes and by Season 6 she is wearing military style colours in navy blue and olive greens, with very limited detailing in brass buttons, contrast seaming, or French cuffs (to show off her presidential cuff links).

Such 'effortless' elegance demonstrates a powerful will, because its very flawlessness requires determination and precision as well as planning, focus and discipline. The perfect outfit for every occasion, maintaining the figure and complexion to carry it off, the requirement to be perfectly groomed at all times are all tied to 'rituals of beauty' that are intended to keep women subordinate to male approval, but Claire's appearance of perfectly executed femininity is camouflage, making it subversive because she is melding masculine *and* feminine visual cues for power. Like Inanna who adorns herself in jewels and make up to seek An's help, Claire ensures that she appears as the patriarchally acceptable woman, and yet this is a performance, and a concealment of the steel beneath, perhaps most evident in her body language. As noted, Claire does not fidget or wave her hands about and she seems to have an emotional self-control that only very occasionally breaks, such as in Episode 3.12 when Francis tells her that a political rival is threatening to publish an old journal of Claire's, which contains details of an abortion. During the phone call with Frank, along with the threatening music, there are more than the usual number of cuts in the editing, and close ups of Claire's face and of her hands shaking, as her voice seems to lose its authority and belong to a much younger woman. It is a relatively brief moment but one which suggests Claire still has one or two chinks in her armour. Season 6 plays more openly with expectation and assumptions about Claire's emotional control. In Episode 6.5, Claire pretends to have an emotional breakdown to draw out her enemies in the cabinet, but then makes it clear to the audience that she is in full control. After listening to her vice president pleading with her, she turns to the camera with her tear streaked face suddenly dead pan to say "Don't worry, I have a plan." In Episode 6.6, in a more ambiguous moment, Claire enumerates the number of her enemies that she has eliminated either politically or actually through assassination, but must then leave the room to vomit, leaving the audience on screen and off to wonder if it is horror and guilt at her actions, or merely a side effect of her about-to-be-announced pregnancy?

Despite these moments of emotion, Claire's narrative trajectory within the show demonstrates ever more clearly that discipline and desire for power.

Although she has little political experience, in Season 3 she is appointed to the UN as ambassador by Frank who has become president, but she is then forced to give up that job when Frank trades her resignation for a diplomatic agreement with Russia and she becomes only the First Lady again. She wants more but Frank is unwilling to accommodate her. In a brutal exchange in the Season 3 finale, she finally articulates herself. She explains that she is unhappy that ultimately it is Frank who makes the decisions, and that she had to ask for his help to get the nomination to the UN in the first place. She resents having to ask. Later in the same scene she is even clearer. "Look at us, Francis," she says, "We used to make each other stronger, or at least I thought so. But that was a lie. We were making *you* stronger. And now I'm just weak and small and I can't stand that feeling any longer." Frank's reply is unsparing:

> When we lose [the election] because of you there will be nothing. No plan. No future. We will only be hasbeens. You want to amount to something? Well, here is the brutal fucking truth and you can hate me, you can be disgusted, you can feel whatever it is that you want to feel because frankly I'm beyond caring. But without me you are nothing. You're right. This office has one chair. And you have always known that from the very beginning. And if you can't stomach that, then I'm a fool for having married you in the first place.

He is the president and she is not. The couple who had been such firm allies are now rivals. Like Inanna, Claire's request for help from a more powerful male is turned down, but she resents having to ask for it in the first place. And like Inanna, Claire begins to take the matter into her own hands. In Season 4, she begins looking for a nomination to a congressional seat, and leaking hostile information against Frank. An assassination attempt puts Frank in hospital and Claire into a powerful position with the weak vice president. On Frank's return, she persuades him to make her his vice-presidential running mate. Season 4 ends with a long, slow pan up the incident room table to where Claire and Frank sit together at the head, culminating in Claire joining Frank in looking directly into the camera. Claire is starting to claim the direct address as her own. Towards the end of Season 5, Claire finally speaks to the camera, acknowledging the audience's presence (Episode 5.11), and in the final episode of that season she stands over the desk of the Oval Office, having replaced her husband as president. He is expecting her to issue him with a presidential pardon, but instead, she refuses to take his phone call and announces "My turn" to the camera. The direct address is now hers and, as it turns out, hers alone. In retrospect, it may have looked like Frank's story, but throughout Claire's power is rising. She is younger than Frank, more telegenic, and more flexible, and when interviewed before the premiere of Season 6, Robin Wright intimated that it had always been the plan from Day One to have Claire end up as president: "We knew that that was going to be the final chapter. How she got there was questionable" (*Variety*, 2018).

The final series of *House of Cards* sees Claire consolidate her hold on power in a more effective and ruthless way than Frank had ever managed. By the end of Season 6, Frank is dead, and Claire has arranged to have all her enemies either politically isolated or assassinated, whilst maintaining a public persona as a caring champion of women, for example choosing to replace her disloyal cabinet entirely with women. In Episode 6.7, she even abandons her married name 'Underwood' and returns to her maiden name, becoming President Hale, and further distancing herself from her husband's influence and the last vestiges of his powerbase. Her timely (and surprising) pregnancy also works to soften her public image, helping to cement her caring public persona as 'mother of the nation'. Exactly how Claire becomes pregnant with her dead husband's child, is not directly addressed in the drama, but a 'blink and miss it' moment in Episode 6.5 shows Claire taking a tablet of folic acid, making the suggestion that she used her time out of the spotlight to see a fertility specialist. It is a timely pregnancy because Frank's will, in the event of no direct heir, left everything to Doug Stamper (Michael Kelly), his most trusted *éminence grise* and keeper of his secrets.

The series concludes with a final death. Claire now several months pregnant with Frank's child, is confronted by Doug Stamper. An increasingly distraught and troubled Doug admits that he is the one who killed Frank to preserve his legacy, and he intends to kill Claire for the same reason. Instead, Claire stabs him with the letter knife he threatened her with, and then suffocates him. The final shot of the series is of Claire, a dead Doug in her arms, the last possible challenger to her power gone, as her eyes slide to stare into the camera one last time. There is no one left to confront her, or to comfort her, only the promise of the child to come. Like Inanna she has become the 'foe smasher', alone in the 'temple' of the White House.

Agency, power and the autonomous ego

A Jungian approach to any text (see Miller, in Hockley, 2018) often seeks to pay attention to an echo or a thread of psychological significance, a hint or whisper of unconscious processes revealed within a consciously organised narrative, and then to amplify that whisper, as Jung suggested in his own approach to mythology. As Rowland puts it, the aim is to pay attention to the "fleeting momentary presence of something that forever mutates and reaches beyond the ego's inadequate understanding" (2005, p.3). The whisper being considered here is the unequivocal desire for power from the two protagonists, and their equally unequivocal determination to do whatever it takes to achieve it. The two heroines demand recognition of themselves as powerful individuals worthy of respect, and, perhaps also, fear, and if the function of myth is to throw conscious light upon the workings of the unconscious, these two stories are expressing a route to agency and power for their protagonists through aggressive energies, a route usually denied to women.

In English, the etymology of the word 'power' lies in the Latin verb *posse* meaning 'to be able'. Thus, implied in the word 'power' is an element of agency.

To have power is to have the ability to act. However, there is a complex chain of association around the issue of power and autonomy that makes it difficult territory for women to own because these concepts are a kind of ouroboros. To have power, to be an autonomous individual, requires agency and the capacity to exercise power, but to be a person *with* agency requires external (social) validation of that capacity to act. So although agency is in theory a universal capacity, in reality it is "realised in a variable and unequal fashion" (Mcnay in Disch and Hawkesworth, 2016, p.39) because both agency and power have long been coded as masculine. Men are socially validated from a very young age for displaying them (independence, self-reliance, and even unruliness), while women are, at best, ignored or, at worst, punished for displaying the same traits. Instead, women are socially validated for being 'nice', that is helpful, quiet, and caring, and socially invalidated for being loud, demanding or putting themselves first. Patriarchal power, acting in a myriad of small social interactions, creates gendered subjectivity or selfhood, constituting male subjects in a privileged position with agency, and constituting female subjects who struggle to claim agency. Social affirmation states in so many small ways that women 'are *not* able to'.

Inanna and Claire do not have their request for power validated, but instead of complying they become angry and they rally themselves to fight back. Austin articulates an uncomfortable reality that to feel aggression and hostility contains the seeds of agency, because with it one realises one is not merely 'done to' one can also 'do to others' (2005, p.7–8). She goes on to point out, as noted above, that the links between aggression and agency are more complex for women because of the social construction of femininity, where once again "stroppiness in women is commonly seen as dangerous and negative, while in men it is often seen as an expression of an original and individual mind" (2005, p.23).

This must also affect the idea of individuation, because to achieve growth, to become an autonomous, mature personality, women's sense of self has to disentangle itself both from the unconscious *and* from social expectations. Social adaptation for women is often a limiting factor rather than endorsement. Adaptation to outward reality means, as Pratt put it, "young girls grow down rather than up …[as] the reward of personal power makes the conquering hero a cultural deviant" (1981, p.168).

For a woman to achieve autonomy, therefore, she must work against the weight of social expectation that forms her persona in particular directions. To resist or rebel against this is hard work, creating contradiction and tension between the ego and persona, where the ego is moving towards greater consciousness and separation, while simultaneously the persona requires relatedness and *loss* of ego. This is in contrast to men where socially acceptable masculinity insists on autonomy as essential to the successful performance of masculinity. As Austin makes clear, there are few paradigms that allow the viewing of female aggression as meaningful and important, more usually they are unacceptable, ugly, absurd or indeed irrelevant.

Inanna and Claire challenge these norms. Through fury and violent action, they clear the decks of their challengers and take up the mantle of queendom.

Although for those hearing these stories, the audience, ambivalence may remain. For example, some academics have described Inanna's subduing of the mountain as petulant and capricious – "Inanna decides to subdue Mount Ebih without any real provocation from the mountain. She complains that when she approached it, it did not prostrate itself before her. It is Inanna's hurt pride that makes her want to subdue Ebih" (Karahashi, 2004, p.117) – before concluding that "Inanna's aggression has no legitimate cause, therefore giving the impression that she acts to satisfy her own desire, which is to be taken as one of her many capricious acts" (Karahashi, 2004, p.118). Yet she is a goddess and as such presumably worthy of respect. The mountain *should* prostrate itself before her. It is a direct attack on her position and requires a direct response. It is interesting that many of Inanna's stories feature the goddess acquiring power of some kind through robbery (*Inanna Brings the First Sky House to Earth*), trickery (*Inanna and Enki*), special daring (*The Descent of Inanna*) or, in this case, direct violence. She is a goddess fighting to maintain her place. It is possible to speculate that Inanna, who wears the robes of the 'old, old gods', might trace her origins to a pre-patriarchal period, which could explain her confused family relationships (variations of sister, wife, daughter, grand-daughter to various major gods), fractious relationship with the rest of the *Anuna* and her bold challenges to their authority with her demands for rights, privileges and power at every opportunity.

For the character of Claire, the audience was divided, and websites and discussion boards debated her style, her hair, her interior design choices, and whether she was a psychopath, a sociopath, or just plain evil. Others however were drawn to her style and confidence, but also her ruthlessness. As the feminist campaigning Women's Media Centre put it, "Claire Underwood breaks the rules and does ugly things. She's not there to convince men that powerful women aren't scary, that their rise is somehow good for everybody. She's there to take what she believes to be rightfully hers and she does *not* apologize" (Evdokimova, 2018). On a more personal note, one blogger articulated her reluctant attraction to the character:

> One thing I'm rather ashamed to admit I *like* about Claire is that while she's selfish, she's very clear and intentional about it. It's not that she's against what good may come out of her success for other people, she's just not motivated by it. … There's something about Claire's selfishness that I *yearn* for; it seems odd to say, I suppose, but I have this strange admiration for her because she's just so unapologetically concerned with herself.

The blogger ends her piece "Claire Underwood has to be a villain because we aren't ready for a world where she's a heroine" (Norman, 2016).

Neither of these stories are about 'good girls', that is patriarchally sanctioned, polite and empathetic, who are rewarded with marriage – the breakdown of Claire's relationship with Frank shows how quickly male approval can melt away when challenged – but then to become queen, an autonomous individual in one's own right, requires the acquisition of power. Power is not 'nice' and those with it are rarely 'likeable'. Inanna and Claire are not nice or likeable but they are unquestionably powerful. Inanna's story ends with the building of a temple or palace confirming her divinity, with Inanna "rejoicing in her fearsome terror" (see *Inanna and Ebih*, ETCSL, 2016a), while Claire, having reached the pinnacle of political power, is only able to glance towards the camera, her expression complex. Inanna does not accept the persona of femininity and goes her own way seemingly no longer reliant on An for her position, a possibility that arises even more clearly in another, albeit more fragmentary, story, where Inanna takes the Eanna (a temple in the sky) from An and brings it to earth to become her important temple in the city of Uruk, leaving An bewailing the possibility that Inanna is now greater than he (see *Inanna and An*, ETCSL, 2016d). Claire must adopt a more negotiated stance, using her femininity and motherhood as a disguise for her ruthless acquisition of power, with no celebration at the end of it. Both stories, however, are an expression of an unequivocal assumption of agency – Inanna and Claire take power and become fearsome individuals with power, that is, they are 'able to'.

In comparing an ancient myth with a modern television drama, I hope to bring into focus a powerful and terrifying aspect of the feminine that is rarely directly apprehended in contemporary culture: the female acquisition of power through aggressive means for its own sake. The two stories highlighted in this chapter are extraordinary in the full sense of the word – from the Latin *extra ordinem*, meaning outside the ordinary course of events. Stories about women who become queens through their own actions, not married to the hero who becomes king, not even forced into reluctant heroism to save the world, but simply because they wish it, are rare. The female protagonists in these two stories cannot sit idly by and hope to get the power and respect that they feel is their due. They have done what they were asked, they have been good daughters of patriarchy, but there will be no reward of personal power for them unless they take it for themselves. They must be not nice, not modest, not consensual but ruthless, powerful and autonomous, and in doing so they suggest that to embrace anger, aggression, and demand, and to embrace 'the keen for battle queen' within, is at least one legitimate route to agency for women.

References

Andò, R., 2015, 'Fashion and Fandom on TV and Social Media: Claire Underwood's Power Dressing', *Critical Studies in Fashion and Beauty*, 6(2), pp. 207–231.

Attinger, P., 2015, 'Inanna und Ebih'. In: B Jarnowki and D Schwemer (eds), *Texte aus der Umwelt Des Alten Testaments: Neue Folge, Weisheitstexte, Mythen und Epen*, Gütersloher, Czech Republic: Verlagshaus, pp. 37–44.

Austin, S., 2005, *Women's Aggressive Fantasies: A Post-Jungian Exploration of Self-Hatred, Love and Agency*, Hove: Routledge.

Black, J. and Green, A., 1992, *Gods, Demons and Symbols of Ancient Mesopotamia: An Illustrated Dictionary*, London: British Museum Press.

Cardwell, S., 2005, *Andrew Davies*, Manchester: Manchester University Press.

Chakelian, A., 2015, 'House of Cards Creator Michael Dobbs: "I Must Have Sold My Soul"', *NewStatseman*. Available at https://www.newstatesman.com/politics/uk/2015/07/house-cards-creator-michael-dobbs-i-must-have-sold-my-soul (Accessed: 31 July 2019).

Covington, C., 1989, 'In Search of the Heroine', *Journal of Analytical Psychology*, 34(3), pp. 243–254.

Delnero, P., 2011, '*Inana and Ebih* and the Scribal Tradition'. In: G Frame (ed), *A Common Cultural Heritage: Studies on Mesopotamia and the Biblical World in Honor of Barry L. Eichler*, Pennsylvania, PA: CDL Press, pp. 123–149.

de Shong Meador, B., 2000, *Inanna, Lady of Largest Heart*, Austin: University of Texas Press.

Disch, L. and Hawkesworth, M. (eds.), 2016, *The Oxford Handbook of Feminist Theory*, New York: Oxford University Press.

Doane, M.A., 1980, 'The Voice in the Cinema: The Articulation of Body and Space', *Yale French Studies*, 60, pp. 33–50.

Electronic Text Corpus of Sumerian Literature, 2016a, *Inanna and Ebih*. Available at http://etcsl.orinst.ox.ac.uk/section1/tr132.htm (Accessed: September 2019).

Electronic Text Corpus of Sumerian Literature, 2016b, *Hymn to Inanna C*. Available at http://etcsl.orinst.ox.ac.uk/section4/tr4073.htm (Accessed: 6 September 2019).

Electronic Text Corpus of Sumerian Literature, 2016c, *Hymn to Inanna F*. Available at http://etcsl.orinst.ox.ac.uk/cgi-bin/etcsl.cgi?text=t.1.3.5# (Accessed: 1 September 2019).

Electronic Text Corpus of Sumerian Literature, 2016d, *Inanna and An*. Available at http://etcsl.orinst.ox.ac.uk/cgi-bin/etcsl.cgi?text=t.1.3.5# (Accessed: 3 September 2019).

Exultation of Inanna (Hymn to Inanna B), Translation by Professor Annette Zgoll, 2015. Available at http://www.angelfire.com/mi/enheduanna/Ninmesara.html (Accessed: 28 August 2019).

Evdokimova, T., 2018, 'Claire Underwood obliterates the conventional 'Strong Female Character' Trope, and It's about Time', *Women's Media Center*. Available at http://www.womensmediacenter.com/fbomb/claire-underwood-obliterates-the-conventional-strong-female-character-trope-and-its-about-time (Accessed: 14 August 2019).

Finn, E., 2017, *What Algorithms Want: Imagination in the Age of Computing*, Cambridge, MA: MIT Press.

Fratti, K., 2018, 'Robin Wright's 'House of Cards' Stylist Explains the Key to Dressing the First Female President,' *The Bustle*. Available at https://www.bustle.com/p/robin-wrights-house-of-cards-stylist-explains-the-key-to-dressing-the-first-female-president-1305796 (Accessed: 1 August 2019).

Hallo, W., 1996, *Enki and the Theology of Eridu Journal of the American Oriental Society*, 116(2), pp. 231–234.

Jang, M., 2017, 'Kevin Spacey Accused of Inappropriate Groping, Showing Porn to a Teen in New Claims', *The Hollywood Reporter*. Available at https://www.hollywoodreporter.com/news/kevin-spacey-accused-inappropriate-groping-showing-porn-a-teen-new-claims-1054990 (Accessed 15th July 2019).

Jenner, M., 2018, *Netflix and the Re-Invention of Television*, Cham: Palgrave Macmillan.

Jung, C.G., 1960, *Structure and Dynamics of the Psyche*, Hove: Routledge and Kegan Paul.

Jung, C.G., 1968, 'The Psychology of the Child Archetype'. In: H Read, M Fordham and G Adler (eds), *The Archetypes and the Collective Unconscious*, Hove: Routledge & Kegan Paul Ltd, pp. 1511–1581.

Karahashi, F., 2004, 'Fighting the Mountain: Some Observations on the Sumerian Myths of Inanna and Ninurta', *Journal of Near Eastern Studies*, 63(2), pp. 111–118.

Miller, C., 2018, 'A Jungian Textual Terroir'. In: L Hockley (ed), *The Routledge International Handbook of Jungian Film Studies*, Oxon: Routledge, pp. 7–25.

Norman, A., 2016, 'The Villainization of Claire Underwood', *Medium*. Available at https://medium.com/@abbymnorman/the-villainization-of-claire-underwood-59c1c c51d18 (Accessed: 25 August 2019).

Pratt, A., 1981, *Archetypal Patterns in Women's Fiction*, Bloomington, IN: Indiana University Press.

Rowland, S., 2005, *Jung as a Writer*, London: Routledge.

Samuels, A., Shorter, B. and Plaut, F., 1991, *A Critical Dictionary of Jungian Analysis*, London: Routledge.

Samuels, A., 1994, *Jung and the Post-Jungians*, London: Routledge.

Stein, M., 2006, *The Principle of Individuation*, Asheville, NC: Chiron Publications.

Strauss, R., 1962, The Archetype: 2nd International Congress for Analytical Psychology, Zurich 1962: Proceedings Base, *The Archetype of Separation*. Basel: Karger, pp. 104–112.

Tylor, E., 2010 (1871), *Primitive Culture: Researches into the Development of Mythology, Philosophy, Religion, Art and Custom*, New York: Cambridge University Press.

Vanstiphout, H.L.J., 1984, Inanna/Ishtar as a Figure of Controversy. In: HG Kippenberg and I Finkel (eds), *Struggles of Gods: Papers of the Groningen Work Group for the Study of the History of Religions (Religion and Reason)*, Berlin: Walter de Gruyter, pp. 225–238.

Variety, 2018, 'Robin Wright on Directing and Final Season of 'House of Cards''. Available at https://variety.com/video/robin-wright-house-of-cards-final-season-int erview (Accessed: 20 August 2019).

Wolkstein, D. and Kramer, S.N., 1983, *Inanna: Queen of Heaven and Earth: Her Stories and Hymns from Sumer*, New York: Harper & Row.

Chapter 7

Gender and the political in Antigone

The need to listen to others

Terence Dawson

André Lardinois (2012) suggests that critical responses to Sophocles' *Antigone* (*c.* 442 BCE) are of three kinds: (1) those who argue that Antigone is predominantly in the right (the 'orthodox view'), (2) those who seek to balance the views of Antigone and Kreon and see the tragedy in terms of a tension between family/ religion and law/the polis (the 'Hegelian view'), and (3) those who are trying to move beyond these two positions (see also Hester, 1971; Holt, 1999). Almost all of these responses assume that (a) whatever the differences in status and gender between Antigone and Kreon, they belong to the same kind of reality; and (b) the tragedy is primarily about the ethical and/or legal merit of the views they each express. In literal terms, both assumptions are almost incontrovertible.

Athenian tragedy, however, is not to be understood literally. Like myth, on which it is usually based, its language is that of *metaphor*—and metaphors are always about something *other* than the literal.

According to Jung, our deeper dreams express themselves in the language of metaphor (1968, p.157). They express tendencies of our personality, often those that are problematic or misguided. They implicitly challenge the dreamer to come to terms with such tendencies, and/or to depict the possible consequences of not doing so (1969, p. 250ff.). In a dream, the carrier of the dreamer's personality is the *dream I*, usually just a perceiving consciousness. The situation in which it finds itself represents a concern pertinent to the dreamer at that moment in their life. The other figures in the dream reflect different aspects of a difficulty or challenge confronting the *dream I* and, by extension, also the dreamer. By definition, they are *others* and, as such, they 'belong' to a different kind of reality from the *dream I*. By engaging with the tensions represented in their dreams, individuals can identify and come to terms with their own problematic or misguided tendencies.

Applying these views—that is, regarding *every moment* in the play as a representation of a challenge implicitly facing *one* character—generates a surprisingly coherent reading of *Antigone*. Sometimes building on, and sometimes recasting Jungian theory, these pages argue (1) that the play's effective protagonist is Kreon, and (2) that his differences with the other main characters (Antigone, Haimon and Teiresias) explicate the specific nature of his misguided tendencies.

Jung argues that our perceptions about *others* provide the key to the nature of our own problematic attitudes (1969, p. 266). *Antigone* was written long before it became usual for writers to explore their own personal difficulties. Most narratives composed earlier than the enlightenment reflect collective rather than personal (autobiographical) concerns. It is highly unlikely that *Antigone* expresses a challenge facing Sophocles as an individual; it is equally unlikely that Kreon is intended to represent any specific individual. Rather, he is the *carrier* of a concern that intrigued (and may have troubled) Sophocles at the time of writing—a concern that was far less psychological than it was political.

In *Antigone*, the psychological *represents* the political. In the first half, each episode represents an aspect of a challenge facing Kreon; in the second half, the episodes represent the inevitable consequences of his failure to meet this challenge. Kreon's hubris represents the hubris of the city's political leaders. The play suggests that a similar hubris was keeping Athens in a state of perpetual hostility with its neighbours. It offers a scathing critique of the political leadership of Athens and expresses a worry that their leaders might be leading the polis to disaster.

The argument is in three parts. The first suggests that the fascination aroused by 'mythical' or 'archetypal' material reflects a (pre)disposition in the *subject*. The second demonstrates how all the key moments in the play refer to an implicit challenge facing Kreon and how this challenge reflects political difficulties facing Athens at the time the play was written. The third considers the recent tendency to consider its eponymous heroine as a representation of the female self.

The origins and history of interest in *Antigone*

According to Jung, the experience of archetypal images in a dream invariably produces a powerful and destabilising emotional response (1969, p. 205; Samuels, 1986, p. 26). Something similar can be illustrated by the reception history of *Antigone*, for many of the claims made about the tragedy, and especially about its eponymous heroine, harbour an unusual emotional insistence. Jung sometimes attributed the numinosity of archetypal images to the *object* (the image experienced); and sometimes to an emergent notion in the *subject* (the dreamer). These pages lend support to the *latter* view.

During the long middle ages, the Athenian tragedies were all but forgotten. The seven extant plays of Sophocles were first published in print during the renaissance (1502). Slowly they began to stir the imaginations of a broader readership, and toward the end of the eighteenth century, *Antigone* began to be singled out.

The enlightenment is sometimes decried for promoting an over-emphasis on 'reason'. This is daft. The term does not describe a specific philosophical propensity or programme. It is best understood as a loosely defined cultural period which did indeed place a new insistence on logical reasoning, empiricism, and the organisation of knowledge—that is, on what we now call scientific thought. But important as these developments were, they were accompanied by others of just as great a consequence.

The enlightenment also witnessed a new interest in the past, in history, and national identity. New ideas about education, the rights of the individual, and the value of personal liberty redefined the relation between the individual and the state. The emergence of political parties, new religious movements, and a new sense of social responsibility redefined social values. Fresh ideas about the importance of sensibility, about the rights of women and children redefined not only the family, but also society. And a new concern with subjectivity, the private self, and the imagination redefined the individual (Pinker, 2018). The enlightenment is characterised by various attempts to correct previous misconceptions and better understand our relation to the world. And it was during the enlightenment—for the first time since antiquity—that *Antigone* was recognized as a great work.

Two very different but equally deeply felt responses to the play illustrate this. The earlier finds *tyranny* at its heart. It was written by a fiery Italian aristocrat who, during his life, was best known for his love of horses and his amours with married women, including the young wife of the aging Charles Edward Stuart, *aka* Bonnie Prince Charlie (Alfieri, 1877; Lee, 1884). Today, Vittorio Alfieri is remembered as a Piedmontese poet and as the foremost writer of Italian neo-classical tragedies. Like Voltaire before him, he was a typical intellectual of the enlightenment: a man from the privileged class who angrily denounced the abuses characteristic of his class.

Alfieri claimed that he wrote for "generous and free men, men who seek virtue and reject violence, who love their country and know their rights" (1985, p. 35, cited in Salis, 2010, p. 90). The early 1770s witnessed several works based on *Antigone*, including operas by Tommaso Traetta and Josef Mysliveček. Alfieri's play was published in 1776, the year of the American *Declaration of Independence*. Its protagonist is Creonte, whom Alfieri depicts as an ambitious, self-centred, hypocritical and ruthless tyrant obsessed with power (Salis, 2010, pp. 87–90). The myth was a vehicle through which he could express his driving concern for nobility of spirit and freedom from oppressive government. The following year, he published *Of Tyranny*, in which he reflects on how the upper classes take advantage of the fears, cowardice, and petty ambitions of the people in order to govern tyrannically (1961).

The second major response to the play was by a French scholar of classical antiquity, best known as an authority on numismatics and for having deciphered, in the 1750s, the Palmyrene and the Phoenician alphabets. In his seventies, Jean-Jacques Barthélemy published a pedagogical work deeply rooted in late-eighteenth-century *sensibility*.

Travels of Anacharsis the Younger in Greece in the Middle of the Fourth Century before the Common Era was published on the eve of the French Revolution (1788). It was a huge success and almost immediately translated into German, English, and Russian. It tells the story of a young descendant of the philosopher Anacharsis, a Scythian reputed to have had a knack for seeing Athenian customs in an unexpected light. Some have described it as a rambling novel, but this is to misclassify it. Barthélemy's work offers a wide-ranging, highly imaginative, and easily accessible introduction to classical Greece and its culture for the privileged and educated classes. Volume two, chapter 11, is given to 'A Performance at the Theatre', that is, at the Theatre of Dionysos in Athens—and the first play on the programme is Sophocles' *Antigone*.

Barthélemy describes the arrival of his hero at the theatre, expresses his surprise at the size of the crowds, and offers a succinct account of the plot. Unlike Alfieri, his emphasis is not on tyranny, but on the depth of feeling aroused in him by the words that Sophocles gives to Antigone. Anacharsis hears her weep: "Alas! At this fateful moment I find myself abandoned. The Thebans are indifferent to my troubles. I have no friend to weep even a tear. I hear death calling for me, and the gods say nothing. But of what am I guilty?" (1790, p. 223; my tr.). He responds as a typical eighteenth-century 'man of feeling'. He is physically overwhelmed by Antigone's fate: he has 'no more tears to weep'. He cannot think of attending another play. He returns home to record his experience in his diary and reflect on it.

He is shaken by his response to Antigone's predicament. But, as a typical product of enlightenment thought, he also wants to *understand* it, and his attention is fixed not only on what is happening on the stage, but also on his own *subjective* and *affective* response to this:

> What kind of art is this which arouses in me, simultaneously, such pain and such pleasure? Which makes me vividly experience adversities which in reality I would not be able to bear? What a wonderful fusion of illusions and realities! [...] Thirty thousand spectators melting in tears increased my emotions and my enthusiasm.
>
> (p. 222)

That is, he wonders what it is about the events of an Athenian tragedy that engender such powerful emotions in him. It is an issue that continues to intrigue scholars (Taplin, 1978; Nuttall, 1996).

Ever since the publication of Barthélemy's work, writers have responded to *Antigone*—and especially to its heroine—with the same immoderate enthusiasm as Anacharsis. For example, about 1814 Percy Shelley read Alfieri's *Tragedies* (including *Antigone*) in English translation. In 1818, while briefly settled in Bagni di Lucca, Mary Shelley devoured Barthélemy's historical recreation of classical Greece in French (M. Shelley, 1947, pp. 218–219; also 100–101 and 229). And in 1821, her husband Percy admitted to being so fascinated by the character of Antigone that she coloured his real-life relationships: "Some of us have in a prior existence been in love with an Antigone, and that makes us find no full content in any mortal tie" (P. Shelley, 1964, vol. 2, p. 364).

Hegel was twenty when Barthélemy's work appeared in German translation, and he too came to see *Antigone* as one of the consummate works of European literature. In the 1820s, he described it as "one of the most sublime and in every respect most excellent works of art of all time" (1975, p. 464). In surprisingly unphilosophical language, he refers to its heroine as "the heavenly (*himmlische*) Antigone, that noblest of figures that ever appeared on earth" (1955, p. 441). In similar vein, in 1888 the eminent classical scholar, R. C. Jebb, described Antigone as "the noblest, and the most profoundly tender, embodiment of woman's heroism which ancient literature can show" (1891, p. v).

The mid-twentieth century witnessed a new wave of creative interest in *Antigone*, both for its depiction of tyranny and for the character of its heroine. Catalan poet and playwright Salvador Espriu wrote his *Antígona* in 1939, although it was not published until much later (1955), and he later revised the text to include a new character called Lucid Counsellor. Meanwhile, Jean Anouilh had adapted the play for performance during the German occupation of Paris (1944). His work cleverly plays realism and irony against the pattern of events demanded by the myth. Almost immediately, other writers began to adapt *Antigone* for their own political and/or activist ends. They include German dramatist Bertolt Brecht (1948), the Puerto Rican Luis Rafael Sánchez (1968), the South African Athol Fugard (1973), the Nigerian Femi Osofisan (1999), the Peruvian poet José Watanabe (2000), and, to protest the American invasion of Iraq, Irish poet Seamus Heaney (2004). In short, in the face of any form of perceived oppression or tyranny, a well-meaning activist-writer will soon appear with a new adaptation of *Antigone*.

From the 1950s, psychoanalysts, scholars interested in psychoanalysis, and feminists were also writing about *Antigone* in highly charged terms. In 1959, Jacques Lacan argued that Antigone was motivated by a death wish. He identified the central conflict of the play as "the effect of beauty on desire" (1986, p. 291). In 1984, Luce Irigaray described Antigone as 'anti-woman', the production of "a culture that has been written by men alone". In 2000, Judith Butler argued that Antigone is "the occasion for a new field of the human, achieved [...] when gender is displaced, and kinship founders on its own founding laws" (Butler, p. 82; see also Söderbäck, 2010).

In short, current fascination with Sophocles' *Antigone* stems from three periods associated with unusually significant change—periods when previous assumptions were overthrown by new modes of thinking and being: (1) the renaissance, when the rediscovery of classical literature promoted the exploration of new ideas and new topics in fiction; (2) the enlightenment, whose heady mix of politics and sensibility-cum-social responsibility laid the foundations of modernity, and dramatically expanded the concerns of literature; and (3) the call for a new kind of political and gender activism which emerged in the mid-twentieth century, which has impacted forcefully on political thinking and writing ever since. In short, the fascination exercised by this myth may stem less from its ostensibly archetypal properties (whatever these might be) than from the emergent ideas with which individual writers happen to be grappling at the time. Writers find in the myth corroboration of *their own emergent concerns*—that is, of the ideas or notions that fascinate them.

The psychological *represents* the political

Jung was amongst the first to note that dreams are dialogical both in their content and in relation to the dreamer (1969, pp. 248–249). He thought every dream, whatever its ostensible subject, reflected an aspect of the dreamer (1970, p. 151). He sought to understand why a specific dream was experienced by a specific individual at a specific moment in their life (1977, p. 110). He is best known for having attributed the *form* of a myth to the collective unconscious; that is, to an autonomous tendency inherent to the psyche (1977, p. 163). Nonetheless, and far more usefully, he also conceded that both the content of a myth and its implications arise in response to specific cultural tendencies. If this is so, then in effect a myth is never *about* the story it ostensibly tells. It constitutes a response, in the language of metaphor, to the specific tendencies which triggered it. Its function is to provoke the society in which it emerges to reflect on its implications.

Athens' most important civic festival was the City Dionysia. It featured a prestigious three-day drama competition (*agon*) in which each of the three 'finalists' had to present a tetralogy: that is, three more or less closely related tragedies followed by a satyr play. Given the occasion, one would expect all four play to contain topical references. Each spectator (*theoros*) would have been awake to the possible civic relevance of the material presented.

The events of *Antigone* are imagined as following soon after those of the closing scene of Aeschylus' play, *Seven Against Thebes* (467 BCE). Initially, this focused on mourning the brothers, Eteokles and Polyneikes. About fifty years after the poet's death, however, owing to the popularity of *Antigone*, its ending was changed in order to anticipate the events of Sophocles' play. After the death of Oedipus, his sons agree to rule Thebes in alternate years. Eteokles is the first to assume power, but when Polyneikes claims his turn, Eteokles refuses to step aside. Polyneikes then rouses the help of an army from Argos and attacks Thebes. The brothers are killed fighting each other; the Argive army promptly abandons hostilities; and Kreon (Oedipus's brother-in-law) seizes the throne for himself.

Antigone is set in Thebes ('*not*-Athens') and unfolds in the timeless world of myth ('*not*-now'). The characters wear masks to indicate that they do *not* belong to the social reality of the spectators. They are emphatically *other*. No earlier mention of Kreon's proclamation, which triggers the plot, or of Antigone's response to it, has survived. Although Sophocles borrowed his characters from myth, he may have devised the story of Antigone. He is certainly responsible for choosing the unexpected imagery of the odes. The origins of most myths are lost in the mists of time. The story of *Antigone* may have been born at a specific moment in the history of Athens in response to political issues specific to this moment.

Jung insisted that every dream reflects an aspect of the dreamer. In similar fashion, might there be a character to which all the events of the play can be related? If so, it will be revealed by the structure of the play:

Prologue   Antigone and Ismene argue about Kreon's proclamation
Episode 1   Kreon and chorus leader; then Kreon and Guard
Episode 2   Guard and Antigone; Kreon and Antigone + Ismene
Episode 3   Kreon and Haimon; Kreon and the Chorus
Episode 4   *kommos*: Chorus and Antigone; then Kreon and Antigone
Episode 5   Kreon and Teiresias
Exodos   Messenger; Kreon enters to learn consequences of his actions

Antigone features only in the prologue, episode two, and episode four. She is referred to, either implicitly or explicitly, in the other episodes, but is barely mentioned in the closing scene. In contrast, Kreon not only issues the proclamation which triggers the plot; he is *central* to all five episodes; and the *exodos* is about him. He is the effective protagonist.

Kreon's centrality is further suggested by the probable distribution of roles between the three actors. The actor who played the part of Antigone probably also played the parts of Eurydike and the domestic in the Exodos, and possibly also Teiresias. If this is so, the actor who played Ismene would also played the Guard, Haimon, and the Messenger. In contrast, the actor who played Kreon is unlikely to have had any other part.

The play begins with Antigone and Ismene, the daughters of Oedipus, advancing out of the palace doors onto the stage. Because Eteokles was king, and he was killed defending Thebes against a 'foreign' army, Kreon has decreed he is to be buried with full honours. But because Polyneikes was attacking his own people, Kreon has issued a public proclamation announcing that anyone caught offering his corpse burial rites will be put to death. Antigone is outraged: she cannot accept that her brother's body be left to the mercy of wild dogs and the elements. She tells Ismene that she is determined to perform the funeral rites for him. Not to do so, she insists, would be to dishonour both herself and the gods (Segal, 1995). She appeals to the laws of kinship and of the gods.

In the opening line of the play, she places an exaggerated emphasis on her kinship with Ismene ("My very own sister, Ismene herself"; see Brown, 1987, p. 136). She wants—indeed, she *expects*—her sister's help. But Ismene hesitates to defy the laws of the polis, the community of citizens of which she is a part, whereupon Antigone derides her. The irony is evident: she is so determined to honour her *brother* that she does not realise how brutal she is being toward her *sister*.

The prologue introduces the key terms of the play. Ismene acknowledges that the law of the polis takes precedence over personal considerations. To borrow from *King Lear* (II, ii), Antigone believes that righteous anger "hath a privilege". Her single-mindedness is compelling, because righteous anger allied to courage and determination usually is. But her treatment of Ismene raises questions: it is clearly unbalanced.

The personal grief and outrage expressed in the prologue give way to a hymn of collective thanksgiving sung by the chorus of elderly men as they enter (the *parodos*). They explain how the Argive army was soaring threateningly over Thebes 'like an eagle' when Zeus 'who-turns-the-enemy-to-flight' decided in favour of Thebes. The enemy having withdrawn, the Theban elders now invite Bacchus to lead their celebrations. Many of those in the audience would have noted the subject and imagery of the ode. They would have remembered the recent revolt of the Euboeans; and that as soon as the Athenians sent an army to quell the rebellion, a Spartan army surrounded Athens—and, albeit briefly, threatened it (Thucydides, 1996, I.114, p. 63). It was a brutal reminder to the Athenians that their aggressive policies were increasingly *resented* by their erstwhile allies, and that they *depended* on neighbouring regions for much of their food.

The focus of the first episode is on Kreon. His claim to the throne is probably legitimate: even his name suggests this, for Kreon means 'king', or 'master'. And yet, like Claudius at the outset of *Hamlet*, he is strangely ill at ease (cf. Kitto, 1956; Stilling, 1976). He is afraid that someone might take up Antigone's cause or otherwise rise in revolt against him. He sees threats where none exists. He is paranoid. He bullies the Theban elders so as to ensure their support. He tries to persuade them that he has the qualities of a good king by identifying the qualities he associates with a poor leader:

> in my view, anyone who, while responsible for the whole city, fails to follow through on the best advice, but owing to some fear does nothing, is now—and always has been—the most despicable of men.
>
> (1994, p. 21, ll. 178–180, my trans.)

As the play unfolds, 'owing to some fear' Kreon repeatedly rejects the well-meant advice of others: for example, in his confrontations with Haimon (episode three) and with Teiresias (episode five). Following his confrontation with Teiresias, he also rejects the advice of the chorus leader—a decision followed almost immediately by the catastrophe. According to his own definition, Kreon is the worst possible kind of leader: he is defined by his reluctance to *listen* to others.

In the second part of the episode, one of the guards, tasked with preventing anyone trying to conduct burial rites for Polyneikes, admits that someone managed to slip past them, and to lightly cover the corpse and sprinkle water on it. Kreon is irate. He berates the guard for having succumbed to the worst of all evils. If they don't find the person responsible, he will punish them for having accepted bribes. The charge is revealing, for the guard clearly hasn't taken any bribe. As he insists, Kreon is too willing to believe "what is not true"—that is, he is surrendering to misplaced fears (l. 323).

Later, he will accuse Teiresias of taking bribes. But why, in a play which is *not* obviously about money or bribery, are there such insistent references to illicit gain? They would have reminded the audience that several of Athens' recent leaders had been thought guilty of bribery. In 471, Themistocles, the victor at Salamis, was ostracised, ostensibly because he had taken bribes (Thucydides, I.135–136, p. 76). In 463, the young Pericles tried, unsuccessfully, to have Kimon ostracised for bribery (Azoulay, 2014, p. 25). And yet in 446, following the revolt in Megara,

Pericles also resorted to bribery in order to persuade the Spartans to negotiate (Plutarch, 1916,'Pericles', 23, p. 67).

The scene underlines parallels between Kreon and the guard. Just as luck has made Kreon king, so luck has allowed the guard to redeem himself with Kreon. Both are delighted to be able to take Antigone prisoner. Neither gives any thought to the hurt they inflict on her by doing so; and even less to the possibility that they might be offending the gods by their actions. Neither is intrinsically perverse; they are 'human, all too human': their primary concern is their own advancement.

As Kreon and the guard leave the stage separately, the chorus begin their first ode. Although the odes of *Antigone* are widely admired for their poetry, scholars still do not agree about their relevance to the play. As we shall see, they harbour images that would have carried strong political associations.

The elders credit the various achievements of human beings not to the gods, but to human ingenuity. And yet, for all the intelligence, imagination, and ingenuity that humans manifest in practical matters, they seem to be incapable of choosing the best path for their own life. When human beings adhere to "the laws of the earth and the justice the gods have sworn to uphold", they are respected by their polis. But if, either from stupidity or recklessness, a person fails to take account of civic laws and divine justice, they will be cast out from their polis.

It might seem as if the elders are referring to Antigone. But as the play progresses, it becomes increasingly clear that these lines primarily refer to Kreon. By denying the corpse of Polyneikes something which is due to it, he is misapplying "the laws of the earth" and ignoring "the justice the gods have sworn to uphold". His thoughts are not on the welfare of the polis. He is bent on his own personal agenda. Thucydides, the leader of the aristocratic faction, had recently accused Pericles of this same offence (Plutarch, 'Pericles', 14, p. 47).

Pericles was a quiet, level-headed, and well-educated man who enjoyed the company of philosophers and artists. He was a democrat. His dream was to rebuild Athens so that it would be the marvel of the Mediterranean world. He was responsible for many of the buildings one can see on the Acropolis today, as well as for the Odeion, the Temple to Hephaistos, and for redesigning the Agora. But Thucydides was almost certainly correct. His building programme was both extravagant and an aggressive assertion of power by Athens. And many in the audience would have wondered whether either was in the best interests of the polis.

The second episode begins with a guard leading Antigone, a prisoner, onto the stage. He feels a genuine pity for Antigone, but his kinder instinct is smothered by a deeper thirst for advancement, and the joy he feels at being able to recover the king's regard is very similar to the joy that Kreon experiences when he discovers that he has caught Antigone in his "net" (ll. 341–342).

Kreon appears from the palace. Whilst he is taken aback to learn that Antigone has disobeyed his proclamation, she boldly admits having returned to her brother's corpse, because his proclamation "does not have sufficient force" to overrule the timeless, "unwritten and unfailing edicts of the gods (ll. 450–457; my tr.). She rests her case on cultural tradition; that is, on what is *known* and *believed* by every adult in Thebes (i.e. also in Athens), but has never been made into law. Not trying to bury her brother would not only pain her, it would bring upon her the anger of the gods. She would rather accept her fate. This shocks the chorus leader, who would like to sympathise with her, but as a representative of the polis he cannot accept that Kreon's proclamation be flouted.

Afraid that she is laughing at him, Kreon reminds her that "over-stubborn wills are the most apt to fall" and that "spirited horses are controlled by a tight rein", for pride is impossible "for anyone who is another's slave" (ll. 473–478). He is referring to Antigone, utterly unaware that his metaphors also apply to him. He too is over-stubborn, and because he is afraid that her strength of will emasculates him ("Indeed, now I am no man, but she is a man", ll. 482–485), he feels compelled to crush her. She retorts by affirming that she cannot think of hatred, but only of love (see Blundell, 1989, pp. 106–148). And yet she contradicts herself almost immediately, for Ismene appears and announces that, because she shares Antigone's guilt, she wants to share her fate. Once again, Antigone shows her contempt for her sister, whom she says can only love in 'words'. In a final attempt to prevent Antigone's execution, Ismene turns to Kreon: "Will you kill your son's bride-to-be?" Yes, he assures her insultingly, for Haimon will easily find other women.

The second ode hinges on the question: What can humans do to check the power of Zeus? Humans often strive for more than Zeus allows them to accomplish. Even dreams reveal a controlling factor which the Greeks called Zeus. The implication is that the care with which we pursue our goals must be complemented by self-understanding. Only this can help us to live free of unrealistic objectives. This clearly relates to Antigone, but far more importantly, as the sequel will show, it relates to Kreon. Human beings might determine the challenges they set themselves, but Zeus—or Fate—will always decide their outcome.

The following episode focuses on the qualities necessary for good leadership. It is a literary *tour de force*. Kreon and Haimon are given *exactly* equal parts to present their views. Appealing to his filial nature, the king tries to persuade Haimon to abandon Antigone, to which his son replies that *if* his guidance is good (*kalós* = beautiful), it will guide him even after he marries. Kreon is stymied; he begins to bluster about the need for people always to retain their 'good sense' (φρένας)—and then promptly contradicts himself by making increasingly insulting suggestions about Antigone.

Haimon responds by telling his father that his 'good sense' comes from the gods, but it rests with him whether he uses it. He reminds him that people murmur their criticism of him only out of his hearing, and that many Thebans are upset by the charges he has brought against Antigone. He should not assume he is always right, for people who claim to hold the only view possible are invariably found to be braggarts, and their claims, vacuous. It isn't shameful to be flexible and adaptable.

The chorus leader thereupon asks each to learn from the other, but Kreon is outraged by the suggestion that he should learn from his son. The ensuing argument is conducted in rapid-fire one-liners (*stichomythia*). Kreon expresses an increasing obsession with having his way. Haimon calmly attempts to persuade him that he should be more concerned with what is best for the polis. His father retorts:

Kreon: Am I to take my orders from the polis?
Haimon: Can't you see, you're arguing like a schoolboy?
Kreon: Should I rule for others rather than for myself?
Haimon: Yes, for a polis does not belong to any individual.

(ll. 734–737)

Kreon is incensed:

Kreon: You scoundrel! Putting your own father on trial!
Haimon: Because I think you are offending justice.
Kreon: Am I wrong to exercise the rights that belong to my position?
Haimon: No rights allow you to trample on the honours *owed* the gods.

(ll. 742–747)

Kreon assumes his son is speaking on Antigone's behalf. But Haimon's primary reason is not to defend an *individual*, least of all to fight for his *personal* interest. As the sequel makes clear, he loves Antigone, but their love is incidental to the issue Sophocles foregrounds. Haimon represents a genuinely filial son who is also deeply concerned for the welfare of the polis. He is concerned the gods below might cruelly punish Thebes.

Their argument hinges on the need to maintain sound judgement (φρήν = the heart-cum-mind as the source of passion, perception, and thought) in order to govern with justice and wisdom, and in accordance with custom. A person cannot rule with φρήν unless they not only listen to others, but also are prepared to learn from what others have to say. Because Kreon won't listen to both sides of a case—as the audience have just done—he offends both justice and wisdom.

This brings the play to its climax. Kreon calls to have "the hateful creature" (Antigone) brought in and killed in front of her bridegroom. Does Haimon respond to this with any gesture? He says nothing; he exits. He is no longer able to reason with his father, whose sole thought is to assert his power. Kreon decides to kill both his nieces. "Both?" the chorus leader asks. Kreon pauses, and then decides to punish only Antigone. He will seal her in a cave, providing her with just enough food so that anyone finding her will think she died not of hunger, but from other natural causes (ll. 773–780). Not even Hades would be able to save her. The cruelty is shocking and the disrespect of Hades signals monstrous hubris.

The third ode comes as a surprise, for it is about the power of Eros. Its relevance to the play is not immediately evident, for the only lovers (Haimon and Antigone) do not exchange so much as a word, even a glance. Whilst *eros* means *sexual love*, here it refers to all passionately held desires that tear the mind from its proper channels. In the first strophe, these include the desire to dominate and to appropriate wealth that belongs to others. In its antistrophe, first it is identified as the cause of the preceding quarrel between Kreon and Haimon; then it is associated with Aphrodite.

At the mention of Aphrodite, Antigone re-enters—and the Chorus Leader chants the compassion he feels at seeing her on her way to her death. This introduces the *kommos*: an affect-charged lament (the word means a striking or beating of the head or breast) for someone who has died or been killed. The irony is chilling, for Antigone is lamenting *her own death*. She is not feeling sorry for herself; nor is she regretting her action. She is reflecting on the consequences of her defiance of Kreon. Earlier, she had insisted on assuming responsibility for her *action*; now she must assume responsibility for its *consequences*.

The *kommos* marks the climax of the play. Antigone has lost any expectation that she will ever come to marry and thereby know sexual love. The angry, stubborn, and bullying, but nonetheless vital teenager has become a young woman who knows she now has to face the consequences of her earlier behaviour. She asks the chorus—and, by extension, *also* the audience—to bear witness to her final journey: that is, to grasp its full horror.

Instead of marrying into an expanded social world, she will become the bride of Acheron (Death). She will never enjoy any of the pleasures of life. She will never be loved. She will never marry. She will never bear children. She will never take pleasure in watching her offspring grow and fall in love and bear children in their turn. She likens her punishment to that of Niobe, whereupon the chorus leader reminds her that, like Niobe, she will become a figure from myth.

Antigone can hardly believe he can be so obtuse. She does not want to be remembered as a heroine from myth—that is, to be remembered for *an instinctive and courageous gesture*. She does not want to be robbed of life when she is about to marry. She is devastated by the thought of losing the mortal life to which she was looking forward. She asks the Theban elders to bear witness not to her conviction, but to her *punishment*. This is why she cannot be compared, as R. C. Jebb suggested, to a Christian martyr (1891, p. xxv). Her highest value is not the afterlife, but life lived to its full within her polis—and both have been stolen from her. She has been cast into the indeterminate zone of the alien—the migrant worker who is a resident, but not a citizen of Athens. She feels neither dead, nor alive.

The remainder of the fourth episode is given to the second *agon* between Kreon and Antigone. Although impatient to see the last of her, Kreon's primary concern is to insist that whatever happens to her, his motives were, and continue to be pure. Antigone then delivers her farewell to the world, and its primary concern is to insist that *her* motives were pure. She clings to one point: Heaven does not forbid anyone to mourn a member of their immediate family and so she broke no law of Heaven. Whilst she takes comfort in the prospect of meeting her family in the underworld, she is nonetheless outraged to be descending there before her time, and regrets that her dreams of marriage, happiness, and children will come to nought.

The emphasis Antigone gives to this suggests that one of the fundamental duties of a polis is to ensure that all its citizens are able to enjoy the partnerships they desire and the pleasures arising from these, especially the joy of having children and grandchildren. Although predominantly or exclusively male, the audience would have understood immediately that her lament was meant to recall the laments of all the young wives whose husbands had been killed or brutally maimed in the course of Athens' incessant quarrels with her neighbours. She ends with a wish that either a *god* would tell her she has done wrong so that she could accept it or, if her impulse was justified, that those who have made her suffer will be made to suffer in similar fashion.

The dominant theme of the complex ode that follows is the impossibility of resisting a divine force immeasurably more powerful than oneself. The elders still want Antigone to *accept* not only that she was at fault, but also her fate. To illustrate their view, they refer to mythological figures either mastered or tamed by a god (Danaë, Lycurgus, and Phineus).

But as they sing, they finally realise that Kreon is also at fault and that his determination to have Antigone put to death is a form of self-defeating jealousy. His φρήν (good sense) has been 'wrenched' from a 'just' course by the power of a misguided desire. Dionysos will soon punish him. More importantly, they are suggesting that, until now, Fate has allowed Athens to browbeat her neighbouring colonies and 'master' them. But Fate may one day turn against her "dark ships" (ll. 951–954), and Fate cannot be resisted, either by Antigone, or by Kreon, or by the wealth or walls of Athens. Fate may no longer protect the polis from her irate neighbours, including Sparta and Boeotia.

We now realise that the *eros* referred to in the third ode is the compulsive drive responsible for the empire-building ambitions of Athens and her obsessive desire to extend the number of its colonies. It wrenches 'good sense' and 'justice' from their proper course. The quarrels it stirs between kin (Keon and Antigone) are also the quarrels of Athens with her neighbours. Athens has lost sight of what is 'just'. She has become a bold, adventurous, and aggressive sea-faring nation which likes to plunder the wealth of others. The wits of her citizens have been unsettled by desires stirred in them by the power of Aphrodite

Led by a boy, Teiresias now enters and tells Kreon categorically both to listen to him, and to 'obey' him. For at his seat of augury, he has been horrified by the portents. The gods are rejecting the city's prayers and sacrifices. The whole city is sick, and this sickness stems from Kreon's φρήν—his heart, his mind, and his perceptions. Even now, however, it is not too late for him to acknowledge his error and reverse his decision. Everyone makes mistakes; only stubbornly persisting in them is wrong.

Kreon is in no mood to listen. He berates the prophet's mantic skills and taunts him for being interested in financial gain. Teiresias can only bemoan how little human beings value sound judgement (εὐβουλία). Drunk on his own hubris, Kreon now scorns all prophets as greedy. Were his eagles to rip the flesh from the corpse of Polyneikes and deliver it to the throne of Zeus, he would still be convinced that Teiresias had contrived the event to discredit him. Teiresias would rather not pronounce a prophecy. He warns the king not to provoke him, but Kreon goads him into doing so. It is a terrible moment.

Teiresias tells Kreon that the implacable Furies and the gods below are lying in wait for him, ready to trap him for crimes he has brought upon himself. Before many days are past, because he has dishonoured and confined 'below' a living soul who belongs in the 'upper world' (Antigone), and has kept in the 'upper world' a corpse which belongs to the gods in the world 'below' (Polyneikes), Kreon will lose one of his own children. He then turns to his assistant boy and exits.

Kreon is stunned. The chorus leader advises him to release Antigone. Kreon hesitates. The chorus leader reminds him that, once they have decided something, the gods move swiftly. Kreon relents. He concedes that Antigone might have been right. And yet he continues to dither, and as the sequel makes clear, this final hesitation seals his fate. Not until the chorus leader urges him to decide quickly does he make a move to free Antigone.

The Theban elders now begin their fifth ode: an invocation of Dionysos, the god of liberation and healing, whose help is sought to end the plague brought about by Kreon's hubris. In the second antistrophe, as if they were in a trance, they invoke the young Dionysos, begging him to appear as Iakhos, giver of blessings—as he probably did at a highpoint of the Eleusinian Mysteries. They assume that because Kreon has changed his mind, all will be well, and everyone will be reconciled. But Sophocles is using one of his favourite devices (cf. the earlier *Ajax* and *Women of Trachis*; also, the later *Oedipus the King*): the enthusiastic celebratory ode comes immediately before the catastrophe.

No sooner have the chorus invoked Iakchos, than a Messenger enters. Incongruously, he develops a commonplace: that the life of man is subject to chance and constant change. He is referring to Kreon. Only when the chorus leader impatiently cuts him short does he finally tell the Theban elders that Haimon has committed suicide. As he speaks, the Queen, Eurydike enters and asks him to continue his story. He tells her how he took Kreon and his men to the badly decomposed corpse of Polyneikes, where they offered what rites they could. Then they proceeded to a cave where they found Antigone hanging from a noose, and Haimon at her feet, his arms wrapped around her, bewailing his lost bride. When Kreon began to bluster, first Haimon tried to kill his father; then, failing to do so, he committed suicide.

On hearing this, the Queen slips away. The know-all Messenger reassures the chorus leader that she is too level-headed to do anything silly; that she has gone inside to lead her maids in private mourning.

Kreon re-enters and there follows a *second*, and unusually elaborate *kommos* in which Kreon *sings* his lines while the chorus leader interrupts either in speech or recitative. The reversal of the usual form heightens the tension. Kreon has finally understood that responsibility for the disaster lies with him. At last, he admits that the loss of his son was caused by his own poor judgement, and he ascribes his error to an irresistible fate leaping down on his head. The chorus leader pities him for not having seen this until too late.

Like Macbeth, Kreon reflects in striking poetry. He does not regret his treatment of Antigone. Rather, he wonders how Hades might be able to destroy him further. By having to witness his son's suicide, he has already been killed once: how can he be killed a second time? The answer is immediate. The palace doors open and servants emerge carrying Eurydike. A domestic tells the elders how the Queen held Kreon responsible for the deaths not only of Haimon and herself, but also of Antigone and Megareus (their older son, killed during the brief siege of Thebes). She has killed herself.

Kreon is totally crushed. He admits full responsibility. He wonders why no one strikes him dead. The last words are given to the chorus—and they clearly apply to Kreon:

> By far the most important part of happiness is to have sound judgement, and never to be irreverent toward the gods—for those whose words are overhasty and arrogant will suffer cruel blows, which as they grow old, will teach them wisdom.
>
> (ll. 1347–1353)

Kreon's punishment is shattering. It mirrors the one he imposed on Antigone. Just as he stole her hope of marriage and children, he now loses both his wife and his son. That is, he loses those who are more important to him even than his love of power. Like Antigone at the end of her farewell, although still alive, he feels as if he were dead.

The relation between law and divine justice is central to the play, and scholars still tend to focus on this. In contrast, this reading shifts the focus to suggest that the narrative hinges on an issue which is emphatically *psychological*: how the φρήν (good sense) of a civic leader is 'wrenched' from its proper channels by *compulsive tendencies* that stem from a ruthless desire (*eros*) for power matched by paranoia derived from insecurity. The most obvious manifestation of Kreon's mistaken attitudes is his reluctance to *listen to others* which is, of course, a form of hubris. With hindsight, he realises that he should have listened to Antigone, Haimon and Teiresias. Too late, he learns the consequences.

Sophocles and Pericles were well-acquainted with each other. At the first performance of *Antigone*, they probably sat within a few yards of each other. Pericles, however, had little patience with views that differed from his own. The real tragedy of the play is that if he had fully grasped its implications, he might have been far more careful not to continue provoking the anger of Sparta; and Athens might have avoided the calamitous Second Peloponnesian War—a war from which she never fully recovered.

When is a female self not female?

In sociological terms, every female character in a text can tell us something about a society's or a writer's attitudes toward women. In psychological terms, however, not every female character is a representation of the female self.

In sociological terms, whilst *Antigone* rests on social and gender stereotypes (men represent the polis/women are confined indoors; men bully/women are victimised), it also persistently undermines them. Antigone may never think to challenge Kreon's right to the throne, and yet *he* is deeply afraid that she might, while *she* is unafraid to walk outdoors, alone and at night, to where her brother's body lies.

In psychological terms, the play explores the relation between Kreon and the *others* with whom he engages—all of whom reflect an aspect of the challenge facing him. Ismene and Antigone are equally loyal, determined, and courageous: but whereas Ismene is level-headed, Antigone is not. And yet her excessive tendencies, although related to stereotypes about hysteria, have nothing to do with female psychology. They both *compensate* and *mirror* the tendencies of a man who is behaving equally excessively and in a very *un*-manly way. Antigone does not represent a young woman; she personifies views and tendencies to which, because Kreon is unsure of himself, he is reluctant to admit.

In episode four, harrowing though it is from *her* point of view, Antigone's farewell to the world both represents and anticipates the consequences of Kreon's mistaken attitudes. Sophocles has imagined her plight vividly; nonetheless, it is triggered by Kreon's failure to rise to the challenge implicitly facing *him*.

Antigone is a female character imagined by a male author whose primary interest is to explore the relation between ambition, fear of failure, and political tendencies. Her role in the play is (1) to simultaneously mirror *and* challenge Kreon's misguidedness, and (2) to personify the consequences of *his* brutality. But it is doubtful whether she can tell us very much, if anything, about a specifically female self.

The same probably holds for the heroines of all the recent adaptations of the play written by men, including those by Anouilh and Seamus Heaney. In recent years, however, many women writers, working in different fields, have also been drawn to the myth: for example, in psychoanalysis, Luce Irigaray (1984) and Bracha Ettinger (2010); in cultural and literary criticism, Martha Nussbaum (1986), Masako Hirai (1998) and Julia Kristeva (2010); and in recent fiction, Ali Smith (2015) and Kamila Shamsie (2017). Through them, and many others, an imaginal 'Antigone' has gradually become assimilated into what *might* be called the female self—but is there such a self?

We often refer to literary characters as if they were individuals with a definable 'centre' to their personality. We do so as shorthand. But with individuals, such shorthand is seriously misleading. Although Jung used the term *Das Ich* (= the I) to describe the 'centre' of the conscious personality, he was amongst the first psychologists to realise that personality may not have a fixed centre. In the standard English translation of his works, *das Ich* is rendered as 'the ego', which suggests something more fixed than the *I*. This is misleading, for the Jungian *I* is not fixed. It is only a mode of perceiving or of expressing ever changing concerns. The 'real me' is a unicorn. We are composed only of combinations of behavioural-cum-psychological *tendencies*. This suggests, paradoxically, that Jungian theory might have more in common than is widely appreciated not only with behaviourism but also with recent theories about a multiple self (e.g. Chater, 2018; Rowan, 1990; Lifton, 1993; Carter, 2008). Whilst *combinations* of such tendencies might reveal typical gender-based propensities, the *tendencies* themselves are probably found in men and women alike.

The author is grateful to Professor Richard Seaford for his many useful cautions and suggestions.

References

Alfieri, V., 1877, *Life of Vittorio Alfieri*, ed. W.D. Howells, Boston: James R. Osgood.

Alfieri, V., 1961, *Of Tyranny*, tr. J.A. Molinaro, B. Corrigan, Toronto: Toronto University Press.

Alfieri, V., 1985, *Tragedie*, vol. 1, Firenze: Sansoni.

Anouilh, J., 1944, *Nouvelles Pièces Noires: Jézabel, Antigone (1944), Roméo et Jeannette, Médée*, Paris: La Table ronde, 1946.

Azoulay, V., 2014, *Pericles of Athens*, Princeton: Princeton University Press.

Barthélemy, J.-J., 1790, *Voyage du jeune Anacharsis en Grèce, vers le milieu du quatrième siècle avant l'ère vulgaire* (1788), 3rd ed., Paris: De Bure L'Aîné.

Blundell, M.W., 1989, *Helping Friends and Harming Enemies: A Study in Sophocles and Greek Ethics*, Cambridge: Cambridge University Press, pp. 106–148.

Brecht, B., 1948, *Antigonemodell 1948*, ed. R. Berlau, Berlin: Gebrüder Weiss.

Brown, A. (ed), 1987, *Sophocles: Antigone*, Warminster: Aris & Phillips.

Butler, J., 2000, *Antigone's Claim: Kinship between Life and Death*, New York: Columbia University Press.

Carter, R., 2008, *Multiplicity: The New Science of Personality, Identity, and the Self*, London: Little Brown.

Chater, N., 2018, *The Mind Is Flat: The Illusion of Mental Depth and the Improvised Mind*, London: Allen Lane.

Espriu, S., 1955, *Antígona*, Palma de Mallorca: Editorial Moll.

Ettinger, B.L., 2010, 'Antigone with(Out) Jocaste'. In: S.E. Wilmer, A. Zukauskaite (eds), *Interrogating Antigone in Postmodern Philosophy and Criticism*, Oxford: Oxford University Press, pp. 212–228.

Fugard, A., 1973, 'The Island'. In: A. Fugard, J. Kani, W. Ntshona (eds), *Statements*, London: Oxford University Press, 1974.

Heaney, S., 2004, *The Burial at Thebes*, London: Faber and Faber.

Hegel, G.W.F., 1955, *Hegel's Lectures on the History of Philosophy* (1892), tr. E.S. Haldane, London: Routledge & Kegan Paul.

Hegel, G.W.F., 1975, *Lectures on Fine Art*, tr. T.M. Knox, 2 vols, Oxford: Clarendon Press.

Hester, D.A., 1971, 'Sophocles the Unphilosophical: A Study in the *Antigone*', *Mnemosyne*, 24(1), pp. 11–59.

Hirai, M., 1998, *Sisters in Literature: Female Sexuality in, Antigone, Middlemarch, Howards End and Women in Love*, Basingstoke: Palgrave Macmillan.

Holt, P., 1999, 'Polis and Tragedy in the *Antigone*', *Mnemosyne*, 52(6), pp. 658–690.

Irigaray, L., 1984, *Éthique de la Différence Sexuelle*, Paris: Minuit; *An Ethics of Sexual Difference*, tr. C. Burke, G.C. Gill, Ithaca: Cornell University Press, 1993, sections 115F, pp. 118–19E.

Jebb, R.C. (ed), 1891, *Sophocles: Works: Plays and Fragments, vol. 3, The Antigone* (1888), Cambridge: Cambridge University Press.

Jung, C.G., 1968, *The Archetypes and the Collective Unconscious*, London: Routledge & Kegan Paul.

Jung, C.G., 1969, *The Structure and Dynamics of the Psyche*, London: Routledge & Kegan Paul.

Jung, C.G., 1970, *Civilization in Transition*, London: Routledge & Kegan Paul.

Jung, C.G., 1977, *The Symbolic Life*, London: Routledge & Kegan Paul.

Kitto, H.D.F., 1956, *Form and Meaning in Drama: A Study of Six Greek Plays and of, Hamlet*, London: Methuen.

Kristeva, J., 2010, 'Antigone: Limit and Horizon'. In: F. Söderbäck (ed), *Feminist Readings of Antigone*, New York: SUNY, pp. 215–229.

Lacan, J., 1986, *Le Séminaire: Tome 7: L'Éthique de la psychanalyse* (1959–1960), ed. J.-A. Miller, Paris: Seuil.

Lardinois, A., 2012, 'Antigone'. In: K. Ormand (ed), *A Companion to Sophocles*, Chichester: Blackwell, pp. 55–68.

Lee, V. [Violet Paget], 1884, *The Countess of Albany*, London: W.H. Allen.

Lifton, R.J., 1993, *The Protean Self: Human Resilience in an Age of Fragmentation*, Chicago: University of Chicago Press.

Nussbaum, M.C., 1986, *The Fragility of Goodness: Luck and Ethics in Greek Tragedy and Philosophy*, Cambridge: Cambridge University Press.

Nuttall, A.D., 1996, *Why Does Tragedy Give Pleasure?* Oxford: Clarendon.

Osofisan, F., 1999, *Tegonni, an African Antigone*, Ibadan: Opon Ifa.

Pinker, S., 2018, *Enlightenment Now*, London: Allen Lane.

Plutarch , 1916, '*Pericles'*, *Plutarch's Lives*, tr. B. Perrin, vol. 3, London: William Heinemann.

Rowan, J., 1990, *Subpersonalities: The People Inside Us*, London: Routledge.

Salis, L., 2010, 'Italian Antigones: Fortunes and Misfortunes of the Antigone Myth in Italy 1515–2006', *Classics Ireland*, 17, pp. 85–102.

Samuels, A., with B. Shorter and F. Plaut, 1986, *A Critical Dictionary of Jungian Analysis*, London: Routledge & Kegan Paul.

Sánchez, L.-R., 1968, *La Pasión Según Antígona Pérez*, Río Piedras [San Juan, Puerto Rico]: Editorial Cultural, 1974.

Segal, C., 1995, *Sophocles' Tragic World: Divinity, Nature, Society*, London: Harvard University Press.

Shamsie, K., 2017, *Home Fire*, London: Bloomsbury Circus.

Shelley, M., 1947, *Mary Shelley's Journal*, ed. Frederick L. Jones, Norman: Oklahoma University Press.

Shelley, P., 1964, 'To John Gisborne' (22 October 1821). In: F.L. Jones (ed.), *The Letters of Percy Bysshe Shelley*, 2 vols., Oxford: Clarendon Press.

Smith, A., 2015*The Story of Antigone*, London: Pushkin Children's Books.

Söderbäck, F. (ed), 2010, *Feminist Readings of Antigone*, New York: SUNY Press.

Sophocles, 1502, *Σοφοκλεους Τραγωδιαι επτα μετεξηγησεων* [*Sophoclis Tragaediae septem cum commentariis*]. ed. J. Gregoropoulos, Venice: Aldus Manutius.

Sophocles, 1994, [Vol. II:] *Antigone, The Women of Trachis, Philoctetes, Oedipus at Colonus*, ed. H. Lloyd-Jones, Cambridge, MA and London: Harvard University Press.

Stilling, R., 1976, *Love and Death in Renaissance Tragedy*, Baton Rouge: Louisiana State University Press.

Taplin, O., 1978, *Greek Tragedy in Action*, London: Methuen.

Thucydides, 1996, *The Landmark Thucydides*, ed. R.B. Strassler, New York: The Free Press.

Watanabe, J., 2000, *Antígona: Versión Libre de la Tragedia de Sófocles*. Lima: Yuyachkani/ Comisión de Derechos Humanos.

Chapter 8

Earth, ecology and the feminine

Furrows in a ploughed earth

Sulagna Sengupta

In the Berlin Family Lectures of 2015 at the University of Chicago, author Amitav Ghosh talked about Climate Change and the tangled global story of carbon economy, capitalism, empire, and the crisis of imagination, calling this postmodern catastrophe *The Great Derangement* (Ghosh, 2016). Ghosh, a social anthropologist by training and literary writer for over three decades, has conducted cutting edge research on the Opium Wars (Ghosh, 2015) and written about diaspora, communal violence and the experience of being colonized (see www.amitavghosh. com). Portraying uncommon relationships, crisscrossing distant lands in search of that elusive truth that binds humans together, Ghosh's novels are etched with a tenderness that belies his shrewd and relentless pursuit of facts. Ghosh insists that climate change has been excluded from literary imagination, and says that it was research on his book *The Hungry Tide* that showed him the magnitude of the situation (Ghosh, in Paulson, 2017). A writer, scholar, teacher, homemaker, environmentalist, Ghosh wears many hats and argues gently and fearlessly about the 'politics of sincerity' in an academia swathed in denialism. Morphing gender stereotypes with his yin-yang style, straddling multiple cultures and geographies, and rationalizing the discourse around ecology, Ghosh maintains that denialism, militarism, free markets and a moral framework underlie this collective imperilment, and are at the crux of a real debate.

Interestingly, Ghosh's literary origins are in a land whose ancient myths symbolize the earth as feminine. The discovery of infant Sita in the furrows of a ploughed field in the epic story of *Ramayana*, ties the feminine to myths of fertility, and to coexistence and coevolution – the moral framework that underpins the climate discourse. The *Ramayana* is a fourth-century Indian epic about Rama, the warrior prince of Ayodhya, and his wife Sita, their exile into the forests, Sita's abduction by the demon king Ravana and Rama's battle against him to rescue her. The epic narrates Rama's adventures in the forests, his friendship with the animal world, and his return to Ayodhya after the battle. The story ends with his cruel abandonment of Sita after their return. The narrative portrays Sita's deep affinity for nature. When she first steps into the forests with her warrior husband, she dissuades him from hunting innocent forest creatures (Griffth, 2008):

Thou with thy brother, bow in hand,
Beneath those ancient trees wilt stand,
And thy keen arrows will not spare
Wood-rovers who will meet thee there ...

Mayst thou, thus armed with shaft and bow,
So dire a longing never know
As, when no hatred prompts the fray,
These giants of the wood to slay:
For he who kills without offence
Shall win but little glory thence
The bow the warrior joys to bend
Is lent him for a nobler end,
That he may save and succour those
Who watch in woods when pressed by foes ...
Pure in the hermit's grove remain,
True to thy duty, free from stain.

(Griffith, 2008, *Ramayana,* Sita's Speech,
Book III, Canto IX, p. 839)

Sita is rescued by Rama in due course but subjected to humiliating tests of chastity on her return. Heartbroken, she finally invokes her mother Bhumi, the earth goddess, who plunges with her into the depths, to the sacred womb of the earth where she came from. The deep earth is not a place a death, but where nature lies buried, waiting to sprout and be born and reborn cyclically.

Jung said:

Here I must go rather more closely into the nature and structure of the unconscious if I am to deal adequately with the conditioning of the mind by the earth. It is a question that concerns the very beginnings and foundations of the mind – things that from time immemorial have lain buried in the darkness, and not merely the banal facts of sense-perceptions and conscious adaptation to the environment. These belong to the psychology of consciousness, and as I have said, I do not equate consciousness with psyche. The latter is a much more comprehensive and darker field of experience, than the narrow and brightly lit area of consciousness, for the psyche also includes the unconscious.

(Jung, 1964, pp. 30–31)

What Jung is suggesting is a realm where conscious sense perceptions do not extend, where unconscious psychic contents lie buried. The departure of Sita from the narrative suggests a separation from nature, a repression of the feminine, the end of her earthly ties, where she had once asked her husband to stop stalking innocent forest creatures. In the complex labyrinth of science, humans and the Anthropocene, the feminine is the ruptured earth, the dark woods, the soil beneath, and if we are to consider the myth of Persephone and her journey between the two worlds, then it is what ties earth and the depths, spirit and matter, conscious and unconscious – realms that become whole when they come together.

The idea of a connected and coexistent world is found not in Indian myths alone but in ancient Vedic texts such as the Arthashstra (science of political economy), Rigveda, Manusmriti, Caraka Samahita, and the Bhagavad Gita (Bhattacharya, 2014). Principles of biodiversity, protection of forests, sacred groves, water bodies, are in Arthashastra dating back to 150 BCE (Kangle, 1986). Concepts of flood, disease, rainfall, famines, pollution, flora, fauna, river courses, hydrological cycles, soil erosion, irrigation, afforestation are referred to here. In an early classification of living beings, the Arthashastra states that organisms born of eggs, earth, womb and moisture are impelled by prajnaman (consciousness). Given this backdrop, the resurgence of ecological consciousness in modern India is not surprising. Contemporary Indian environmentalists have argued that colonially initiated practices of deforestation ruptured existent links with land, displaced indigenous people, induced poverty and alienated people from their ecology (see Guha, 2016; Gadgil, 1992).

The feminine looms large in this ecological resurgence. Spearheaded by women who have been saving forests, seeds, homestead farms and perennial ecosystems (Shiva, 1988; Narain, 2017; Seema, 2014), rural women's overriding presence in ecological initiatives in India stems from her struggle to ensure food security for her family – the forests, rivers, ponds are integral for her food, fuel and fodder supplies. Surprisingly, Ghosh has not counted this wide-ranging environmental consciousness as hopeful in offering a way out of the looming climate predicament. Jung would have signified this as archetypal – a spontaneous collectivization that has gathered intense scale and pace. "I would like to suggest that every psychic reaction which is out of proportion to its precipitating cause should be investigated as to whether it may be conditioned at the same time by an archetype" (Jung, 1964, p. 32). We will examine nuances of the feminine in India's contemporary environmental movement, in myths and ancient texts, adding to this some reflections on mind and earth and the Anthropocene.

Ecology, the feminine and Jung

As an imperial discipline that began with studies in geology, botany and zoology, ecology emerged as a separate field in the twentieth century when it attempted to go beyond disciplinary boundaries in understanding the natural world, using conservation as a guiding principle. Cambridge-trained Albert Howard, broadly considered the founder of organic agriculture in Britain, cut his teeth in early 1900s in colonial agricultural institutions in India and Africa, learning about soil fertility, crops and conservation, conducting scientific experiments and observing indigenous farming traditions (Beinart & Hughes, 2007). An ecological approach in India combines ancient knowledge with scientific experiments, blending colonial science and indigenous agricultural wisdom, aligning ecology with traditional livelihoods and local economies.

Jung referred to the feminine in anima and animus, describing these as sub-jective, a priori categories in the unconscious psyche of men and women (see Jung, 1968, pp. 54–72), that help mediate the conscious with the unconscious. The anima and animus characterize psyche's contra-sexuality – something that has no comparable terminology in Indian knowledge. But a variety of symbols, myths and rituals denote the masculine and feminine in analogous ways, offering a basis for understanding these ideas in cultures outside the west. Jung gave objec-tive descriptions of these contra-sexual symbols – the feminine according to him is "the inherited collective image of woman that exists in a man's unconscious with the help of which he apprehends the nature of women" (CW, 1953, p. 190). Jung's idea of contra-sexuality, or the unconscious feelings, images, associations that are evoked when one encounters the other was a pioneering thought, but in describing them he viewed the feminine from a fixed and culturally reductive standpoint, ignoring the fluid, overlapping and multifaceted nature of these enti-ties. Jung's characterization of the anima and animus has therefore elicited many criticisms in the Jungian field (see Ulanov and Ulanov, 1994; Young-Eisendrath, 2004; Douglas, 2000; Rowland, 2002; Samuels, 1985, amongst others). Naomi Goldenberg's *A Feminist Critique of Jung* (1976) points toward the patriarchal, religious orientation in Jungian psychology as well as the sexist bias in Jung's writings in privileging men and in stereotyping women as the Eternal Feminine. Goldenberg questions the inherent inequities in the anima-animus dyad and asks if the primary libido is not same for both men and women and if the anima-animus terminology should be used at all given the inbuilt biases around these concepts.

While Jung pioneered the concept of unconscious contra-sexuality in the indi-vidual psyche, when it came to elaborating on the anima and animus, he revealed essentialist biases:

> When the animus breaks out in a woman, it is not feelings that appear, as in a man, but she begins to argue and to rationalize. And just as his anima feelings are arbitrary and capricious, so these feminine arguments are illogical and irrational. … The animus is irrational thinking.
>
> (Jung, 1964, p. 41)

The question if women have a specific kind of thinking or feeling orientation tied to their gender or if only they have "irrational thinking" has been rightly posed by Jung's critics. Likewise, in describing the unconscious feminine in man, Jung said that these anima feelings are capricious and arbitrary. It is arguable if a man's anima is dominated only by capricious feelings. While culture encourages men to imbibe stereotypical masculine traits and repress his contra-sexual psyche, it is not clear how Jung concluded that this unconscious feminine evokes arbitrary and capricious feelings always. Where does that place the caring, nurturing, spiritual and aesthetic qualities of the anima that are not culturally dominant masculine traits, but seen in men nonetheless? Does Jung's narrow characterization of the feminine warrant a rejection of the terms anima/animus altogether as Goldenberg suggests, or a re-articulation? We will see how the feminine comprises both light and dark aspects, and forms an active ground for engendering consciousness and inducing large transformative changes. We take the feminine as denoting not just women, but orientations and attitudes that are carried by both men and women, historically identified with women, but not limited to them.

Jung's notion of a contra-sexual psyche in a gendered self, ties up with myths and symbols of many cultures, especially epics, sacred texts, art, religious iconography of India, that are pre-psychological in character. These are not defunct, 'lost, buried images of women' as Goldenberg suggests, but ways of imagining the feminine, envisioning the feminine, and as Amitav Ghosh, whose numerous characters are female protagonists suggests, it is imagination that stimulates debate. Ghosh has reminded us that the climate crisis is also a crisis of imagination.

If we look into origins, feminine denotes primal matter and phenomenal world in India's early texts (Schuhmacher and Woerner, 1994). In the Rig Veda, the feminine is called Prithvi, the earth goddess. In the Samkhya school (one of the six philosophical schools), the feminine is Prakriti or matter, which together with the masculine Purusha gives birth to meaning and consciousness. The feminine is represented in the cult of Devi where the deity is sculpted from loamy riverside silt or lutum during the annual autumnal festival of goddess Durga. She is returned to earth when her idol is immersed in the river at the end of four days of sacred invocation – a ritual that is celebrated annually in India on an epochal scale. The advent of the goddess is mythologized in her slaying of the buffalo demon (Bhattacharya, 1995). Battle against evil, or encounter with it, is considered necessary for preserving cosmic order - a function that the masculine Shiva also performs, making gender connotations fluid and interchangeable in Hindu religious pantheon.

In yoga philosophy, the feminine and masculine energies are symbolized in Ida and Pingala (IJAPC, 2019). They represent dual consciousness, of intuition and reason, solar and lunar, extroversion and introversion. The nadis or pathways through which Ida and Pingala flow are subtle channels which help integrate both kinds of consciousness. The feminine is denoted as lunar, intuitive and reciprocal in contrast to the masculine solar consciousness, but neither is hierarchized over the other. In rural India, the feminine is also symbolized in serpent deities of fertility. In Vedic texts, the feminine is symbolized as knowledge (goddess Saraswati), death and destruction (goddess Kali) earth mother (Bhumi), as anima figures such as Parvati, Lakshmi and Kali and in psychic states like Chhinnamsata (the bleeding and truncated feminine) and the androgynous syzygy, Ardhanareshwara (Kinsley, 1988). In the Ramayana, feminine is embodied in earth principles, in Sita and other anima figures. Varieties of feminine agency seem represented in these myths. The diversity and complexity of the symbols point towards its many-sided character – of war and destruction, alliance and partnership, knowledge, fertility, turmoil, death and rebirth and syzygy (Bose, 2018).

In a reference to the feminine in 'The Worship of Woman and the Worship of Soul', (Jung, 1971, p. 221ff), Jung alluded to the feminine as spirit, honor, justice, wisdom, devotion, counsel and gladness, symbolized in the Virgin Mother. This description leaves out the feminine that is in the body, the erotic, dark, destructive, and defiant, that co-exists with spirit. Jung wrote that

> Earth bound desire, sensuality in all its forms, attachment to the lures of this world, and the incessant dissipation of psychic energy in the world's prodigal variety are the main obstacle to the development of a coherent and purposive attitude.
>
> (1971, p. 231)

In Indian mythology, the erotic is tied to spirit – gods are both sensuous and spiritual. In a myth of Parvati, we find that the goddess creates her son Ganesha from the clay she has used to anoint and exfoliate herself during a ritual bath. Hence, Ganesha was born not from her womb, but from the surface of Parvati's body. This curious antecedent notwithstanding, Ganesha is designated as the god of wisdom and prosperity in Hindu pantheon, considered no less important than other gods. Parvati is imbued with erotic and divine potency. A separation between spirit and body is not characteristic of the feminine in the Hindu context – this is an important cultural variation between eastern and western religious symbols.

In another myth, we are told that Parvati is pursued amorously by two demons, Shumba and Nishumba. When they continue to torment her despite her protestations and warnings, she is infuriated and transforms into Kali, the dark and naked goddess, who destroys the demons in a flight of rage (Bhattacharya, 1995). Archetypally, a complex is activated that sets the goddess on a murderous rampage, gripped as she is by an unstoppable destructive instinct. It is only when her consort Shiva obstructs her path and she unheedingly steps on him, that her rage is defused and she returns to her senses. The fury of the goddess does not diminish her beauty or honor; in fact, the dark Kali is ritually offered prayers and worshipped across India. In tantric philosophy, the erotic feminine is at the root of the chakras (consciousness centres) and is considered sacred (Flood, 2006). The notion of an immaculate feminine sans its dark, fiery, sensual aspects as denoted in the Virgin Mother of Christian symbolism is rare in Hindu religious myths.

It is not myths alone where the feminine can be located. The spontaneous acts of compassion, courage, dissent, solidarity, justice that characterize India's environmental campaigns reveal the fullness of the feminine in a contemporary setting. Radical Indian environmentalist Vandana Shiva's pioneering work *Staying Alive* (1988) was instrumental in bringing India's ecofeminist philosophy into global discourse. Shiva placed women at the center of production and reproduction processes in a predominantly agricultural country like India where a significant number live below the poverty line. Her argument that women's organic links to nature were destroyed by colonially initiated, market-driven agricultural practices, forms the keystone of contemporary ecofeminist discourse (Leach and Green, 1997). According to Shiva, women's ancient links to earth, seeds, crops, seasons, water cycles and climate have helped communities live in relation to nature for centuries as opposed to modern production systems that have alienated people from their ecology. Based on her own experience of seeing forests, seeds and indigenous food crops vanish in the mountain habitat where she grew up, Shiva, who originally trained as a physicist turned her attention to environment and ecology, spearheading a crusade to revive indigenous ecological knowledge. Navadanya, the organization she founded in 1987 in the Himalayan region are the fruits of scientific inquiries on biodiversity, seed conservation and farming technologies. It mirrors hundreds of green initiatives in India, where ecologically sustainable models are being experimented with, tested and adopted. Shiva's work has catalyzed ecological consciousness on a global scale and although she has been critiqued by development scholars for categorizing all third world women as one, ignoring men's role in ecology and offering a limited understanding of the complexity of colonial science, her work with Marxist sociologist Maria Mies (Mies and Shiva, 1993) defined Indian ecological concerns as rooted in concerns of poverty, distinct from environmental concerns in the west. Shiva has argued for a reappraisal of the notion of poverty in her ecological framework:

> People are perceived as poor if they eat millets (grown by women) rather than commercially produced and distributed processed foods sold by global agri-business. They are seen as poor if they live in self-built housing made from natural material like bamboo and mud rather than in cement houses. They are seen as poor if they wear handmade garments of natural fibre rather than synthetics. Subsistence, as culturally perceived poverty, does not necessarily imply a low physical quality of life. On the contrary, millets are nutritionally far superior to processed foods, houses built with local materials are far superior, being better adapted to the local climate and ecology, natural fibres are preferable to man-made fibres in most cases, and certainly more affordable. This cultural perception of prudent subsistence living as poverty has provided the legitimisation for the development process as a poverty removal project. As a culturally biased project it destroys wholesome and sustainable lifestyles and creates real material poverty, or misery, by the denial of survival needs themselves, through the diversion of resources to resource intensive commodity production. Cash crop production and food processing take land and water resources away from sustenance needs, and exclude increasingly large numbers of people from their entitlements to food.
>
> (Shiva, 1988, p. 59)

Shiva's radical stance against globalization, capitalist ideology and seed multinationals is well known. At Navadanya, a rich body of biodiversity research, legal and political campaigns, crop patents, livelihood experiments and women-led initiatives symbolize the feminine. A political ideology that is infused with reason, perspicacity, anger, reflecting not Jung's notion of the animus as irrational thinking, but a feminine impulse imbued with concern for the earth and the poor.

The decade of the eighties in India also saw a young social worker from Mumbai plunge into mass protest against the construction of Narmada dam, a project that had deluged hundreds of villages in central India (Nielsen, 2010). Medha Patkar had conducted studies in the Naramada river basin as part of her research and encountered gaping loopholes in a World Bank project – it convinced her that the developmental model adopted in India was anti-poor, anti-women and anti-environmental. Mobilizing thousands of protestors across riverbanks, Patkar's long struggle over three decades in stalling the construction of the dam, that has jeopardized hundreds of farming communities by appropriating their land and displacing them, drew worldwide attention on the pitfalls of lopsided development funded by international agencies. Patkar has camped near the Narmada bank with tribal communities, working on a mammoth scale, questioning the idea of development itself – a movement that is not just ecological and political. Seeking reparation for the displaced and disbanded through hundreds of national tribunals and court battles, Patkar's work evokes images of earth goddesses who are provoked into anger to counter largescale transgressions and violence. Shiva and Patkar's environmental crusades encompass diverse attributes of the feminine – reason, justice, compassion, dissent, struggle and solidarity. Jung's basic premise that a woman's conscious attitude is characterized by the quality of Eros and not by discriminative consciousness of Logos, needs considerable overhauling.

Amitav Ghosh's significant views on climate debate notwithstanding, the crux of India's environmental crusade lie in the work of the ordinary poor, grassroots women and men, and activists such as Sunderlal Bahuguna, Sunita Narain and Arundhuti Roy. Bahuguna was instrumental in flagging the Chipko, a movement against felling of trees in the fragile Himalayan region, an erstwhile colonial practice that commercialized India's precious forest wood. The familiar image of Bahuguna embracing a tree that was about to be felled (Chipko – to hug) became a symbol for the green movement in India, of earth, ecology and the feminine. Like many other green activists, Sunita Narain and Arundhuti Roy bring uncommon scientific wisdom and literary imagination to the climate discourse. Narain has led rigorous campaigns against global multinationals through her empirical research, using it to confront large conglomerates, pressing for transparency and accountability in environmental policies (Narain, 2017).

Roy's activism and literary scholarship on the other hand perform an entirely different function in the collective – it disrupts status quo in a 'shrill' manner (Palit, 2001) speaking the unspeakable, upsetting stereotypical notions of a benign and subdued feminine, shredding the image of establishment. It is a Cassandra syndrome, where her truths, however well-researched are habitually rejected and she is labelled as hysterical. Roy has backed Patkar's Narmada Andolan with her ruthless critique of national politics – a dark and feisty feminine that is contemptuous of status-quo and unyielding to what is truly gloomy, fragmented and subversive of the climate politics.

Interestingly, Jung talked of feminine wholeness in his experience of Africa, where he encountered an Elgonyi woman in her homestead shamba. During that meeting, Jung noted that the woman's husband was referred to in distant, ambiguous tones, while she herself appeared settled in her commune, living with her children and family members. Exuding power, beauty and stability, she appeared to Jung to be in sync with her physical surroundings, conveying a fullness of being in the earthy centeredness of her home (Jung, 1989, p. 253ff). This image of the feminine is important in understanding Jung's impressions of Africa and its unique cultural traditions, and mirrors his own feelings of closeness to nature and pastoral life. However, it appears that Jung located feminine wholeness only within the precincts of home and hearth, in women's domestic and reproductive roles, and not in the vast public sphere where the feminine has for centuries played vital roles across the world, sustaining, transforming and engendering societies.

Mind and earth as distinct and connected entities

In a lecture of 1941, Jung said that 'loss of roots':

> is a disaster not only for primitive tribes but for civilized man as well. ... If they get lost, the conscious mind gets severed from the instincts and loses its roots, while the instincts unable to express themselves, fall back into the unconscious and reinforce its energy, causing this in turn to overflow into the existing contents of consciousness. It is then that a rootless condition of consciousness becomes a real danger.
>
> (Jung, 1954, p. 216)

Jung's allusions to psyche in 'loss of roots' or soil of psychic injury' (Jung, 1954, p. 216) is not uncommon in his writings. Jung defined unconscious as "the contents that have vanished into darkness" (Jung, 1964, p. 30), active through their symptoms, things which are not dead relics but have "grown out of the dark confines of the earth," (Jung, 1964, p. 32).

He viewed loss of roots as psyche's dissociation from instincts and thought that a relation between instinct and spirit is helpful and necessary.Transpersonal psychology, Ecopsychology and Deep Ecology are movements where the link between biological and psychological self is proposed through a nondual ontology (Rust & Totton, 2012).

Jung nurtured this instinctual link in himself, (see Sabini, 2002) in the Tower he built and the pastoral life he led at Bollingen. David Tacey comments that Jung while elaborated on the chthonic aspects of the psyche in his essay 'Mind and Earth' (Tacey, 2009), he revealed his difficulty in linking primordial nature with the objective psyche. This is not just Jung's individual dilemma about two discrete worlds of mind and earth, but a fragmentation of knowledge between science and spirit, conscious and unconscious, with its history in Western Reformation and Enlightenment. Jung's attempt in bringing the worlds of psyche and matter into a relationship with each other signifies this history, and Tacey rightly notes that

Jung struggled to link the two worlds, lingering tentatively in both mythopoetic and scientific, unable to establish a clear correlation.

My contention is that the two categories of mind and earth are distinct, in the sense that knowledge of one does not automatically explain contents of the other. This insight comes from my own experience of the biodynamic world which I encountered in the ecological wisdom of a personal mother. The circadian care and knowledge needed to keep the elements of the natural world in sync with one another came spontaneously to her, unknown in origin but steadfastly present. The family's ancestries were in erstwhile East Bengal (now Bangladesh) where they had lived on fertile acreages near river belts and tended large farming estates, before a large-scale ethnic crisis forced them to migrate to a neighboring state, thereafter a separate nation. Despite the intricate knowledge of nature my mother carried because of her early childhood , which she effortlessly recreated in a new land, it was a struggle for her and the family to cope with the aftermath of Partition that she and the larger immigrant community had experienced. The Partition of Bengal into a Muslim Bangladesh and a Hindu India in the early decades of the twentieth century, forced lakhs of people to flee their homeland due to large-scale communal riots, leaving behind inter-generational psychic trauma of violence, dislocation and uprooting. The communal scars, loss of homeland and memories of diaspora that were experienced could not be contained or fathomed, even though knowledge and instincts about a biodynamic universe remained intact in her, and flowed seamlessly from one geographical location to another.

Pertinent to recall that ecology has ancient roots in India when compared to the scientific psychology of the unconscious, which is a relatively modern historical development with the distinctive feature of having evolved systematically in Western intellectual tradition (Shamdasani, 2003). Knowledge about the unconscious is distant ken in India, although the concept of consciousness is richly elaborated in various Indian philosophical schools. As Jung's correspondence and conversations highlight, the notion of psychological unconscious is not analogous with Indian philosophical notions of consciousness. This history, both personal and objective, suggested to me that earth and psyche do not correspond in exact ways, and even if they parallel each other or synchronize, they have distinctive set of operative principles. The difference between the two realms does not imply a dissociation, but an acknowledgement that they cannot be explained through interchangeable terms. What is often bemoaned is their dissociation, the split between nature and spirit, but what is not acknowledged is their distinct epistemic origins and structuring principles, which could help in better understanding their links and relatedness.

Anthropocene

Climate discourse is perhaps inconceivable today without an understanding of Anthropocene and its various implications. In a round table organized by the Journal of Asian Studies (JAS) to discuss Ghosh's *The Great Derangement:*

Climate Change and the Unthinkable (see JAS Round Table, 2016), contemporary historian Julia Adney Thomas talks about the importance of merging disciplines to understand climate change and the physical transformation of the planet from Holocene to Anthropocene epoch. The term Anthropocene, formulated by atmospheric chemist Paul Crutzen to mark geological epochs, signifies the transformation of the planet through geologically induced changes, from the relatively stable Holocene to the Anthropocene. Adney emphasizes that the term did not initially signify human impact on planetary degeneration but denoted instead the irreversible rupture of earth and the overshooting of planetary boundaries, that is fast making the earth unsuitable for human habitation. Its implications, she says citing Ghosh, are in redefining the Anthropocene not just through ecology, but human factors that influence ecology, factors such as geopolitical relations, production processes and wealth. Ghosh's own argument is that there is a crisis in the arts and in literary imagination with ecology left out, and that the arts should discuss climate degeneration. Ghosh alludes to a liminal nonhuman realm, the human factor in the geopolitical debate, but makes no reference to the unconscious psyche that determines human behavior on the planet. Thus the scientific and literary, in this instance, have both failed to take cognizance of the psychological unconscious.

Jungian scholar Susan Rowland has taken the nonhuman, unconscious psyche as central in her discussion on ecocriticism. She challenges the exclusive, masculinist geological and geopolitical explanation of Anthropocene in current discourse, challenging this in her paper, 'Against Anthropocene: Transdisciplinarity and Dionysus in Jungian Ecocriticism' (2017). Rowland believes that the schism between human and nonhuman, culture and nature, masculine and feminine, rational and irrational is a colonial legacy that characterizes Western science, and it is an ecocritical approach that breaks this rigid division by bringing in the language of symbols to understand nature as a whole. She argues that ecocriticism and Jung's language of the unconscious bring the mythical, poetic and aesthetic aspects of non-rational (Ghosh's nonhuman) into the rational, in order to re-plot modern consciousness because human nature and nature are not separate but entwined in each other, expressed through metaphors and images. There is no objective nature, she says, as Jung's notion of synchronicity demonstrates, and there is explicit dualism if human action is signaled as separate from nature. Rowland cites Basarab Nicolescu and Transdisciplinarity in affirming that knowledge is derived from various sources, present at many levels, and there is no testable form of ascertaining all truths in a homogenized manner.

This approach integrates the human and geological in the concept of Anthropocene and reflects Ghosh's concerns about the schism between science and arts and the absence of climate change themes in literary imagination. Rowland's discerning analysis is helpful in telling us that unconscious psyche and Transdisciplinarity are useful bridges in understanding the nonhuman. However, human nature and nature as one is an idea that needs further exploration. Examples cited before in this paper reveal that while knowledge of ecology has evolved in

distinctive ways in India since ancient times, expressing itself in rich and powerful activism around environmental issues, knowledge of psyche and the unconscious has not had a similar trajectory. The psychological unconscious is strongly
contested in Indian schools of philosophy. The fields of nature and human nature
are not anchored around the same principles, though they may relate and parallel
each other. In what ways do matter and psyche synchronize and diverge, remain a
vast ground of experimentation and inquiry.

Jung's description of the unconscious psyche as an archaic layer that consists of primordial images can be evidenced in the myths and symbols of other
cultures. While the archetypes themselves do not suggest universal truths, they
offer a rich ground of envisioning the feminine in its complexity and depth.
Jung's notion of the feminine needs to be realigned to include the dualities of the
archetypes, the significance of light and dark, spirit and body, instead of a single
explanatory frame of a dominant Eros and a compensatory Logos, an irrational
animus or feminine as spirit without body. The rational, humane, combative,
sensual and fiery aspects of the feminine that reflect psychic complexity and
wholeness and places the feminine in the wider field of transformative change,
needs to be emphasized. While the exclusion of climate change in the arts is
being rightly questioned and lamented upon, it is helpful to understand that the
relationship between psyche and earth is not straightforward, and that nature and
human nature are not the same – historically these fields have evolved in discrete
ways and need to be explained through specific principles. Ghosh's question if
we are deranged because we do not bring imagination, arts and the literary into
climate talks could be ours as well about analytical psychology – and the vex-
ing absence of any reference to the unconscious psyche in mainstream earth and
ecology debates.

References

Beinart, W. and Hughes, L., 2007, *Environment and Empire, the Oxford History of British
Empire, Companion Series*, New York: Oxford University Press.
Bhattacharya, S., 1995, *The Legends of Devi*, Calcutta, India: Orient Blackswan.
Bhattacharya, S., 2014, 'Forest and Biodiversity Conservation in Ancient Indian Culture:
A Review Based on Old Texts and Archaeological Evidences', *International Letters of
Social and Humanistic Sciences*, 30, pp. 35–46.
Bose, M., 2018, *The Oxford History of Hinduism: The Goddess*, Oxford: Oxford University
Press.
Douglas, C., 2000, *The Woman in the Mirror: Analytical Psychology and the Feminine*,
An Author's Guild Backinprint.Com Edition, published by iUniverse.com NE, USA.
Eisendrath, P., 2004, *Subject to Change: Jung, Gender and Subjectivity*, Hove: Routledge.
Flood, G., 2006, *The Tantric Body: The Secret Tradition of Hindu Religion*, London, I.B.
Tauris.
Gadgil, M. and Guha, R., 1992, *The Fissured Land*, New Delhi, India: Oxford University
Press.
Ghosh, A., 2015, *Sea of Poppies*, Delhi, India: Penguin Books.

Ghosh, A., 2016, *The Great Derangement: Climate Change and the Unthinkable*, Delhi, India: Penguin, Random House.

Paulson, S., 2017, 'Where's the Great Climate Change Novel?: A Conversation with Amitav Ghosh, A 2018', *Los Angeles Review of Books*, https://lareviewofbooks.org/article/wheres-the-great-climate-change-novel-a-conversation-with-amitav-ghosh/ (Accessed 11 October 2019).

Goldenberg, N., 1976, 'A Feminist Critique of Jung', *Signs: Journal of Women in Culture and Society*, 2(2), pp. 443–449.

Griffith, R., 2008, *The Ramayan by Valmiki*, Translated into English Verse, London: Trübner & Co., Benares: E. J. Lazarus.

Guha, R., 2016, *Environmentalism: A Global History*, Delhi, India: Penguin Random House.

Jung, C.G., 1953, *Two Essays on Analytical Psychology*, Hove: Routledge & Kegan Paul Ltd.

Jung, C.G., 1954, *The Practice of Psychotherapy*, Hove: Routledge & Kegan Paul Ltd.

Jung, C.G., 1964, *Civilisation in Transition*, London: Routledge & Kegan Paul Ltd.

Jung, C.G., 1968, *The Archetypes and the Collective Unconscious*, Hove: Routledge & Kegan Paul Ltd.

Jung, C.G., 1971, *Psychological Types*, London: Routledge & Kegan Paul Ltd.

Jung, C.G., 1989, *Memories, Dreams, Reflections*, New York: Random House.

Kangle, R.P., 1986, *Kautīlya Arthaśāstra*, Part II, Delhi: Motilal Banarasidass.

Kinsley, D., 1987, *Hindu Goddesses: Visions of the Divine Feminine in the Hindu Religious Tradition*, Delhi, India: Motilal Banarasidass Publishers Private Limited.

Leach, M. and Green, C., 1997, 'Gender and Environmental History: From Representation of Women and Nature to Gender Analysis of Ecology and Politics', *Environment and History*, 3(3), pp. 343–370.

Mies, M. and Shiva, V., 1993, *Ecofeminism* (Critique. Influence. Change), New York: Zed Books.

Narain, S., 2017, *Conflicts of Interests: My Journey through India's Green Movement*, New Delhi: Penguin Viking.

Nielsen, A.G., 2010, *Dispossession and Resistance in India: The River and the Rage*, Abingdon: Routledge.

Palit, C., 2001, 'The Historian as Gatekeeper', *The Hindu*, Volume 17, Issue 26, https://frontline.thehindu.com/static/html/fl1726/17261160.htm (Accessed 9 October 2019).

Rowland, S., 2002, *Jung: A Feminist Revision*, Cambridge: Polity.

Rowland, S., 2017, 'Against Anthropocene: Transdisciplinarity and Dionysus in Jungian Ecocriticism', *Revue Internationale de Philosophie*, 282(4), pp. 401–414.

Rust, J.M. and Totton, N. (eds), 2012, *Vital Signs: Psychological Responses to Ecological Crisis*, London: Karnac.

Sabini, M. (ed), 2002. *C.G, Jung on Nature, Technology and Modern Life*, Berkeley, CA: North Atlantic Books.

Samuels, A., 1985, *Jung and the Post-Jungians*, London: Routledge.

Schuhmacher, S. and Woerner, G., 1994, *The Encyclopaedia of Eastern Philosophy and Religion*, Boston, MA: Shambala.

Seema, 2014, 'Eco-Feminism and Environmental Movements in India', *International Journal of Current Research*, 6(01), pp. 4656–4660.

Shamdasani, S., 2003, *Jung and the Making of Modern Psychology*, Cambridge: Cambridge University Press.

Shiva, V., 1988, *Staying Alive: Women, Ecology and Survival in India*, New Delhi: Kali for Women.

Tacey, D., 2009, 'Mind and Earth: Psychic Influence Beneath the Surface', *Jung Journal: Culture and Psyche*, 3(2), pp. 15–32.

Thomas, J., Parathsarathi, P., Linrothe, R. et al. 2016, 'JAS Round Table on Amitav Ghosh, the Great Derangement: Climate Change and the Unthinkable', *The Journal of Asian Studies*, 75(4), pp. 929–955.

Ulanov, A. and Ulanov, B., 1994, *Transforming Sexuality: The Archetypal World of Anima and Animus*, Boston, MA: Shambala Publications.

Chapter 9

The modern ancients

Intrinsic feminism in precolonial
Philippine culture

Mary Gayle Certeza-Narcida

According to Paulo Freire, in his book, *Pedagogy of the Oppressed*, "Cultural invasion is on one hand an instrument of domination, and on the other, the result of domination" (1970, p.150). In most colonised countries like the Philippines, there is a lack of precolonial knowledge attributed to the decimation of the culture during the conquest and the subsequent cultural domination after the subjugation. This chapter is an in-depth look into the imagery, idea, and customs surrounding women in the Philippines before the Spanish colonisation, exploring the premise that the Philippines' ancient culture was intrinsically and precociously feminist. This chapter will also delve into the myths of precolonial Philippines and seek to find the connection between them and the position of women within the structures of precolonial society, by utilizing a combination of a feminist perspective; guided by the postcolonial framework of Paulo Freire; Jungian ideas on mythology by Joseph Campbell, and reviewing native mythology and folklore.

In the United States and Europe, the earliest voices for gender equality began in the fifteenth century with women who had access to learning, like Christine de Pizan of France. In the 1800s, Elizabeth Cady Stanton in the United States championed the education, property rights, and full citizenship of women and Mary Wollstonecraft of the United Kingdom advocated for education. In the twentieth century, suffragettes led by Emmeline Pankhurst put feminism in the forefront by actively fighting for women's right to vote. The Second Wave of Feminism espoused ideals that went beyond enfranchisement to sexuality and reproductive rights alongside a campaign for social and cultural equality (Freedman, 2007, p.xiii). In contrast to these struggles, the precolonial Filipino women were already in possession of full equality more than 1,300 years ago.

Framework and definition of terms

This chapter makes use of three interwoven frameworks: feminism, a Jungian mythological perspective, and postcolonial philosophy with focus on a people's loss of culture and reclaiming of identity. These frameworks are interrelated with the three main premises of this chapter. First, feminism, as defined by feminist philosophers especially Mary Wollstonecraft, was already nascent in the Philippines millennia ago. Second, one of the reasons Philippine culture was innately feminist was based on its myths –wherein women were portrayed as equals, or sometimes, even better than men. And, last, through a postcolonial lens, this chapter seeks to add to the body of work on the forgotten Philippine precolonial history and be part of the process of cultural reclaiming.

Feminism is the advocacy of women's rights on the basis of the equality of the sexes. As Mary Wollstonecraft, English writer and one of the earliest feminist philosophers, declared in her treatise, *A Vindication of the Rights of Woman*, that "I love man as my fellow; but his scepter, real, or usurped, extends not to me, unless the reason of an individual demands my homage; and even then the submission is to reason, and not to man" (Wollstonecraft, 1996, p.33).

Joseph Campbell, an American teacher and author, studied comparative mythology and examined the universal functions of myth in various cultures and literatures around the world. He postulated that more than merely stories, myths embody the human narrative and they have a number of functions in human society. Its sociological function is that myths support and reinforce the social structures of their place of origin. He said that myths serve as a mirror of culture and social structure, and they help in the legitimization of social institutions (Campbell, 1973, p.38).

Postcolonial philosophy explores the consequences of colonisation, in this case, the culture of a colonised people. Paolo Freire's social concept of *conscientização* or conscientization is particularly useful in this context. Conscientization or critical consciousness is a process for colonised cultures to develop awareness of their existing social situation through critical thinking and intervention or action (Freire, 1970, p.100). This process is crucial because the damage caused by colonisation is two-fold. First is the destruction of the land and, second, imposition of the dominant culture. In a colonised environment, reality is obfuscated, "The oppressor consciousness tends to transform everything surrounding it into an object of its domination. The earth, property, production, the creations of men, men themselves, time – everything is reduced to the status of objects at its disposal" (Freire, 1970, p.44). The definition of culture used here is that of Edward Tylor, who defined culture as, "The complex whole which includes knowledge, belief, art, law, morals, custom and other capabilities and habits acquired by man as a member of the society" (Tylor, 2016, p.1).

Philippines: introduction & history

Most of the historical facts detailed on this paper came from the book, *History of the Filipino People* by Teodoro Agoncillo, the standard textbook for Philippine history. The Philippines is an archipelago of more than seven thousand islands located in Southeast Asia. It has three main island groups: Luzon, Visayas, and Mindanao. The country is bordered in the west by China, Japan, Vietnam, and Taiwan; Malaysia and Indonesia in the south; and Palau in the east. This central geographical location played a crucial role in the development of the country, as it opened the island nation to waves of migrations, colonisations, and the cultural influences they brought with them. The earliest human settlement in the islands was 22,000 years ago, during the Paleolithic era (see Agoncillo, 1990). Recent archeological finds revealed that a specie of small-bodied hominin lived on the island of Luzon around 50,000 to 67,000 years ago (Greshko & Wei-Hass, 2019). It is clear that the islands already had an ancient civilization before coming into contact with western countries like Spain.

The basic unit of settlement in precolonial Philippines was the *barangay,* a village of around a hundred families or approximately 500 people. The word came from the Malay word for the boats that used to ply the seas and travel between islands (Scott, 1994, p.4). Early Filipinos were primarily engaged in traditional shifting cultivation. Aside from agriculture, they had other industries such as hunting, fishing, poultry, stock raising, lumbering, weaving, shipbuilding, and mining. The inhabitants had extensive trade relations with numerous foreign merchants. From 900 CE to the fourteenth century, the archipelago remained a disparate collection of islands existing independently; sometimes, at war with each other. Millennia of trading with neighboring islands brought about cultural influences from all over the region and beyond, such as: Indo-Malay writing and governance, language from India, food and pottery from China and Islam from Saudi Arabia.

During this period, the position of women in society was equal to that of men. They were in possession of the same rights as men. Women could own and inherit property, engage in trade and industry and aspire to leadership in the community in the absence of a male heir. A woman had the exclusive right to give names to her children and she had the right to divorce her husband (see Mangahas & Llaguno, 2006).

However, this inter-island co-existence was disrupted by the arrival of Spain in 1521. Spain sent numerous expeditions until it completely colonised the archipelago in 1564. A Spanish soldier Miguel Lopez de Legazpi named the archipelago Philippines, in honor of the reigning monarch at that time, King Phillip II. The 300-year Spanish colonisation disrupted social classes as all natives were made second-class citizens and destroyed property rights as Spain now held the rights to most of the land. Indigenous culture and religion were wiped out. The rights of Filipinos, women included, were removed.

Unlike other countries, the Philippines did not have the opportunity to develop a centralised government ruling over a large portion of the archipelago, or evolve into a dominant culture before it was colonised. The colonisation and the subsequent revolution became the catalysts of the scattered islands to become a nation and the prolonged colonisation led to loss of freedom. Under Spanish rule, Filipinos were heavily taxed. They were asked to perform compulsory labor for the galleon trade. They could not hold leadership positions in government as these were open only to Spaniards. In their capacity as spiritual guides, the friars used their power to control the natives. They controlled the educational system and they owned vast tracts of arable land.

The Spanish colonisation was not just political and economic. It was also cultural. Ancient Filipinos used materials from nature to mark history – bark of trees, leaves and bamboo tubes. They used knives, daggers, pointed sticks or pieces of iron as pens with colored saps of trees as ink. Aside from the destructive work of the elements, the early Spanish missionaries destroyed many manuscripts in their zeal to propagate the Catholic religion.

The inhabitants of the islands did not capitulate entirely and there were isolated insurrections against Spain from the start of the colonisatio. These sporadic rebellions were easily quelled as the country is an archipelago and it was difficult to unite people. Andres Bonifacio, a revolutionary leader, wrote how the lives of Filipinos changed:

> The Filipinos who in early times were governed by their own countrymen before the coming of the Spaniards were living in great abundance and prosperity, [and] young and old, including women, knew how to read and write in our autochthonous alphabet.
>
> (Agoncillo, 1990, p.104)

After more than 300 years of colonisation, the hardships, loss of equality, and erosion of national identity all led to a revolution. The first battle cry was sounded in August 24, 1896, and it spread like wildfire throughout the islands. After a fierce and bloody series of battles, the Filipinos won and the revolutionary government of the Philippines declared independence from Spain on June 12, 1898.

Myth as reflection and embodiment of social structure

The main premise of this chapter is that Philippine precolonial culture was precociously feminist because the myths of its early society included women in the process of creation, created them as equals to men, and portrayed them as independent goddesses and strong ordinary women, but before delving further into specific precolonial myths, it is important to discuss the meaning of myth being utilized in this instance.

William Bascon defines myth as prose narratives accepted by the society in which it is told as historical accounts of the past. They account for the origin of the world, phenomena of nature, human beings, birth, death, and more. Most important, they are held to be sacred (Bascon, 1965, in Dundes, 1984, p.9). However, Joseph Campbell posited that myths have four functions. The first function is mystical. Myths allow people to experience the mystery of the universe. The second function of myth is cosmological. It helps people to imagine an idea or image of the universe. The third function is sociological, which is all about supporting or validating a social order. The stories serve to bind people to their tribe, enforce rules, and give meaning to the culture. The last function is psychological. Myths help guide people to live (see Campbell and Moyers, 1991). This chapter however focuses on the sociological function of Campbell's scheme as it connects precolonial myths to their society and to the privileged status of women in that community. There are two reasons for this. First, myths carry the spirit of an epoch. "Myths are therefore like reflections or mirroring of certain cultural situations of mankind, they contain deep intuitions and anticipations of further developments and thus they can be considered as milestones in the development of human consciousness" (Kluger, 1991, p.17). Second, myth reinforces and strengthens the social structures of their society. Joseph Campbell noted this significant aspect of the myth by saying, "It would not be too much to say that myth is the secret opening through which the inexhaustible energies of the cosmos pour into human cultural manifestations" (Campbell, 1973, p.3).

Every land has its own myths and the Philippines is no different, though it has a great diversity of storytelling being made up of thousands of islands, home to hundreds of ethnolinguistic groups with their own respective myths, legends, and stories. These myths tell stories about different kinds of creators, but a significant number are creation stories that are gender-equal while others are legends about brave goddesses, or strong ordinary women.

The various creation stories and myths came predominantly from two notable books. The first is, *Philippine Folk Literature: An Anthology* by Damiana Eugenio. This is a pioneering work in Philippine folklore studies. The second book, *The Soul Book*, is an academic and an art book in one. The stories are culled from rare books on reserve shelves, esoteric journals, anthropological field reports and graduate theses. The artworks are from a prominent Filipino artist.

In the Judeo-Christian tradition, God is traditionally considered a male being, who created a man in His own image. This God is omnipotent and complete unto Himself. The Philippine precolonial view of a creator was more varied. Ancient Filipinos believed in a deity who created the world. This deity was called different names in different places such as Bathalang Maykapal, Lumikha, Laon, Manama and Kabuniyan. These were creators who had warrior aspects but they were more known as benevolent gods. Bathala was the grand conserver of the universe, the caretaker of things, from whom all providence comes. The creator was viewed as the supreme teacher who taught humans to plant rice, make fire, and create rituals (see Demetrio and Cordero-Fernando, 1991). However, contrast with Islam and Judeo-Christian narratives wherein a single God created the world, the precolonial pantheon of creators was more complex and the precolonial gods were not all-powerful.

For some, their reason for creating the world was because they were prone to loneliness. A creation myth from the Visayas told of a god, Tungkung Langit who was married to the goddess, Alunsina. They had a good marriage although Alunsina had a jealous nature. When Tungkung Langit had to journey to fix the chaotic disturbances in the flow of time, Alunsina sent the breeze to spy on him. This angered him so much that upon his return, he asked her to leave. Alunsina promptly left. As the months passed, Tungkung Langit grew more desolate. He found the world too lonely without Alunsina. So he made the sea and the earth. He planted the earth with trees and flowers. He took Alunsina's jewels to decorate the skies. Her necklace became the stars, her comb the moon, and her crown the sun. He created all these hoping Alunsina would return. She never came back. The myth related that up to now, Tungkung Langit is so miserable that when he cries, his tears fall down to earth as rain and his sobbing can be heard as thunder reverberating across the earth, asking Alunsina to come back (see Eugenio, 2007). For the Kapampangans, however, the earth was created by Mangetchay in remembrance of his beloved daughter. She died in a battle where the gods fought each other for her hand (Jose, 1974, cited in Gaverza, 2014, p.59).

In the main island, Luzon, however, the creation story was about three gods. They were: Bathala, a giant human, Ulilangkalulua, a giant snake who could fly and Galangkalulua, a winged-head god. Bathala and Ulilangkalulua were enemies. They fought and the latter was killed. Many years later, Galangkalulua, became sick. Before he passed away, he asked Bathala to bury his head in Ulilangkalulua's grave. From the grave grew a coconut tree from which Bathala created the first humans (Mangahas and Llaguno, 2006).

A triumvirate also created the world according to the inhabitants of southern Mindanao. One was a Good Being who looked like a man, Diwata na Magbabaya. The second one, was a Bad Being who had a human body with ten heads, Dadanhayan Ha Sugay. And the third was a hawk-like being, Agtayabun. Creatures, including a human, were created using materials from both the Good and the Bad Beings, cooled by the wings of the Hawk-like Being. This is the reason why humans are both good and bad (Demetrio and Cordero-Fernando, 1991).

The B'laan tribe has an interesting creation story. The god Tasu Weh created humans who had both sexual organs – the penis in one knee and the vagina in the other. Another god, Fiu Weh, separated the organs and became the humans we know of today (Lutero, 1986, cited in Gaverza, 2014, p.100). The Warays, meantime, who lived in the islands of the Visayas had a creator who was both male and female. This creator had two aspects or two personas. One aspect was Malaon or The Ancient One, a mild and understanding woman. The other aspect was Makapatag or The Leveler, a severe and fearful male (Demetrio and Cordero-Fernando, 1991).

Other traditions included women as co-creators. For the Bagobos, in the beginning, a god created the first man and woman out of corn meal. There were some design flaws in the beings he made. The humans were too small, the god forgot to put joints in their bodies, their noses were tiny and their eyes were covered with scales. The goddess consort saw their flaws and intervened to fix them. She re-did their faces, confined the scales to the tips of their fingers and toes, and created joints so they could move (Demetrio and Cordero-Fernando, 1991). Likewise, the supreme deities of the T'boli were a pair of married gods, Kadaw La Sambad and Bulon La Mogoaw (Casal, 1978, cited in Gaverza, 2014, p.98). While in the southwestern Mindanao highlands lived the Tirurays. Their creation myth was a bitter fight between a brother named Sualla and his sister, Sinonggol. They were powerful deities who could change themselves into any form. The way Sualla created the first humans echoed the creation story in the Bible's Book of Genesis. The first man was made from the pith of a very hard wood. A woman was created from his ribs to keep him company. From there, the story diverged. The first man and woman had a son who got very sick. The parents appealed to Sualla for help. He sent a medicine man who was intercepted by Sinonggol under the guise of a demon. Sinonggol changed the medicine and the boy died. Sulla buried the boy in the center of the world whose soil came from heaven. From the body of the boy came vegetation – his teeth became corn, his hands became bananas and from his navel sprouted the first rice. Sinonggol was so jealous of her brother's work that she sent pestilence. She threw down her comb and it became the first pig, and it destroyed the bananas. Her spit and her saliva became the first rats to eat the rice and corn. The Tirurays worshipped both Sulla and Sinonggol even if the latter was evil as her actions made the world better (see Eugenio, 2007).

The Visayans told the story of how two primordial giants created the earth. Bayi, the female giant and Laki, the male, appeared out of nowhere and started the process of creation. Bayi caught a female earthworm which excreted the earth. Bayi also gave birth to the wild animals inhabiting the world (Jocano, 1967, cited in Gaverza, 2014, p.73).

Some myths even featured women as creators on their own. The Manobos in Mindanao had a creation story wherein the world was created by the goddess Dagu who lived at the four pillars of the world. She lived with a giant python. When human blood was spilled on earth, she commanded the python to wrap itself around the pillars of the earth and shake them, causing earthquakes and destruction. When she was angry, she cursed the earth or made rice disappear from the granary (Garvan, 1931, cited in Gaverza, 2014, p.89). And the Mandaya believed that the earth is flat but was pressed into mountains by a mythical giant woman (Demetrio and Cordero-Fernando, 1991).

The materials out which the world was made are also interesting. In one of the creation stories in the Bible and in the Qur'an, man was created from soil and woman from the rib of the man. In precolonial Philippine creation myths, both man and woman were made from the same material and they were created the same time. One was not made after, or for the other, and there are a wide variety of materials from which humans are made. In a Tinguian creation myth, the first human man and woman came from a reed. And when the woman, Cavahi, first gave birth, she brought forth a great number of children at once (see Eugenio, 2007). From the Manobos, humans were created from clay with strands of abaca for veins. In the B'laan myth, the creator god Melu who always cleans himself. From his discarded dead skin, he created the first humans. The first human couple of Bikol evolved out of two strands of hair from the cut arm of Bulan, the moon god. The Ilokanos wrote that when the creator god spat, his sputum became the first man and woman. The Negritos claimed that the first human beings were made out of blades of grass woven together. In some legends, the first humans were sculpted from wood. Among the inhabitants of Mindanao, the first man and woman were hatched from the eggs of a sacred bird (see Demetrio and Cordero-Fernando, 1991).

There is even a creation myth that can be considered gender neutral. In this creation myth which was widely known on many islands in the country, in the beginning, there was no land. It was just the sky and the water. A hawk was fly-ing, trying to find a place to land. There was nowhere to alight. The hawk turned the water against the sky. The offended sky scattered islands on the water. Now, the hawk had someplace to rest. While the hawk was resting, the water threw a piece of bamboo at its feet. The hawk pecked at the bamboo until it opened up in two. From one side came a man, from the other side a woman. The woman was named Maganda meaning beautiful and the man was Malakas or strong (Scott, 1994).

Aside from creators, early Filipinos also had a pantheon of gods, goddesses, and spirits. The goddesses were notable for being strong, stubborn and hav-ing minds of their own. For example, there was the story of Bayani and Maria Sinakuan. The latter was more powerful than her lover. When she set him a task to complete a bridge and he failed, she caused a stream to engulf both Bayani and the unfinished bridge. The stream became the mighty Pampanga River (Fansler, 1922, cited in Gaverza, 2014, p.54). The Ifugao told of the tale of the goddess Bugan and her marriage to a mortal. Bugan was the daughter of Dakaue and the god Hinumbian. She lived with her parents in the uppermost part of heaven or Skyworld. When she came of age, her relatives asked her repeatedly to get mar-ried. She steadfastly refused and to get away from them, she went down to explore the many levels of Skyworld. When questioned by a chieftain why she did not wish to marry, Bugan answered, "I shall take care to marry at my pleasure, when I see someone of my liking."

Bugan continued exploring until she reached the earth where she saw and fell in love with a mortal, Luktag. She went up to Skyworld and informed her father, the god Hinumbian, that she had fallen in love and wished to marry. He gave her his permission. She went down to earth and married Luktag. She bore him a child, Balituk. The people of the earth were jealous of Bugan and disliked her ways. Their hatred was so intense that it caused her to become sick. She decided to go back to heaven. Bugan asked her husband to come with her back to heaven. She even made a rope to help him climb up. Though Luktag wanted to accompany her, he could not because of his intense fear of heights. Bugan divided their son Balituk into two and left the upper part with her husband, so Luktag would not be lonely. But he didn't know how to take care of his son, so Balituk's body quickly decomposed by the time his mother found out. Bugan came down again, and cre-ated beings and vegetation out of her son's body parts. She changed his head into an owl, his nose became a shell. From his bones came a great serpent and from his heart, a rainbow. After creating these, she returned to Skyworld to live with the remaining half of her son (see Eugenio, 2007).

In the same region, there was another story of a goddess, Gaygona who fell in love with Aponitolau, a married man from earth. She sent a basket to fetch him and had him brought to heaven. They lived together and had a child. After sometime, he started missing earth. So the goddess Gaygona allowed him to go down and spend half of the year on earth and the other half of the year in heaven (Demetrio and Cordero-Fernando, 1991).

Bontoc region had a deity named Ob-oban. Her name meant white hair. In her white hair lived ants, insects and vermin. She once punished a rude man by sending him a basket filled with all the insects, and reptiles of the world (Almendral, 1972, cited in Gaverza, 2014, p.49). In other islands, the moon was thought to be a goddess and the phases of the moon were caused by her putting on or removing her garments. When the moon was full, she was thought to be entirely naked (Demetrio and Cordero-Fernando, 1991).

In Bohol there was a goddess of mercy named Sappia (on other islands, her name is Bugan). She emptied the milk from her breasts into the weeds and the weeds turned into white rice. When her milk ran out, blood came and that was the origin of red rice (Eugenio, 2007).

In another myth, the god of winds over the earth, Captan, saw a beautiful maiden and did not know that she was Maguayen, the goddess of winds over the sea. He approached her in a cheeky manner to which Maguayen replied, "Who are you that dare hold conversation with me? Do you not know that with my softest breath I can raise waves in the vast ocean that can sink inlets?" In response, Captan created an enormous lightning accompanied by great thunder to show him her power. Angered, the goddess sent a towering wave which dragged the brash Captan out of the island. Since he was a god, he overcame the colossal wave and returned to the island in no time. He apologised to the goddess and she accepted. She said, "I myself wanted to know if there was a being who had power equal to mine." He declared his love for her and she reciprocated his feelings. From then on the land and the sea were in harmony with each other. In other versions of this myth, Captan and Maguayen planted a seed, which grew to a huge bamboo. And it was from this bamboo that the first man and women came from (Demetrio and Cordero-Fernando, 1991, p.34).

Long ago, the powerful Bagobo god Lumabat had a quarrel with his sister. He told her, "You shall go with me up to heaven." His sister replied, "No, I don't like to do that." She decided to go down to Gimokudan or the underworld. Riding on a rotating mortar she slowly went down until she reached the lower world. Above the earth, she was only known as "sister of Lumabat." But under the earth, she became Mebuyan. Mebuyan became the leader of a town called Banua Mebuyan or Mebuyan's Town where she took care of all babies who died while they were still nursing. Mebuyan's whole body was covered with nipples. The dead babies remained with Mebuyan until they stopped taking milk from her breasts. Then they went to their own families who were in the underworld (Demetrio and Cordero-Fernando, 1991, p.111).

In the Pampango myth, Bathala, ruler and creator of the world had two children, a son, Apolaqui and a daughter. The children's eyes were so bright that they shone light on the earth. When Bathala died, he did not name his successor. Apolaqui wanted to be the sole ruler. She refused to consent to his plan. Apolaqui and Mayari engaged in a long and bitter war for sole power to rule over the earth. A long and bitter war ensued between the two siblings. In one of the battles, Apolaqui wounded his sister in the eye. Realizing what he had done, he stopped fighting and agreed to exercise equal power on earth with his sister, by ruling at separate times. Apolaqui became the sun and ruled during the day. Mayari became the moon, as her light is fainter – she has but one eye (Eugenio, 2007).

Even ordinary women in Philippine precolonial myths were powerful. There was a world where the earth and the sky were too close to each other. Pounding the pestle against the mortar to remove the chaff from the rice became very difficult. One day, an old woman named Tuligbong, commanded the sky to rise up. It did so although reluctantly. In some versions, the woman placed her comb and earrings on the clouds. She pounded the pestle so powerfully that the earth and sky separated. Her comb became the moon and her earrings turned into stars (Demetrio and Cordero-Fernando, 1991).

In one of the stories of the Yligueynes, the husband Pandaguan was killed in a battle with another god. After he died, his wife became a man's concubine. After thirty days in the infernal regions, the gods took pity on Pandaguan and sent him home. After he arrived, he looked for his wife who was out attending a feast. Pandaguan summoned her but she refused to come saying, the dead do not return to the world. The angry Pandaguan returned to the infernal regions. The Yligueynes believed that had the wife obeyed his summons, all the dead would return to life (see Eugenio, 2007).

In all, women were well-represented in Philippine precolonial myths. They were created as equals to men – made from the same materials and created at the same time, in what Fe Mangahas called an "egalitarian creation myth" (Mangahas and Llaguno, 2006, p.26). The portrayal of women in the pantheon of goddesses was comprehensive: creator, co-creators, an heiress fighting for her right to rule the earth, a sister who chose to rule the underworld, maidens who wanted to marry at their pleasure or with their equals, and more. In the stories, even ordinary women could command the sky or refuse the summons of a dead god-husband.

Moving from myth to law

As noted earlier, Campbell wrote that, "It would not be too much to say that myth is the secret opening through which the inexhaustible energies of the cosmos pour into human cultural manifestations" (Campbell, 1973, p.3). With creation myths where woman was created and whole as the man from the beginning and with strong representation in the pantheon of deities, it followed that Philippine precolonial society placed women in an equal position with men. This worldview helped shape a society where women are respected, revered and regarded as equal to men.

Elizabeth Cady Stanton in the United States championed the education, property rights, and full citizenship of women and Mary Wollstonecraft of the United Kingdom advocated for education. Both asserted the equality of all men and women and that both sexes should be given unalienable rights to property, life, and liberty. Feminism fought for the right to suffrage, participation, and representation in the government, addressing inequality in education and employment opportunities (Freedman, 2007). Philippine precolonial society, which historians dated to have started in 900CE, already gave women the right to be equal to men in every way.

For example, in precolonial Philippines, women could own and inherit property, and engage in any trade and industry they chose. They could succeed in chieftainship of a *barangay* in the absence of a male heir, though lineage was recognised equally through the male and female lines when it came to inheritance and succession (Agoncillo, 1990, p.37). A good exemple is *Paninilbihan* or the custom requiring the man to work for the woman's family before marriage was practiced. Women could choose whom to marry, and separate from their spouses at will for reasons of incompatibility, childlessness, incapability to provide for the family, and even a husband's refusal to do housework (Mangahas and Llaguno, 2006). A woman could also keep her property after divorce. She had a say in how many children they were going to have. Women had the exclusive right to give names to their children, and her children could carry her name. Abortion was widely practiced (Agoncillo, 1990, p.37).

In terms of laws around sexual conduct, in precolonial times, adultery was not regarded as a crime. It was simply a personal offense that could be settled. The wife was not punished at all. Premarital sexual mores were lenient and relationships between single men and women were allowed. There appeared to be no specific term for virginity. The Filipino word, *dalaga,* meant a young maiden of marriageable age whether she was a virgin or not (Scott, 1994).

In precolonial Philippines, women could take on leadership roles in society. She could be a chieftain, as daughters of the chieftain were part of the line of succession. She could also be a warrior. A Moroccan traveler and scholar, Ibn Battuta, stopped at Tawalisi (northern Luzon) on his journey to China in 1345. His accounts included a precolonial warrior princess named Princess Urduja. She spoke his language and welcomed him to her kingdom. She told him of the battles she won with her regiment of women. She remained unmarried because she supposedly said, "I will marry only the man who can defeat me. My husband must be braver, stronger, and wiser than myself." No one dared to challenge her to a tournament (Sotelo, 2017).

Women also held important and respected positions in communities as healers and priestesses, called *babaylan*. The religion in precolonial Philippines was shamanism. Eliade defined a shaman as, "He who 'sees', because he is endowed with a supernatural vision. He sees just as far into space as into time. He can perceive what is invisible to the layman – spirits, gods, the soul" (Eliade, 1971, p.19). In the case of the Philippines, the shamans or *babaylan* were predominantly women. When occasion arose that a man would take this role, he needed to dress up as a woman (Demetrio and Cordero-Fernando, 1991).

The *babaylan* was the spiritual leader of the community. She was not subservient to the datu or the chieftain; she worked with him in the upkeep of the community. The *babaylan* was in charge of the rituals in relation to agriculture and hunting. She was knowledgeable in astronomy and she set the clearing, planting, and harvesting cycles of the clan. She was also the community doctor, using her knowledge of plants and the spirit world to heal her people. She was the keeper, responsible for the transmission of the wisdom and knowledge of her tribe (see Mangahas and Llaguno, 2006). More important, she communicated with ancestral spirits. During rituals, she goes into a trance became a conduit to the gods (see Demetrio and Cordero-Fernando, 1991).

During the Spanish colonisation, the missionaries perceived a formidable rival in the *babaylan*. For the new religion and political order to take root, the *babaylan* had to be subverted and destroyed. The *babaylan,* as keepers of the community's culture, led many of the earliest and violent resistances to Spanish colonisation. Unlike the chieftains and the warriors who cooperated and were given positions in the new colonial order, the predominantly female *babaylan* defied the order to relocate people to the newly created towns, opting instead to stay in the mountains. The *babaylan* urged the people to resist and preserve their own native beliefs and practices, instead of submitting to evangelization. This valiant stance of the babaylan angered the Spanish friars who engaged in widespread vilification campaigns, calling the *babaylan - brujas* (witches), *anitera maldita* (evil idol worshipper), *male mujer* (bad woman) and *diabolica* (satanic) (Mangahas and Llaguno, 2006, p.37).

In 1609, a *babaylan* named Cariapa, warned against the incoming decimation and colonisation in a *dalit* or lament. The prophecy was delivered with such power that the Jesuits in attendance were moved to record it.

> This land will be changed
> other people will possess it
> with another culture, other practices
> This town is to be utterly destroyed
> This province with the rest of the islands
> are to be subjugated
>
> (Mangahas and Llaguno, 2006, p.36)

From 1596-1778, there were a number of *babaylan*-led rebellions. Filipino history books, in the process of reclaiming history and culture, had just started recognising these women leaders by their individual names and assumed titles. These were some of the *babaylan*-led revolts against Spain. Dapungay led a celebrated revolt in Cebu, Negros, and Panay in 1599. Caguenga, the provocative "idol worshipper," led the battle of Nafoltan, Segovia in Cagayan Valley. In 1646, Yga, from Nueva Ecija, assumed the title Santa Maria and angered Fray Juan de Abaca who ordered the troops to take down the *babaylan* even by blood and fire. In 1664, a *babaylan* who called herself Santissssima, was put to death by impalement on a bamboo pole, as punishment. Then her body thrown in the river for crocodile feed (Mangahas and Llaguno, 2006). These women-shamans were isolated and hunted down by the colonisers. A number of them were murdered and as if to make sure their bodies would never return, their bodies were chopped and fed to crocodiles (Mangahas and Llaguno, 206). After the *babaylan* were destroyed, it ushered in a monotheistic, male-centered, colonised culture which lasted for more than three centuries. The death and disappearance of the *babaylan* were the symbolic "transitus from the realm of the mother to the realm of the father" (Kluger, 1991, p.137).

From empowering myths to the Babaylan to now

Joseph Campbell wrote that a myth is, "A mask of God – a metaphor for what lies behind the visible world" (Campbell and Moyers, 1991, p.xviii). In precolonial Philippines, this mask of God had many aspects where hundreds of creation myths presented a profusion of creators – gods, goddesses, creators who were of both genders and even creators with animal aspects. Therefore, the imagery of the creator was not just that of a man. There was an egalitarian creation process wherein both man and woman were made of the same materials, either from deities or from nature. Both man and woman were created at the same time; one gender was not preferred over the other. Last, there was the presence in the myths of goddesses and ordinary women who were strong, decisive, and confident.

This created a society which placed women in equal footing with men – the dream of feminists. Wollestonecraft predicted that, "with sound politics, diffuse liberty, mankind, including women, will become more wise and virtuous" (Wollstonecraft, 1996, p.35). Historical evidence supported her claim as precolonial Philippine culture produced women rulers, warriors, and healers from precolonial, all the way to the revolution. In the revolution against Spain, women warriors, like Gabriela Silang took reins of the revolution. When her husband was assassinated, she led the rebel movement for four months before she was captured by the colonial government and executed by hanging (see Mangahas and Llaguno, 2006). Continuing this thread of resistance, in 1986, Corazon Aquino took the mantle of a massive peaceful revolution against President Ferdinand Marcos. The latter's 21-year rule ended with the election of Aquino. She became the first female president of the country and Asia's first. In the 2018 Global Gender Gap Index which ranked 149 countries on health, education, economic and political indicators, the Philippines ranked number eight in the world and number one in Asia (Okutsu, 2018).

The Philippines has embarked in the process of reconnecting with the past before colonisation and along the lines of Freire's conscientization. There is a "deepening of the attitude of awareness characteristic of all emergence" (Freire, 1970, p.101). In 1991, in one of the meetings with indigenous people around the country, a T'boli healer echoed the voices of millennia past. She said, "D'wata (God) has no image. ... But now we see pictures of God as a man. Still, we believe that God has no image, because D'wata is all" (Mangahas and Llaguno, 2006, p.56).

References

Agoncillo, T., 1990, *History of the Filipino People*, 8th edition, Quezon City: C & E Publishing, Inc.

Campbell, J., 1973, *The Hero with a Thousand Faces*, Princeton, NJ: Princeton University Press.

Campbell, J. and Moyers, B., 1991, *The Power of Myth*, New York: Anchor Books

Demetrio, F. and Cordero-Fernando, G., 1991, *The Soul Book*, Quezon City: GCF Book.

Dundes, A. ed., 1984, *Sacred Narratives: Readings in the Theory of Myth*, Berkeley and Los Angeles, CA: University of California Press.

Eliade, M., 1971, *The Forge and the Crucible: The Origins and Structures of Alchemy*, New York: First Harper Torchbook.

Eugenio, D., 2007, *Philippine Folk Literature: An Anthology*, Quezon City: University of the Philippines Press.

Freedman, E. ed., 2007, *The Essential Feminist Reader*, New York: Modern Library

Freire, P., 1970, *The Pedagogy of the Oppressed*, New York: Herder & Herder.

Gaverza, J. K., 2014, *The Myths of the Philippines*. Bachelor Dissertation, University of the Philippines. Available: https://www.academia.edu/36248979/THE_MYTHS_O F_THE_PHILIPPINES_2014_.

Greshko, M. and Wei-Haas, M., 2019, 'New species of ancient human discovered in the Philippines', *National Geographic*. Available: https://www.nationalgeographic.com/science/2019/04/new-species-ancient-human-discovered-luzon-philippines-homo-luzo nensis/ (Accessed 18th September 2019).

Kluger, R. S., 1991, *The Archetypal Significance of Gilgamesh: A Modern Ancient Hero*, Einsiedeln, Switzerland: Daimon Verlag.

Mangahas, F. and Llaguno, J., 2006, *Centennial Crossings: Readings on Babaylan Feminism in the Philippines*, Quezon City: C & E Publishing, Inc.

Nono, G., 2008, *The Shared Voice: Chanted and Spoken Narratives from the Philippines*, Pasig City: Anvil Publishing Inc.

Okutsu, A., 2018, 'Philippines tops WEF's gender equality ranking in Asia', *Nikkei Asian Review*. Available: https://asia.nikkei.com/Economy/Philippines-tops-WEF-s-gende r-equality-ranking-in-Asia (Accessed 24th August 2019).

Scott, W. H., 1994, *Barangay Sixteenth-Century Philippine Culture and Society*, Quezon City: Ateneo de Manila University Press.

Sotelo, Y., 2017, 'A princess story with a twist', *Inquirer, Net*. Available: https://newsinf o.inquirer.net/urduja-a-princess-story-with-a-twist (Accessed 24th August 2019).

Tylor, E. B., 2016, *Primitive Culture: Researches into the Development of Mythology, Philosophy, Religion, Language, Art and Custom*, Vol. 1, New York: Dover Publications.

Wollstonecraft, M., 1996, *The Rights of Women*, London: Phoenix.

Chapter 10

The Peony Pavilion

A story on obstacles and solutions to the path of individuation for a Chinese woman

Huan Wang

The story of *The Peony Pavilion*

Most Chinese romance stories share a common element – the active role of women in love relationships. The principal female character actively approaches the male character and displays her interest in him. The Ming dynasty (1368–1644) story of *The Peony Pavilion* by Tang Xianzu vividly portrays this natural, ingrained arousal of female desire for love and sex.

The story first appeared as an opera and then as a published script and, since the Middle-Ming dynasty, Chinese people not only watched the opera on stage but also read the scripts at home which in the years after *The Peony Pavilion* was published, had become a bestseller. All literate families in the late Ming and Qing dynasties kept a copy, while many scholars produced commentaries and reviews of it (Hua, 2015, pp.107–108; Liang, 2017). Thus, by the late days of imperial China, its popularity had prevailed for many years.

In this story, Du Liniang was the teenage daughter of the city Mayor, Du Bao. As the only child in her family, her parents raised her very strictly and wanted her to become a virtuous lady. One day, however, her maid told her about a large garden in her home with a beautiful vista, which she was forbidden to visit alone. At that time, ladies were expected to remain in their chambers, and spending time outdoors, even in the garden of their own homes, was considered disrespectful. However, when her father was out, Liniang snuck into the garden, and became infatuated with the spring scene there – the flowers blossomed and butterflies and birds flew in pairs. She felt something inside her move deeply and emerged with a strong desire to have a romantic relationship with a man. She dreamt of a handsome young man, a student, and in her dream made love with him. Upon waking, she missed him, and lamented that it had only been a dream. Realising her suffering, her parents invited her tutor, Chen Zuiliang, who was also a doctor, and a nun named Sister Stone to treat her, but they failed. Eventually, suffering from lovesickness and sadness, she dies.

After Liniang's death, her father is promoted and becomes an important provincial official but as a result has to move with his family to another location to defend against an intrusive enemy. He buries his daughter in the garden and built a temple near the tomb, inviting Sister Stone to live in the temple and guard Liniang's tomb. At first, Liniang's ghost was sentenced in the underworld by the judge of the underworld. However, when the judge of the underworld discovered the reason for her death, he was touched by her beauty and vivacity and decided to keep her body fresh, asking her to come back to life at an appropriate time.

Meanwhile, the man in her dream is a student, called Liu Mengmei. When he was on his way to an imperial examination, he fell ill just in the city where the garden was located. Seeing this, Chen Zuiliang (the doctor who treated Liniang) saves him and sends him to live in the temple near Liniang's tomb for his recovery. Mengmei visits the garden and finds a portrait of Liniang. He immediately fell in love with her and gazes at her portrait from morning until night. Soon, Mengmei calls upon the ghost of Liniang and they meet night after night. Eventually Mengmei proposes to Liniang, but she tells him she is a ghost, and asks him to open her tomb which could help restore her to life. With the assistance of Sister Stone, Mengmei opens Liniang's tomb and miraculously she comes back to life.

Mengmei goes to the capital with Liniang so he can complete his examination, though the results take a long time to be revealed. During this waiting period, Liniang asks Mengmei to meet her father, hoping to gain his blessing for their marriage. However, the doctor Zuiliang had already reported that Liniang's tomb had been opened by Mengmei and he is accused of being a grave robber. Liniang's father, accepts this accusation against Mengmei, refusing to accept his daughter's resurrection and accusing Mengmei of robbing his daughter's tomb and insisting on his imprisonment. However, when the result of the examination come out, Mengmei is recognized by the government as a 'number one scholar' and released. The couple then set about proving to Liniang's father that she really is his resurrected daughter. However, even though the emperor himself gives his blessing to the marriage of Mengmei and Liniang, her father remains upset, begging Liniang to choose her natal family over her husband, but she refuses to do so.

From the start, the story had a very strong and profound effect on readers and traces of the story were evident everywhere in Chinese culture in subsequent years, in other plays and novels. In particular, female readers in the Ming and Qing (1644–1912) dynasties were deeply moved by the story. Some reports even suggested that some female readers tried to court the author, Tang, to become his wife or even his concubine because of his deep understanding of women (Liang, 2017). Some women felt that they were the embodiment of Liniang when they felt erotic desire but had to face disappointment in their own marriages, and even mimicked her death. Finally, a female actress died of a broken heart when playing Liniang on stage. During those years, female writers published commentaries and reviews and tried to interpret the story from their own perspectives, which was quite rare at that time in China (Xu, 1987, pp.213–217; Li, 2007; Xie, 2008, pp.19–25, p.43; Liang, 2017). Thus, it appears that this story has resonated greatly with Chinese women since its first public performance.

It is evident that Liniang's story was an idealized pattern for these women. Her experience deeply touched them because few of them had the opportunity to be her. Liniang was an only child whose father was a government official with no concubine or other children. Hence, it appears that he valued her greatly, which was quite unusual in China. Usually, because of the son-preference and the emphasis on the number of offspring, a man in Liniang's father's position would have had several wives and children. Furthermore, Liniang was educated and had her own tutor, while many girls, even those born to rich families, were illiterate due to the common belief that 'innocence is a virtue for women' and that reading would damage that innocence. Therefore, even Liniang and her family had to follow certain mainstream rules of the time; however, under further examination, her characteristics and her relationships with others, in particular with her father, were quite modern. Liniang represented the idealized image for Chinese women of the period while her self-awareness and behaviour resemble more a modern woman, in particular the only daughter in contemporary China and her story could be seen as a process of individuation for a Chinese woman.

Obstacles to the path to individuation

Stein noted that the core of female individuation is for a woman to rid herself of her identification with the controlling inner mother (2005, p.97), but this Chinese story is about how the heroine fights against the patriarchal system. On the surface, Stein's statement and what happened in this story go in different directions. However, Neumann points out that even when experienced as a patriarchal uroboros, the phallic-chthonic gods still belong to the realm of the Great Mother (1951/2017, p.12). The uroboros is a heavenly serpent eating its own tail. It is a mythical creation in ancient Egypt that was later applied to Western alchemy. Neumann applied this image to depict the undifferentiated state of early development of the psyche (Neumann, 1954/1989, pp.5–38). Hence, beyond the biologically assigned roles of the mother and father, the patriarchal principle might be the conscious order of a society, but beneath this, in the deep unconscious realm, the power of the Great Mother cannot be neglected, and it has secretly dominated people's psychological lives.

In China, such power is very obvious. Taoism believes 'Yin' to be the primary power in the universe. Chinese scholars think that although Chinese women have not had political power in our long period of traditional patriarchal society, mothering has been highly valued and pregnancy and fertility are the most important family issues. Hence, it is often the mother who takes charge in her son's family and her son must be filial to her, admire her and obey her will (Ye, 1997, pp.40–55, p.202; Yi, 1998, p.364; Sun, 2010, pp.351–354; Wu, 2016, p.23). The dominating Great Mother is the foundation of a traditional Chinese family and further, the deep root of Chinese ethics, in which people value the privilege and power of a grown-up son's mother and put her in the highest position in the son's family.

The mother figure in China is quite one-sided, in other words, only the good mother exists. In many cultures which refer to the Great Mother, there are two typical figures: the good and the bad mother. Sometimes, the most important Great

Mother can be both nurturing and destructive. However, there is rarely an image of an evil or terrible mother in Chinese culture. Almost every mother in Chinese myths and legends is good, nurturing and inspiring. Some provide moral models and enlightened figures for their sons. Sometimes they cause damage, but they do so for good reason, not out of malevolence. Although there are some well-known mothers-in-law who have treated their daughters-in-law badly, they are still good mothers to their sons and all their actions are for their son's benefits. This one-sided mother is difficult to protest against and fight because she is so nice to her children on the surface, but at the same time she has the power to secretly devour her children's wills and to prevent them from gaining independence.

Therefore, on the one hand, Liniang stands against her father's will and challenges the patriarchal system for which her father stands; on the other hand, if we explore the story in more depth, beneath this system, Liniang must also struggle with and separate from her identification with the devouring mother who has unconsciously constellated her image in Chinese culture.

The oppression of sexuality

In imperial China, while people recognized the primacy and power of female sexuality, they also adopted strategies to limit this feminine power and to control women's sexual desire. In the Ming and Qing dynasties, a common way to do so was to confine women within a very limited space. Idema considered the garden in *The Peony Pavilion* to be a symbol of sexuality (2005, pp.291–297). Liniang, who was forbidden from entering the garden and had to remain within her chamber, was not only cut off metaphorically from her connection with her sexual nature, but was also literally confined, which was a requirement for young ladies at the time.

As Mann points out, there occurred at this time segregation of the sexes within the household while, at the same time, the practice of foot-binding cloistered women within their own chambers to limit their interaction with others, from outside men in particular (2011, pp.7–12). Therefore, Liniang and other young ladies of her era had to remain indoors and shut off their feminine awareness, a primary and latent factor in women's nature, which, of course, cannot be shut off.

A deep chamber looks like a deep well. Liang (2017) describes how such chambers were usually on the second floor of buildings and had just one window high up on the wall, which was solely for ventilation and lighting. The position of the window guaranteed that young ladies would not be seen by others, nor could they look outside. Thus, such chambers were a kind of prison. Chinese people thought that if a woman's beauty was seen by a man, he would be seduced, or even conquered, by following the woman's sexual power. Therefore, the best way to avoid such a situation was to cloister women in deep chambers.

When Miles discussed 'the body politic', she said, "[s]ince women were seen as reproductive beings, any and every disorder they experienced was treated by treatment of the reproductive organs". She further mentioned the practice of "female circumcision, the excision of the clitoris and external genitalia" to cure women's disease (1988/2001, pp.244–245). In Chinese culture, there is no record of female circumcision, but there is a long history of foot-binding. Both practices are attempts to control women by torturing their bodies and objectivising them. Nevertheless, the aim of excising the clitoris is to eliminate women's sexual pleasure, while foot-binding limits women's mobility and confines their power within the household. Ironically, in the sense of Chinese aesthetics, foot-binding, as a typical Chinese fetish, increased a woman's sexual attractiveness as an object.

Furthermore, Chinese people of these eras understood that controlling feminine power, either through confinement in a deep chamber or through foot-binding, was not sufficient. Besides literal and physical confinement, their minds were also confined. Luxun (1918) pointed out that in China in that period, women were encouraged to be 'Jie' and 'Lie'. 'Jie' means that a woman maintains fidelity to her dead betrothed or husband, while 'Lie' means that a woman commits suicide after her betrothed or husband has died, or if she is raped. In sum, women should maintain their chastity and sexual purity. Mann named such women "faithful maidens" (2011, p.122). Liang (2017) noted that in the record of *History of Ming* the number of such 'faithful maidens' was four times the total number in the records of previous history. He explains this increase stemmed from the increased population in the Ming and Qing dynasties, which also increased the risks of their damaging an over-populous society. Women were the core and foundation of the family; thus, if women were deemed 'stable' in the family with a high level of morality, they could manage their husbands and sons well.

In contemporary China of the 2010s, people face another round of issues related to the vast population and skewed sex ratio (excessive males in Chinese marriage market). The terms 'Jie' and 'Lie' are no longer used, but emphasis on the importance of women's chastity and purity has returned. In 2015, a university in Xi'an asked its female students to sign a pledge not to have sex before or outside of marriage. In 2017, a female lecturer, Dingxuan, aroused a huge debate in China for offering lectures on 'female morality', in which she taught women how to be 'faithful maidens' and to maintain their love for their husbands even if they encountered domestic violence. She recruited many students and her lecture can be found on YouTube (www.youtube.com/watch?v=A08oYsDKAzI). In the same year, the BBC reported on the 'Chinese virginity debate', triggered by the popular TV show *Ode to Joy 2*. In this show, a girl was dumped by her boyfriend when he discovered that she was not a virgin. These voices, which should have disappeared from modern society, continue to haunt China. Such strategies are still effective, making many Chinese women hide their sexual desires and forming a stereotype of their passive sexuality.

This oppression of sexuality does not just pertain to women, however. After all, if most women must value their chastity and retain their virginity, then, due to the skewed male/female gender ratio (because of the son-preference, sex-selective abortion and female infanticide have always exists in China, plus polygamy in ancient periods, and there have been always excessive men in marriage markets), it would also be difficult for men to fulfil their sexual desires. Furthermore, in traditional values, the idea of sexual activity for pleasure has not been welcomed and further, it is also believed that a man's sperm is his vital essence and that he should keep his sperm within his body to maintain his health; hence, sexual activity which is not for the goal of reproduction would harm his vitality. A man of noble character should be abstinent and fulfil his desires through aesthetic activities (Ye, 1997, p.204; Mann, 2011, pp.39–46, p.58). Hence, even in today, in a typically traditional Chinese romance, the hero is always a young, innocent student, like Mengmei. While before meeting Juliet, Romeo had had a physical relationship with another woman, there is no evidence that Mengmei had been intimate with a woman before meeting Liniang. Although meeting several young nuns in the temple, those relationships were innocent.

Not only is the sexuality of young men and women oppressed, but parental figures also do not demonstrate overt sexual activity. In *The Peony Pavilion*, the story is initiated by a girl's sexual desire, but no sexual trace is found in the mother and father figures. Liniang's parents only had one child, their daughter, and as was typical of a couple of the elite class from ancient time to today, the relationship was respectful and remote. Following Liniang's death, her mother suggested that her father take a young concubine to bear him a son. Her father, however, rejects this suggestion and focuses entirely on his work to defeat the intrusive enemy from other country. Mengmei was raised by an old male servant, who was single and devoted all his life to Mengmei's family. Liniang's tutor, who saved Mengmei's life, was a single, pedantic old man, who seemed entirely closed off from sexuality.

Another mother figure, Sister Stone, the old nun who protected Liniang's tomb and assisted Mengmei to open her tomb, was named 'Stone' because she had no vagina and she could not have sex. Hence, the sexual hormones are absent from most of these parental figures. Since sexuality would seem essential to reproduction, this absence of sexuality in the story's parental figures is ironic especially in a story full of sexual symbols. However, this is common and understandable in Chinese culture (in a general sense): a typical Chinese family, having finished their task of reproduction, the couple focus on their roles of father and mother: their sexual interaction is no longer important. In Chinese stories all the time, all around China, it is always very difficult to imagine that a mother and father have a sexual life.

'Giant babies' without mature sexuality

It is a widespread phenomenon that in Chinese literature young people of reproductive age have a desire for sex. However, as many have pointed out in discussion of Chinese society, a decent lady should retain her chastity in extreme ways – such as Liniang, seeking death – at least until she meets the 'right' man. And indeed it is to be preferred that a virtuous gentleman should not have sexual experience except in pursuit of reproduction. Sun concluded that in China, sexual activity only serves for reproduction and marriage, since reproduction was not regarded as being for the pleasure of sexuality; the result is that marriage and reproductive sexual activity are entirely removed from the individual's personal sexual desire (1983/2001, pp.238–242). But he pointed out an exception to this: in fact another aim of sexual activity is to nourish life.[1] He considered this to be another way of feeding, whereby sexuality is not a genital desire but a replacement of the oral desire (Sun, 1983/2001, pp.111–115). In sum, traditionally, when sexuality has been allowed, it occurs in forms which do not involve a mature intimacy between two individuals because the relationship is not based on their own choice.

Influenced by Sun, Wu Zhihong studied the national character of Chinese people and concluded that China is a nation of Giant Babies. According to him, all Chinese people remain at the oral stage, with a mental age of less than one year old. Moreover, symbiosis with the mother is also a pattern that is actively encouraged in Chinese culture (Wu Zhihong, 2016, pp.8–15). Both Sun and Wu adopted Freud's and Klein's ideas to make direct interpretation of Chinese culture. Applying this Western-rooted pattern to examine the Chinese psyche brought about an inevitable result: they concluded that Chinese people are less mature than Western people. It is the case, however, that both these scholars applied the conclusions they arrived at in examining extreme cases or from reaction to only parts of Chinese culture to represent all Chinese people and the whole picture in China. However, Liniang and several other female figures in literature, demonstrate a higher level of sexual maturity, in which they chose the way to fulfil their sexual desires by their own will and take responsibility for such choices, and have characteristics of a high developmental phase to show their autonomy. These female figures form a crucial part of Chinese culture and are highly valued. It is the point of this chapter that both Sun's and Wu's arguments are limited by their one-sided assertions and ignorance of the complexity of Chinese culture. Nevertheless, their ideas can help in understanding the problems in China and the conflicts between modernization and traditional Chinese values.

The image of the Giant Baby, a grown-up face with a baby's mental stage, paints a vivid picture to facilitate our understanding of certain issues specific to Chinese culture and the reasons for certain difficulties in Chinese marriage.

There are several rich images in the Peony Pavilion story. When we look at the picture of the deep chamber – a dark, narrow, and sometimes humid place – it seems to be a symbol of a womb. The foot-binding which limits movement, and the brainwashing designation of 'Jie' and 'Lie' in which women are asked to obey moral rules unquestioningly, all demand of women that they be dependent on others and comply with the patriarchal system, foregoing their independence and self-awareness. Wu observes that although some young Western girls date 'sugar daddies', the phenomenon of young girls dating or marrying a man of nearly their own father's age is more common in China. After interviewing these girls, he found that their attraction to older men was not necessarily related to their possession of money and power, but was rather due to those girls' eagerness to be taken care of and their seeking love and attention. In effect, I would claim, they are looking for maternal care from an older man (Wu Zhihong, 2016, pp.57–58).

Obviously, Liniang is not such a girl. She is the only child in her family and is valued and cherished by her parents (her family hire a tutor and a maid for her, and during the period of her illness, her mother is quite sensitive to the reason for her illness and shows her understanding and sympathy while her father denies his daughter's sense of sexuality, and tries his best to save her. Following her death, her parents are very sad and her father even builds a temple to memorialize her and guard her tomb). Hence, Liniang was cherished in her own family. In studying a number of well-known Chinese romance stories, I observed that most heroines who dare to find an appropriate lover by themselves are only children (such as *The Dream of the Red Chamber*), a few have just one sibling, and very small number have several siblings. In all cases, however, the heroine is the youngest and the cherished child. Hence, one of the conditions for separating from the primary care of the mother is to have received enough love. This fits with attachment theory, which states that a secure base with love and attention facilitates the developmental phase of "separation-individuation" (Bowlby, 1973, pp.360–362).

Not only are women under pressure to remain at an early stage of dependence in their development, it is also preferable for Chinese men to remain Giant Babies. In romance stories, Mengmei is a typical male who is pretty and fragile without a moustache or muscles, which are traditionally in the tales, the signs of a mature man. In *The Peony Pavilion*, the figure of Mengmei is not as vivid or lively as the figure of Liniang. He is attractive to women and can easily secure the help of a mother figure. However, he seems unable to defend or protect himself when faced with an accusation from a man. Sun argues that Chinese men are very feminine in the eyes of Western people, because they are too close with the mother and the mother always stands between the father and son; hence, they identify more with the mother (1983/2011, pp.215–219). However, this conclusion is due to Sun's application of the Western culturally assigned models of femininity and masculinity to his analysis of Chinese people. Further, only in romance stories is Mengmei a typical male figure; in stories of political events and novels about brotherhood in China, the leading figures can be strong and aggressive, with heavy hair. Hence, Mengmei's type does not represent all male images of China.

However, a man of his type does have the advantage of attracting Chinese women. A study on sexual preference in China demonstrates that, for many years and even today, Chinese women have preferred pretty boys with narrow shoulders and light hair, while men with muscles are less attractive (Dixson, Dixson, Li and Anderson, 2007). Such boys are not necessarily feminine, however, as such descriptions are culturally dependent; more precisely, they seem immature and their sexuality seems undeveloped, like a child or even a baby. Further, they demonstrate a certain passivity in relationship compared with their female partners. As an active agent, after all, it was Liniang who visited Mengmei, and who led him to open her tomb and guided him to confront her father. In a word, he is less autonomous than she is, and his actions were triggered or motivated by her.

Moreover, Wu's most inspiring idea about the term 'Giant Baby' is that the parents of these Babies – the passive boys and dependent girls – are also Giant Babies and the over-emphasis on filial piety – asking children to obey all their parents' orders unconditionally and placing the parents in the most important positions in their lives – is an attempt to treat parents as such (2016, pp.370–373).

This idea has similar counterparts in both relational psychoanalytic and post-Jungian theories. Benjamin points out that the mother must have the ability to distinguish the real baby from her fantasy, "to set clear boundaries for her child and to recognize the child's will, both to insist on her own independence and to respect that of the child … if she cannot do this, omnipotence continues" (1995, p.38). Hence, the maturity of the mother is the basis of the future development of the child, but if the mother herself is unable to assert her own independence and recognize the potential independence of her baby, she will cause her children to remain in a state of symbiosis. Knox points out that if parents' development remains in the early stage and hence lacks the ability of mentalization, they will treat their children as the absent internal parents and ask them to take care of their emotional needs. Under such circumstances, they cannot treat their children as independent beings and foster their individuation (2004, pp.126–145).

These arguments facilitate our understanding of how parents, as Giant Babies, are unable to foster their children's self-agency and sense of subjectivity, and even become obstacles in their children's path of individuation. Alternatively, we could say that the parents are devoured by the omnipotent Great Mother, and hence, their mental age remains at an infantile level and they unconsciously engage their children in this symbiosis. Wu writes in detail that such symbiosis is the origin of collectivism which opposes individual will and a collectivistic group is the only residence for a Giant Baby (2016, p.90). In China, a dominating mother figure is important for the unity of large families and the mother metaphor is used to represent the community and the state. Although such metaphors exist in other cultures, in China, devoting oneself to the extended family and the state and being filial to one's mother are the two basic ethical principles.

Hence, we can understand why Liniang's father was so stubborn in refusing his daughter's marriage. Idema suggested that this might be due to a form of 'Oedipal complex': the father has a secret, incestuous desire for his daughter (2005, pp.309–312) and if this were a typical Western story, this might indeed be the case. However, in China, I would suggest there is another interpretation. Sexual encounters can be distinguished as between either mother-infant affection or intimate relationships between two adults (Colman, 1994, pp.511–512). As a man who shows no mature sexual desire and devotes himself to his work and his country (the only evidence of his sexual life is that he has a daughter, and after she is born, he had no other offspring and rejected her mother's suggestion to have more other women to be more reproductive), Liniang's father is still at the stage of being a mother's son and wants his daughter to remain innocent about sex and remain at the stage of a baby's asexuality. However, he fails in imposing this restriction. Liniang has a strong determination to rid herself of the intergenerational symbiosis and to remain with the man who had initiated her sexual desires. This is the most extraordinary part of the story: although the parents are Giant Babies and try to keep their child in the same condition, the child takes the opportunity to break free from this intergenerational curse and to enter the path of individuation. Ironically, Liniang's active pursuit of her sexual desire demonstrates her aggression and this aggression is the result of her identification with her father, as the only daughter with a father working for military. Unfortunately, although her father demonstrates strong aggression he has a repressed sexuality; hence, he did not take the same opportunity to break free as his daughter did.

Aggression: a two-edged sword

The split of sexuality and aggression among Chinese men

Samuels points out that the 'monolith of men' needs to be broken up: "some are powerful …; others are manifestly powerless and oppressed" (2013/2015, p.121). Such a monolith called 'men' has not existed in China either where is a long tradition of men being differentiated by their social class and career. Furthermore, even in the elite class, the characteristics of different male images are quite divided; hence, power is not attributed evenly to all men no matter what class or career level.

In *The Peony Pavilion*, both Mengmei and Liniang's fathers belong to the elite class, but Liniang's father obviously has more power and demonstrates strong aggression while Mengmei is vulnerable and demonstrates little aggression. This is a typical split among the images of Chinese men in literature through Chinese history. Usually, sexual desire and aggression are not carried simultaneously by a virtuous man. Hence, the hero of the romance story is Mengmei, the pretty and vulnerable boy who has been well educated. Liniang's father is a different figure. In the eyes of the Chinese mainstream, although he was against his daughter's marriage with Mengmei, he is also not the villain of the story. On the contrary, he represents a good father and husband, a virtuous gentleman in the Confucian value system, who shows no interest in women and has great passion for the state.

As a director of the military, Liniang's father is quite similar to another typical male image, the warrior, who also shows no sexual desire. There is a Chinese saying describing a common belief among warriors: 'you have to treat your brothers as hands and feet and your wife as a piece of clothing. Changing a piece of clothing is easy but replacing hands and feet is difficult'. This implies that a warrior's sexual desire for women is much less important than his sense of camaraderie bordering on brotherhood with other men. A prevalent and influential Chinese novel, *Water Margin* (fourteenth century), which was also written in the Ming dynasty, tells the story of a group of warriors who have muscles and show strong aggression. They are very close to the image of Western masculinity, but most of these warriors show no interest in having sex with women. Some have experience of being cheated or betrayed by women for which reason they hate them, while others have lost their wives at the beginning of the story or their wives are unimportant or almost invisible in the stories. Hence, in this thick tome, it is difficult to find any romance and in the eyes of such heroes, a woman is either a slut who will bring damage to them or a shrew without sexual attraction. However, they admire their mothers and being filial to the mother is a notable virtue.

In contrast, a very important theme for Western heroes is to rid themselves of their mother complexes and to unite with the anima, the contrasexual image, depicted by the slaying of a dragon and rescuing a princess captured by the dragon. This is an important moment in which a hero can express his aggression directly and his aggression is in service of his sexual individuation. The typical image of the Chinese mother is always positive and therefore this theme is lacking in Chinese culture. There are stories of Chinese warriors fighting against monsters or evil spirits, and while such monsters and spirits sometimes represent the evil power of women, such power has nothing to do with motherhood. After annihilating this evil force, if the warrior has the opportunity to marry a girl in gratitude for his service, a man of honour should reject such a marriage to demonstrate his selflessness. Hence, in Chinese romance, there is no image akin to the typical knight of Western literature, an attractive hero who is simultaneously equipped with both aggression and sexuality. In China, an aggressive man with sexual desires has always been a lecher, the villain of the piece who indulges in sex, the trafficking and raping of women, bullying and hurting their fathers and husbands, and is thus exterminated by a warrior by the end of the story. Such figures represent another image of the omnipotent Giant Baby.

None of the male figures in China mentioned above has a sense of separation from the mother. A decent man, whose first identity is as the son of his mother, may choose between either sexuality or aggression. However, if a man is without sexuality, he cannot be mature while if he is without aggression, there is no opportunity for him to overcome the mother complex which fosters a mature sexuality. Under these circumstances, a man remains faithful to his mother but as a mother's baby possessed by his mother complex. Hence, we observe that, in *The Peony Pavilion*, Mengmei is Liniang's contrasexual image, but without any aggression, and he is thereby no equal to the animus of Jung's idea, which designates separation and independence. More precisely, in fact, he initiates Liniang's own will to separate from her natal family and become independent while motivating her aggression and action. He represents the potential for a future from the other sex.

While Chinese people create a split between masculine sexuality and aggression, their traditional attitude towards women's aggression has its own different characteristics.

Women's aggression and the damage caused by their sexuality

As Austin noted, "femaleness has been taken to be synonymous with non-aggression" (2005, p.25). However, women's active role in pursuing the fulfilment of their desires for love and sexuality has been a very common theme in Chinese stories, while the aggression that lies beneath the activeness and damage caused by their sexual power has also been emphasized. Therefore, while it is recognized that a woman can be the subject of desire, her sexuality should be oppressed lest her active sexual desire, her sexual attractiveness and her aggression cause damage.

A typical pattern of Chinese romance stories is that a beautiful woman causes a disaster, and she mostly does so actively and with a certain level of awareness. In *The Peony Pavilion*, Mengmei opens her tomb in order to rescue Liniang. As an intellectual, this was disgraceful and criminal behaviour and, in this story, it has been inspired by a beautiful woman. Liniang had insisted that Mengmei must meet her father, a government officer, and although it was not her intention to bring trouble to Mengmei, he was jailed for this action. To a certain degree, the relationship with Liniang does bring him disaster, although he eventually overcomes it. Nevertheless, this could serve as a lesson for him.

In other stories, sexually active women cause destruction to a single man or even to a whole dynasty. Chinese scholars (Luxun, 1918/2001; Yi, 1998, pp.25–27; Boyang, 2010) have concluded that this pattern shows Chinese men as not responsible for their own actions, always blaming women: a typically patriarchal attitude. From a different perspective, however, Chinese people tend to emphasize the primacy and power of female sexuality and aggression, a recognition that is not obvious in Western literature. There is little, it would appear, that a male figure could do about it.

Boyang (2010) compared the story of Helen in *The Iliad* with the story of Daji in *Fengshen Yanyi* (*The Creation of the Gods*, first published in book form in the sixteenth century). There are certain similarities between the two stories: both occurred in the twelfth century BCE and both heroines were beautiful women who caused a great war, which their current husbands lost. Boyang noted that the difference between them was that the Trojan warriors appreciated Helen's beauty and she returned to the arms of her ex-husband, who had won the war, while Daji was accused of being a fox fairy who had enchanted her husband, causing his demise, and was thus beheaded by the victor. Boyang claimed that these differing ends demonstrated differences in attitude towards women in the West and in China, where, for one thing, the Western attitude is more merciful (pp.44–46). With further examination, however, another conclusion can be reached: in *The Iliad*, the woman, Helen, is the passive victim of a man's desire. She never intended to cause the war; she was the one who was seduced and should thus be forgiven. The appreciation of her beauty implies that she is a trophy of war. However, in *Fengshen Yanyi*, Daji was sent by a goddess to seduce the emperor as a punishment; thus, from the start, as a representative of feminine power, she played an active role in her relationship to the man. She then pushed her husband into war, and even fought in the war herself in an attempt to prolong her reign as queen. She is evil but strong, presenting her negative, destructive feminine power to challenge the patriarchal order.

Thus a Western counterpart more like Daji is Lady Macbeth, an evil woman in Shakespeare's play who manipulated her husband into killing the king and stealing the crown. However, she did not have her own name or identity, and her ambition served her husband; thus, her desire for power was intertwined with his. She is dependent on her husband and is the victim of patriarchy. However, Daji's ambition and desire served herself. Furthermore, Daji seemed quite similar to the male image of the lecher mentioned above, who demonstrates both sexuality and aggression, however, a typical lecher is still a mother's boy, who depends on being taken care of by women while Daji is tougher and more independent. As an evil woman who should be defeated, her failure is inevitable, but her story shows the fear surrounding women's initiative and autonomy which imply an awareness of those attributes in the first place. Hence, we can understand another function of the deep chamber and foot-binding – to confine women's movement and limit the damage that may be caused by their sexuality and aggression.

Aggression turned against the self

Another cost of the deliberate oppression of the female power of sexuality and aggression is the high rate of female suicide in China. Suicide is an exemplary action of turning aggression against the self. After studying the phenomenon of the 'faithful maiden' in China, Mann (2011) came to the conclusion that, for many, the decision to commit suicide was made to avoid moral disgrace and the consequent unbearable lifetime of celibacy. China is among only a few countries where the rate of female suicide is higher than that of male suicide (Philips, Li, and Zhang, 2002; Cui, 2009). Moreover, China has always had the highest rate of female suicide (Wolf, 1975; Lee and Kleinman, 2003, p.292), which is quite unusual. The reason for suicide amongst Chinese women might be due to the dynamics between them and the external world.

There have been two typical types of suicide amongst Chinese women. The first was common in the late Ming and Qing dynasties, and complied with the requirements of the government and the voices of mainstream society – to be the 'faithful maiden' for her fidelity and purity. These women died for 'Jie' and 'Lie' to be the moral model to protect the patriarchal order, allowing their aggression to be used instrumentally by the patriarchal system. This type of suicide has disappeared since 1949. However, there is another kind of suicide among Chinese women – "a deliberate display of protest" (Mann, 2011, p.123). In *The Peony Pavilion*, Liniang also 'actively died' (giving up the will to be alive) in the middle of the story although there is no obvious suicide attempt, and after the story was published, she had female followers. Usually, such a protest is conducted for the sake of autonomy in marriage, which might have been the most available mode of protest for women in Chinese society for many years.

After her dream in the garden, Liniang could not accept an arranged marriage from her parents which seemed to be the only way for a lady to marry at that time, and the only way to escape her parents' arrangement was to die. Mann also points out that after the New Culture Movement in 1919, "young girls would kill themselves to resist arranged marriages" (2011, p.xx). In recent studies of rural female suicide in China, it has been shown that most such suicides comprise impulsive acts due to the conflicts within the women's marital families. Because of China's urbanization, more and more rural women are now migrating and dwelling in cities; thus, they have more choice in a more contemporary urban setting over their own marriages and are less dependent on their husband's families. As a result, the suicide rate in China has decreased dramatically (*The Economist*, 2014; Jin, Wu, and Zhang, 2010). For many Chinese women, death has for many years been the only way to attain freedom from liability to their families and marriages.

Therefore, the recognition of women as the subject of desire and as having aggression has not, in reality, brought more liberation or freedom to Chinese women; on the contrary, they must face severe oppression for many years due to the fear of and defence against feminine power, which shapes the persona of well-known Chinese women – a passive and obedient female image with no evident aggression – and as a consequence, brings their passive aggression and inhibited sexuality into their marital relationships.

Aggression in the context of individuation

The negative aspects of aggression have always been emphasized in both China and the West. However, more recent studies show that aggression can be a two-edged sword bringing both creative and destructive results. Samuels has argued that aggression "is part of life and it is not all bad. … Aggression is part of communication" (2001, p.133). It is clear that aggression cannot be avoided in daily life and in relations with others and can be ambivalent. Austin elaborates the two sides of aggression and says there is a "creative possibility and push towards embodied agency which dwells within aggression, alongside its destructive and annihilatory potentials" (2005, p.10). Such possibility and agency were clearly revealed by Liniang's story and prompted her to move forward, entering the path of individuation, while the contrasting image of Daji demonstrates how aggression can bring damage to others and to herself, and negate self-knowledge.

Here, the key questions are how to facilitate benevolent aggression, allowing creation and agency to merge in service of individuation and to prevent the pure destructiveness of aggression. Let us compare the two different images of women: Daji and Liniang. Daji is sent by an angry goddess. She is the daughter of a Great Mother. From the outset, she represents aggression and punishment deriving from the mother's anger. However, it must be recognized that in *Fengshen Yanyi*, although Daji is an evil woman, the goddess who sent her is an image of a good creating and rescuing mother. By the end of the story, she abandons Daji because she only sent her to punish the emperor who humiliated her and cannot accept Daji hurting others. Daji's aggression is utilized to dominate others and to enslave them for her own benefit. Her husband, the emperor, was used by her instrumentally and she had no intimate connection with a man.

Meanwhile, Liniang has entered a process of individuation in her trajectory. Her aggression serves her in a benevolent and creative way. As Austin describes, "a capacity to hold and direct aggressive energy for the good of relationship is a significant human achievement, and ... an increasing capacity to do so correlates with an increasing capacity to build and sustain lively relationships without compromising oneself or one's values" (2005, p.1). Liniang maintains agency and establishes a solid relationship with Mengmei, showing her loyalty to him despite the pressure she is under from her father at the end. What makes Liniang different from Daji is that she is not only her mother's daughter but also her father's daughter. Her father cares for her very much. As Samuels points out, "fatherly warmth leads to a recognition of daughters as people in their own right. ... Fatherly recognition of the daughter as other than a mother can enable women to break out of the cycle of the reproduction of motherhood", and lead them to other pathways, such as, "the spiritual path, the work path, the path that integrates her assertive side, the path of sexual expression ... maybe the path of celibacy" (2001, p.109). Hence, being recognized by the father and receiving affection from him open various opportunities for the free choice of the daughter and allow her to dare to be herself and to rid her of the solely culturally assigned role of a woman.

Further, as a daughter of a military director, Liniang's aggression is more likely to stem from her identification with her father. Benjamin applies Anna Freud's case to illustrate a daughter's wish to be her father's son and points out that such an identificatory bond can be healthy, having nothing to do with Oedipal compulsion, and can foster the daughter's self-assertion and her "sense of being the subject of the desire" (1995, pp.130–135). Hence, we can understand why Liniang is able to face her sexual desire directly and pursue her love actively. In a certain way, as the only child, she was cherished by her parents as a son and could become the successor to her father. Because of the son-preference in China, there is a tendency to treat the only daughter as the son of her family and the only successor to her father, particularly in modern only-child families. Only daughters have more interaction with their fathers than daughters from non-only-child families. These only daughters and their fathers have more opportunity to mutually recognize that the daughter could be the father's son.

Moreover, Samuels highlights that the daughter's aggression from her identification with her father serves "to validate and reinforce [her] capacity to challenge and fight with men" and extends her "capacity to confront the patriarchy" (2001, p.114). This is exactly what Liniang did. Samuels also proposes "the possibility of an element in fathering that can help to transform antisocial, sadistic, unrelated aggression into socially committed, self-assertive, related aggression" (2001, p.113). This is the key difference between Liniang's aggression and Daji's. Daji's aggression comes from the Great Mother, which is the unconscious realm and thus, once unleashed, it is very difficult to control the damage caused by her. However, Liniang's aggression is identified with her real father. It is used more consciously and instrumentally to serve a clear purpose which is to have a marriage based on free choice with a man she loves, and thus serves a mature sexuality and fosters her sexual individuation.

China is a country where the patriarchal system has dominated the collective consciousness while the power of the Great Mother has occupied the unconscious realm and deeply affected the ethical awareness of Chinese people for many years. To be the mother's child is preferred in China. Chinese men are encouraged to split aggression and sexuality lest they rid themselves of their mother complex. Both women's sexual desire and aggression have been recognized but the dangers of such power have also been overemphasized. Hence, Chinese women have been oppressed for many years. *The Peony Pavilion* delivers an ambivalent attitude towards women in Chinese culture: on the one hand, women's innocence and obedience have been encouraged in daily life, while on the other, in literature, a girl who has awareness and is rebellious is the idealized female image. This might reflect Chinese people's secret eagerness to individuate.

From a psychological perspective, only mature and independent parents can foster their children's development and make their children independent. Immature and dependent parents harm their children's capacity to gain a sense of agency, cut off their opportunities for separation and place obstacles in their path to individuation. However, Liniang's story tells us that with enough love, even if it is from immature parents, the child dares to separate from her natal family and to be herself. In the process of separation and individuation, the affection from the father and identifying with his aggression are the two facilitating elements in an environment that overemphasizes the importance of the nurturing mother. Although Liniang is an image of a Chinese woman, her experience could be borrowed or emulated by others, particularly by Chinese men.

Notes

1   It was believed that under certain guidance by a senior Taoist, the man could gain benefits for his health and longevity by keeping his sperm in his body and sucking the essence released from women during orgasm. This is a Taoist sexual practice, but was opposed by Confucianists and not approved by the mainstream of China.

References

Austin, S., 2005, *Women's Aggressive Fantasies: A Post Jungian Exploration of Self-Hatred, Love and Agency*, London and New York: Routledge.

Benjamin, J., 1995, *Like Subjects, Love Objects: Essays on Recognition and Sexual Difference*, New Haven and London: Yale University Press.

Bowlby, J., 1973, 'Attachment and loss: Volume II: Separation, anxiety and anger', *The International Psycho-Analytical Library*, 95:1–429. London: The Hogarth Press and the Institute of Psychoanalysis.

Boyang, 2010, *The Death of Chinese Queens*, Beijing: People's Literature Publishing House.

Colman, W., 1994, 'Love, desire and infatuation: Encountering the erotic spirit', *Journal of Analytical Psychology*, 39(4):497–514.

Cui, W., 2009, 'Women and suicide in rural China'. *Bulletin of the World Health Organization,* 2009–2012.

Dixson, B., Dixson, A., Li, B., and Anderson, M., 2007, 'Studies of human physique and sexual attractiveness: Sexual preferences of men and women in China', *American Journal of Human Biology,* 19(1):88–95.

Hua, W., 2015, *A Close Examination on Tang Xianzu,* Shanghai: Shanghai People's Publishing House.

Idema, W., 2005, 'Suiqing Shui Jian: Du Liniang, Meigui Gongzhu Yu Ni'a Fuqin de Fannao.' In: W. Hua (ed.), *Tang Xianzu Yu Mudanting* (pp. 289–321). Zhuankan, Zhongguo Wenzhe. Taibei: Zhongyang Yanjiu Yuan, Zhongguo Wenzhe Yanjiusuo.

Jin, J., Wu, X., and Zhang, J., 2010, 'The migration of rural women and the decrease of suicide rate in China', *The Journal of China Agricultural University (Social Sciences),* 4: 20–31.

Knox, J., 2004, 'From archetypes to reflective function', *Journal of Analytical Psychology,* 49(1):1–19.

Lee, S. and Keinman, A., 2003, 'Suicide as resistance in Chinese society'. In: E. Perry and M. Selden (ed.), *Chinese Society: Change, Conflict, and Resistance,* 2nd edn. (pp. 289–311). London: Routledge Curzon.

Li, X., 2007, 'The Peony Pavilion in the eyes of female readers in the Ming and Qing dynasties', *Journal of Southeast University (Philosophy and Social Science),* 9(5):107–123.

Liang, W., 2017, 'A classic causing the suicide of female readers'. https://mp.weixin.qq .com/s?__biz=MzA3MDM3NjE5NQ==&mid=2650820234&idx=2&sn=c3e757d43 88960f8527dd87e81908ce4&chksm=84c920e6b3bea9f092188f9a79f24353113fcd9 ab3f1da588e03cb0fd0b7f27efed1e9cbb47a&mpshare=1&scene=1&srcid=0901k7EzO CQnO74eb7GUZb3C#rd (Accessed 8 January 2020).

Luxun, 1918/2001, 'My opinion on Jie and lie', *'The Tomb',* Guilin: Lijiang Publishing House.

Mann, S. L., 2011, *Gender and Sexuality in Modern Chinese History,* Cambridge: Cambridge University Press.

Miles, R., 1998/2001, *Who Cooked the Last Supper? The Women's History of the World,* New York: Three Rivers Press.

Neumann, E., 1951/2017, *The Fear of the Feminine,* trans. Hu, Q. Beijing, Guangzhou, Shanghai, Xi'an: World Publishing Corporation.

Neumann, E., 1954/1989, *The Origins and History of Consciousness,* trans. Hull, R.F.C. London: Maresfield Library.

Phillips, M., Li, X., and Zhang, Y., 2002, 'Suicide rates in China, 1995–99', *The Lancet,* 359(9309):835–840.

Samuels, A., 2001, *Politics on the Couch: Citizenship and the Internal Life,* London: Karnac.

Samuels, A., 2013/2015, *Passions, Persons, Psychotherapy, Politics: The Selected Works of Andrew Samuels,* London: Routledge.

Stein, M., 2005, 'Some reflections on the influence of Chinese thought on Jung and his psychological theory', *Journal of Analytical Psychology,* 50(2):209–222.

Sun, L., 1983/2011, *Deep Structure of Chinese Culture,* Guangzhou: Guangzhou Normal University Press.

Sun, L., 2010, *The Matricidal Culture of America: A History of the American Ethos in the 20th Century,* Nanchang: Phoenix Media Press and Jiangxi People's Publishing House.

The Economist, 2014, 'Back from the edge: A dramatic decline in suicides', https://ww w.economist.com/china/2014/06/28/back-from-the-edge (Accessed 9 January 2020).

Wolf, M., 1975, 'Woman and suicide in China'. In: M. Wolf and R. Witke (eds.), *Women in Chinese Society* (pp. 111–141). Stanford: Stanford University Press.

Wu, Z. H., 2016, *The Nation of Great Babies*, Hangzhou: Zhejiang People's Publishing House.

Xie, Y., 2008, *The Peony Pavilion and Emotional Education among Women in the Ming and Qing Dynasties*, Beijing: Zhonghua Book Company.

Xu, F., 1987, *Further Examination on the Study of Peony Pavilion*, Shanghai: Shanghai Classic Publishing House.

Ye, S., 1997, *The Goddess of Gao Tang and Venus*, Beijing: China Social Sciences Publishing House.

Yi, Z., 1998, *Chinese Men and Women*, Beijing: China Federation of Literary & Art Circles Publishing Corp.

Chapter 11

Dynamic growth and infinite feminine potential in The Walking Dead

Carol Peletier's narrative journey

Emma Buchanan

Disaster and apocalypse narratives may seem bleak, pessimistic and even hope-less, but, in fact, these stories describe a scenario where the old systems which underpinned society have been stripped away and we see survivors trying to rebuild their lives and experimenting with new types of societies. Since the turn of the century, disaster and apocalypse narratives have enjoyed a surge of popularity. The zombie apocalypse, in particular, has recently become a ubiquitous theme in popular culture. Originally developing via tales of Haitian voodoo folklore, 'zombie' as the sub-genre we know today first enjoyed some success in the 1930s (Bishop, 2009, p.15), then again in the 1960s and 1970s with George Romero's … *of the Dead* film series, starting with *Night of the Living Dead* in 1968, which made the zombie apocalypse mainstream (Bishop, 2009, pp.17–18).

The most popular of these zombie narratives since the turn of the century has been *The Walking Dead* (AMC, 2010–ongoing), which began as a comic book, created by Robert Kirkman in 2003, but has been adapted into a cult television series by AMC. It is difficult to overstate the extent to which this series has been a popular phenomenon. At the time of writing, 193 issues of the comic book, as well as numerous novels have been published, the long-running television series has recently moved into a bold new phase, having written out its main protagonist, in order to set up some new stand-alone features, and a spin-off series, *Fear the Walking Dead* (AMC, 2015–ongoing), has become established.

The key premise of *The Walking Dead* is that, for reasons yet unknown, a significant proportion of the global population suddenly turned into zombies, and that all people, in fact, are infected with an unknown something which causes them to become zombies when they die. They do not call them zombies in the series, however, but 'walkers'. The series follows a core group of survivors as they attempt to continue surviving and build a new society in the face of nihil-ism and chaos, facing threats from both walkers and hostile humans. One of its main themes is the exploration of who is really the 'walking dead' of the title, because although at first glance it is the walkers, the human survivors are little more than nomads, battling to survive until they die, which they do, often and violently. However, a second key theme is 'in a world ruled by the dead, we are forced to finally start living'. A narrative exploring new ways of living allows for a postmodern insight into categories we once saw as fixed, defined and binary, but are starting to consider as blurred and fluid, such as gender, and even death itself.

There are several leading male and female characters in *The Walking Dead*. Nine seasons into the series, there are only two members of the original group from the Atlanta survivors' camp left (though a third, the original main protagonist, Rick (Andrew Lincoln), remains alive but has left the narrative). One is Carol Peletier, a female character played by Melissa McBride; the other is Daryl Dixon, a male character, played by Norman Reedus. Since the departure of the original main protagonist, male and female characters arguably have equal value. Daryl is a complex and untraditional character who challenges gender norms, but here we will focus on Carol, who has gone through an incredible transformation since the beginning.

Having started out an abused, passive housewife who contributes nothing to the plot or even her own character development and is known only in relational terms as a wife and mother, the idea that Carol would become the only female survivor from the original group could have been considered extremely unlikely at best (indeed, in the comic books, which have some key differences, she has died). In her first scenes (1.3, 2010) she is depicted meekly avoiding confrontation, completely under the control of her aggressive husband, Ed (Adam Minarovich), and unquestioningly doing domestic chores. However, she develops into a strong, confident, independent woman who is a dangerous fighter and as such evades the limitations of clear definitions.

The aim of this chapter is to demonstrate, through an analysis of Carol, scope for depth psychology to discover and describe a psychology and way of living which serve women better than currently. This chapter will show how rethinking the dynamic processes behind the psyche and emphasising its cyclical and chaotic nature gives rise to women's infinite potential. Moreover, an approach to Carol using analytical psychology will clarify *The Walking Dead*'s feminist potential and suggest that popular culture is a rich source for Jungian enquiry.

Exploring Carol's heroine's journey

In traditional analysis, a heroine is characterised by sacrifice, (of her life, for example, in order to uphold the patriarchy) and is usually seen as a feminine aspect or version of the hero (Covington, 1989, pp.243–245). Moreover, her journey involves change from one family to another, establishing a new family and sense of belonging: relating rather than discovering, in a world where not belonging to a community is discouraged and dangerous (Bassil-Morozow, 2017, p.137). In some ways, Carol's story is rooted in tradition: although she has not sacrificed her life to maintain patriarchal structures, family and community do play a role for her. She swaps her oppressive real family for 'The Group' – the key group of survivors we follow on the show, always finding a sense of belonging from having a meaningful role building the community. Furthermore, when she leaves The Group's settlement of Alexandria to separate herself from the community, which I will discuss in due course, she is immediately injured, which reinforces the notion that not belonging is dangerous. However, although we must be cautious when female individuation involves "motherly behaviour towards others, community-making" (Bassil-Morozow, 2017, p.150) and "going through a liminal, transitional state between losing the 'old' home' [*sic*] and acquiring a 'new' one" (2017, p.151), there is much more to this complex character's journey. This section will approach Carol's narrative using Maureen Murdock's *The Heroine's Journey* (1990).

Murdock (1990) suggested a woman's journey cycle, in contrast with Campbell's Hero's Journey, with the following stages: separation from the feminine, identification with the masculine, road of trials, finding the illusory boon of success, awakening to feelings of spiritual aridity, descent to the Goddess, urgent yearning to reconnect with the feminine, healing the mother/daughter split, healing the wounded masculine and integration of masculine and feminine. There are some issues to critique with Murdock's theory, which I will come to, but I will first apply these stages to Carol's narrative to illustrate that *The Walking Dead* both supports the empowerment of women and allows women to do things their way.

Carol, a character oppressed by the role of housewife, separates from the feminine following a conversation with other female characters while doing laundry at the side of a lake (1.3, 2010). Some of the other women voice objections amongst themselves regarding the division of labour at the survivors' camp, as well as express sexual agency by lamenting the loss of their vibrators. Carol does meekly support this division, but it is the first time we have seen her engage with others or express an opinion, and she does agree that she misses her vibrator and enjoys a laugh. The solidarity and camaraderie amongst the women in this scene are the catalysts for what comes next, providing a more feminist 'power-with' structure to fight her oppression (Allen, 1998, pp.35–36). This is interesting because it means that the feminine is helping her separate from the feminine, and therefore begin her own journey. In Murdock's work, the separation is caused by negative feelings towards the feminine – the desire to be freer than the mother allows; to be a separate person from the mother, or because the mother rejects the person in question (1990, pp.13–26). However, for Carol, experiencing the collective feminine and how other women's feminine differs from her own starts the individuation process. This already implies that women supporting women gets favourable results. Carol's husband (Ed) interrupts their conversation, mocks them, orders Carol to come with him, slaps her and threatens to hit another female character. The women stand up to him in Carol's defence and Shane, a key male character and former police officer, brutally beats Ed and warns him against harming any of the women in the camp. In the next episode, Carol stands up to a sulking Ed when he tells their daughter to remain in their tent with him, insisting instead that she joins in with The Group (1.4, 2010). This is the first time we see Carol assert herself and refuse to obey Ed. Later, he is killed by walkers and in the next episode Carol cathartically beats his dead body (1.5, 2010). She has begun her separation from the feminine by rejecting her identity as Ed's wife.

The laundry scene by the lake is now infamous. It is widely cited (I will give some examples later) as an obvious indictment of the show's inherent sexism. The issues taken with this scene are, briefly, that it is a man who defends the abused woman; that the sexist division of labour is raised but not dealt with overtly or quickly; that Carol defends the division of labour; that the women are doing laundry yet again (how much laundry can this group possibly have?) and that Shane only attacks Ed because he is annoyed about something else that is going on. Yet more cause to say it is not that simple, however the scene is one of very few in the series which pass the Bechdel test.

However, the facts I have just outlined show that it is not that simple. For Carol, this scene represents the end of her abuse, the beginning of friendships and the emergence of her own agency and identity. It is also this scene which directly causes Ed to be killed: he was sulking alone in his tent when the camp was attacked by walkers. Taken by surprise and alone he was devoured by walkers within seconds. As a result of that scene, then, Carol is not only liberated from his oppression, but she is probably safer now, even during a zombie apocalypse, than she has been for years.

Carol completes her separation from the feminine when her daughter Sophia goes missing (2.1, 2011) and is killed (2.7, 2011). She can no longer define her life based on her relation as mother. She has no semblance left of what feminine meant for her. Indeed, she worries that Sophia's death is her punishment for wishing Ed dead (2.1, 2011), implying that she believes that she, indirectly, chose Sophia's death and, therefore, chose to reject her identity as mother on some level.

Carol then embarks upon the stage of identification with the masculine and gathering male allies. Impressed by Daryl's tireless commitment to the search for Sophia before she was found dead, his kindness towards Carol herself and his ability to remain calm and stay hopeful, she forms a strong bond with him that has turned into the closest friendship on the show. It is a complex relationship which refuses to be limited by definitions: they are best friends, yet also mother and son, yet also suggestively romantic and sexual (though nothing physical has happened). Carol champions Daryl above all other members of The Group, giving his self-esteem much-needed compliments, for example that he is just as good a man as Rick and Shane (2.5, 2011). Daryl is a very valuable fighter and capable survivalist but abuses in his own life and a sense of inferiority arising from being very 'white trash' make him aloof, immature and lacking in self-respect. Having both suffered at the hands of hegemonic masculinity, they form a bond. Understanding his value as an ally, Carol puts him on a pedestal, even to the extent of vehemently trying to persuade him to rebel against their leader, Rick (2.13, 2012). Her keenness to replace Rick, a middle-class proven leader as Sheriff's Deputy, with Daryl, a difficult young man from a 'white trash' background shows that identifying with the masculine for Carol means starting to question and challenge accepted social structures, not upholding them as you might expect (1990, p.34). This shows again how Carol's heroine's journey is different from Murdock's rather limiting description, bringing a sense of positive social change with it.

Later, she develops a good working relationship with Rick, who changes his style of leadership. Despite undeniably favouring Daryl, she makes an ally out of Rick as well, gaining his confidence and esteem.

When The Group moves into the camp Alexandria in season five, Carol is Rick's right-hand 'man', hiding weapons and her true nature in case the people there are untrustworthy.

Starting before stage two has completed, Carol begins her road of trials. Given that the setting is the zombie apocalypse, it is easy to pin-point who the ogres and dragons she meets are: walkers and other human survivors who are hostile. Survival is a repeated trial against the walkers, who are ubiquitous and yet come out of nowhere and from whom a bite means death, and survivors such as The Governor and his camp at Woodbury, who are thriving because they find other survivors, take what they have and kill them. Once, with The Group's encourage-ment, Carol has learned to fight and defend herself and others, she fights the same threats only a man would have fought in seasons one and two and becomes so adept that she moves on in her journey and finds the illusory boon of success (5.1, 2014) when she rescues most of The Group from being cannibalised at Terminus, a camp which had advertised itself as a sanctuary but is actually a trap. In scenes worthy of a traditional male action hero, such as Rambo, Carol disguises herself in walker viscera and harnesses a herd of walkers, which she lets into the enemy camp by shooting the propane tank to cause a fiery explosion which blows a hole in the gate. She then enters and fights the hostile group, adding her weight to the chaos that allows the others to fight their way out. It is truly an outstanding action scene and depicts Carol as an almost inhumanly tough warrior. It is par-ticularly interesting that the rescue is not coloured by the same power relations as a traditional male hero's rescue, i.e. the hero saving someone helpless, but rather Carol, a female rescuer, makes it possible for The Group to 'rescue them-selves' – another excellent example of 'power-with' empowerment (Allen, 1998, pp.35–36). In Carol, in this heroine's journey, have we finally reached the point where heroes help people help themselves?

However, soon afterwards Carol awakens to feelings of spiritual aridity. After The Group move into a survivors' settlement, Alexandria, she gets lost in a 'meek housewife' persona designed to fool the inhabitants and experiences a steady decline in her confidence and ability to function, leading up to a scene in which she and another character, Maggie, are captured by two women during an assault on an enemy camp (6.13, 2016). Upon capture she experiences what appears to be a breakdown fuelled by anxiety over the deaths she has caused and a loss of connection to the divine. The inescapability of the fact that she must kill these women to survive causes her to be unable to act and to mutter incoherently while clutching a crucifix.

Shortly after this Carol begins her descent to the Goddess. Murdock points out that, in the male journey, progress is linear: it is not done to refuse the next task; the only alternative to activity is passivity (1990, p.83). However, there is another option: 'being' instead of 'doing'. Being is not passivity, it is the choice to silence all voices but your own and grow by listening to yourself (1990, p.83) Murdock explains: "[w]omen find their way back to themselves not by moving up and out into the light like men, but by moving down into the depths of the ground of their being" and leaving the male world (1990, p.89) in order to find that which split off when they rejected the feminine (1990, p.90). A woman's descent is a journey to the underworld, darkness and depression triggered by life-changing loss, and not necessarily of a person (1990, p.88). The journey is "filled with confusion and grief, alienation and disillusion, rage and despair" leaving her feeling "naked and exposed, dry and brittle, or raw and turned inside-out", but she must take it to discover truths about herself and it necessitates "a period of voluntary isolation" (1990, p.88). This is a perfect description of Carol between 6.14 (2016) and 8.4 (2017). After the loss of her confidence and dynamism, in what seems to the viewer dramatically out-of-character behaviour, she sneaks out of Alexandria abandoning everybody and seeks out a rural house to live in alone. She refuses to kill, thereby refusing to engage in the predominant patriarchal structure of 'All Out War' which dominates those seasons, and will not accept any attempts to bring her back into any community. It may be argued that the persona of fighter and warrior which she has presented until this moment was just as imposed upon her as that of wife and mother. In order to search for her true self, she remains in the house alone excepting brief interaction with King Ezekiel, a community leader she has recently met, and when Daryl discovers where she is and visits her (7.10, 2017). It is interesting in light of the tendency I have observed for Carol's journey to allow scope for a feminist interpretation, that nobody complains about her choice to isolate herself, claims it is unhealthy or tries to fix it, which Murdock says is the normal reaction to the descent (1990, p.90). Both Daryl and Ezekiel make it clear they want her in their lives but do not complain, pester or otherwise react negatively to her isolation, nor does anyone else. Her choice is respected, there is no suggestion that her 'being' equates to passivity and this necessary part of her journey is allowed to just run its course.

It is also interesting to note that in *The Walking Dead* it is strongly felt that you cannot survive this new world alone. The characters frequently reinforce that you need other people for protection, to share resources and for companionship. The audience believes them – the post-apocalyptic world on screen is brutal, scary and difficult. To prove them right, when we encounter people alone, we usually see that they are not coping well. Even very tough characters like Daryl often end up in desperate situations when alone. However, Carol survives easily and even becomes healthier. Rather than a battle, her time alone functions as a sort of meditation, an appeal to all aspects of her unconscious, and she emerges with more clarity, strength and power than when she went in. Since it is supposed to be essentially impossible to survive outside of a community, let alone thrive, this sub-plot perhaps implies that Carol is the strongest character.

A woman's yearning to reconnect with the feminine is characterised by a need to get to know her own body and sexuality (Murdock, 1990, pp.111–119). Indeed, once she emerges from her descent, Carol forges a bond with King

Ezekiel and soon enters into a relationship with him, also helping to care for a young boy he has informally adopted. Ezekiel is the antithesis of Carol's deceased husband Ed, an overweight, grumpy, sexist white man who epitomised toxic masculinity. Ezekiel is a confident, chatty, cheery black man with dreadlocks who likes animals and the arts, looks after others and lives an unconventional lifestyle, in that his Kingdom is a role-playing community living a historical re-enactment. Clearly, her attraction to him is based upon a yearning to explore the new potentials of her sexuality. Her feelings for the boy, Henry, show that she is re-embracing the notion of mother, especially in contrast to the way she treated Sam, a boy who lived in Alexandria in the run-up to her descent. Carol was mean to him to the point of traumatising him. Her positive relationship with Henry, however, leads her onto healing the mother/daughter split, though in a less conventional sense than Murdock's heroine, who is a woman dealing with feelings for her own mother (1990, pp.130–136). Carol is dealing with feelings *for herself as a mother*. The part of her that split off both when her daughter Sophia died and also when she was forced to execute (or euthanize depending on your view) Lizzie, a young orphaned girl she was caring for who killed her sister Mika due to mental illness (4.14, 2014), she is able to find again through love for Henry.

Empoweringly, healing this split also means reclaiming the agency, strength and inclination to act, fight and kill if necessary. We see that this is the case when she kills a group of hostile people who try to steal from her and Henry and threaten their lives: not only does she kill them, but she sets fire to them (9.6, 2018), which is a clear allusion to the way she disposed of the infected Karen and David's bodies after killing them (4.2, 2013) and the inferno she created when she attacked Terminus and rescued The Group from cannibalism. That she can work with fire again shows she has forgiven and incorporated that part of herself and constitutes the healing of her wounded masculine: fire destroys to make way for creation, and since, archetypally, the creative power is masculine, in wielding fire she is accepting that side of her psyche.

I would argue that in the emerging storylines with the Whisperers, a hostile group of survivors who live like a combination of walkers and wild animals, Carol is currently embarking on the final stage of her journey's cycle: integrating the masculine and feminine, which is the sacred marriage; accepting masculine and feminine as forces within one's psyche, ultimately to give birth to something new (1990, p.160). Towards the end of season nine Henry was killed and Carol and Ezekiel ended their relationship, and their community was displaced by the Whisperers, therefore it is a transitional time for her without a focus on either traditionally masculine (leadership) or feminine (nurturing) roles. The trailer for season ten appears to suggest Carol and Daryl are about to leave together. It is impossible to predict what will happen, and it is likely this scene is not all it appears, but I believe it will involve Carol renewing her alliance with the masculine, yet without separating from the feminine and creating something new, perhaps a new type of society: integrating the two to create a new, third.

I have mentioned that Carol's heroine's journey allows for a more feminist progression that Murdock proposed and, indeed, it is necessary to raise several criticisms of this otherwise valuable work. First, Murdock's heroine's journey is too restrictive and seems to suggest that only women who are drawn to their fathers as girls are likely to make the journey, implying that women without a strong connection to their father or a father-figure (be it positive or negative) lack the creative power and drive towards liberation. Since making the journey equates in Jungian terms to individuation, or the conscious integration of hitherto unconscious aspects of the personality in order to create a unified, aware self, Murdock's restrictiveness would suggest that many women are not able to individuate. However, Jungian psychology does not place such limitations on women: all people are able to individuate by paying attention to the symbols arising from the unconscious, such as dreams.

Second, despite attempts to mitigate it (1990, pp.169–183), Murdock does make assumptions based upon a binary of natural gendered behaviour which I contend does not exist. For example, "[w]omen tend to cluster, they like being related, helpful, and connected" (1990, p.173). Although I do like to be helpful (does anybody not?), I do not enjoy being with groups of other people and avoid lots of connections. Moreover, Murdock admits Joseph Campbell's view that women should be passive, even irrelevant, in their stories is shocking (1990, p.2) but soon after is happy to accept his equally sexist view that a woman's primary function is fostering (1990, p.7).

Finally, Murdock feels that woman's task is to heal the split that tells her her feelings, knowledge and wishes are less valid than patriarchal ones; to be able to live with paradox and with not knowing all the answers; to be willing to listen to the wisdom inside us and of the planet; to understand that the success they have achieved in following the male model is only a part of what we need to be whole (1990, p.11). I would argue that this task should be made available to all people; it is not only women who suffer under patriarchy. Patriarchal society enforces gendered behaviour onto both men and women, the most obvious example of which historically is the heterosexual family with a male breadwinner and female nurturer. Although that particular definition of gender is losing its hold, we are still controlled by patriarchy's pervasive, often more insidious, social conventions. For example, patriarchy's heteronormativity does not just enforce gendered behaviour, as I said above, but even enforces gender as a social category, creating the very definitions 'man' and 'woman' and treating them as universal and inherent to maintain its social norms. As a result, whilst it is especially vital for women, who have been oppressed by patriarchy, any individual's individuation process must allow them to recognise and challenge the wishes and desires which come from patriarchal society rather than from themselves. If it does not, they risk integrating aspects of patriarchy's 'personality' rather than their own, which both prevents true individuation and perpetuates problematic patriarchy, by making its norms appear inherent. Indeed, although Jungians rarely realise (or admit), the very concept of 'Self' links to hegemonic masculinity's tendency to make being 'other' seem normal: as David Tacey has pointed out, 'Self' is an unusual choice of word for something that is actually 'other' to the ego (2006, p.47). As I will explain in the next section, 'Self' is a patriarchal notion which would serve us better if it were revised and conceived of as potential.

The possibility of escaping patriarchy is one of the things which makes apocalyptic settings so rich a line of enquiry: if society has broken down, patriarchy no longer has to exist and women need no longer be constrained by it. Although recent seasons have attempted to explore how women might be different, it has been, at best, a dabbling into post-patriarchal potential. For instance, although the all-female settlement of Oceanside proved a decisive ally in the battle against Negan and the Saviours, turning up at the last moment and effectively winning it (8.16, 2018), the writers have chosen not to explore those characters in much depth. I would suggest that this failing results more from sheer inability to imagine a genuinely un-patriarchal society than from unwillingness to imagine it: patriarchy has us in such a grip that we cannot see beyond it, rather like a goldfish trying to conceive of what it cannot see from its bowl.

The joining of two to create a third: finding unlimited potential

I have shown that Carol has reached the stage of sacred union which begets a divine child: she is likely about to integrate the masculine and feminine by creating something new. I now want to discuss how that act of creation relates to unlimited potential, what role archetypal functions play and what that means for women in particular.

In Jungian terms, we can understand that archetype equates to potential: "[a]n archetype is an inborn *potential* for a certain sort of image" (Rowland, 2002, p.30, her emphasis). Additionally, Jung was clear that archetypal image manifestations have "an almost infinite variety of aspects" (1976, p.15). Thus, archetype is innate, limitless potential. Certainly, Carol personifies as wide a range of archetypal images as we are aware of, often simultaneously. The archetypal roles she fulfils do not necessarily appear in the traditional order, nor are there clear lines between them. A full analysis of her archetypal journey is beyond the scope of this paper, but I will briefly exemplify her archetypal complexity.

In that Carol fiercely protects and cares for The Group as a whole and nurtures Daryl and various children individually she personifies the Mother. Incidentally, Murdock (1990, p.18) pointed out that the Great Mother archetype "embodies *limitless* nurturance, sustenance, and protection" (my emphasis), meaning that if the Great Mother meets someone to nurture, that caregiving has unlimited potential – a point that will be pertinent shortly. In that Carol passes on her wisdom to children, for example when teaching the children at the prison to use knives (4.1, 2013), and withdraws from 'normal' society during her descent to the Goddess, she embodies the Wise Woman. Teaching the children to use knives is also indicative of a Trickster at work, and she does fulfil that role often, for example at

Alexandria when she shape-shifts into an unthreatening housewife and deceives the residents (multiple season five episodes). Of course, there is a very blurred line between the trickster and shadow (Jung, 1976, p.150), and, indeed, those same acts could be attributed to the shadow. Her role as shadow is clear on multiple other occasions, such as killing the infected Karen and David and bullying Sam, the boy at Alexandria who takes a liking to her. Morphing into the meek housewife to deceive the Alexandria residents also exemplifies how persona plays a role in her archetypal identity, as does her position as 'Queen' of The Kingdom in season nine. Given the negative animus' potential to murder (von Franz, 1996, pp.169–170), we might also speculate that that archetypal image is at play at times when Carol kills, and we also see the animus in the perfectionist that 'does' so that she does not have to 'be' (or think) during season four, when she recklessly leaves the prison camp alone to fix a water pump and is almost surrounded by walkers (4.3, 2013) (although wanting to provide water is also a nurturing quality, therefore, she is Mother as well as Animus here). I have already explained how she also personifies the Warrior and Hero, both in fighting for protection on an everyday basis and in rescuing The Group from cannibals.

Interestingly, Black Kultov's (1986) detailed description of the empowering female archetypal image of Lilith reads like a description of Carol. Lilith rejects the masculine consciousness and chooses wilderness, even demons instead (1986, p.24) and chooses 'separation over constraint or submission', often resulting in unrelated, desolate wilderness experienced as madness, as well as a metaphorical menstrual hut where she can heal by connecting with the feminine. Carol suffers a breakdown, then refuses to submit to the demand to kill by rejecting the masculine 'All Out War' and separating herself to live alone in a rural cottage, choosing to expose herself to the threats of the post-apocalyptic world beyond the walls of Alexandria, during which time she heals. Lilith wants to attach herself to the young (1986, p.23) and, though bearing many offspring, she has been known to kill children (1986, pp.35 and 81). Carol finds meaning and happiness in looking after children and comes to love many throughout her narrative, yet she also kills Lizzie and as good as kills Sam by traumatising him so that he cannot escape walkers. Black Kultov mentions repeatedly throughout (1986) that Lilith is hard to pin down, suddenly does unexpected things and is associated with fire. Carol cannot be pinned down to a clear archetypal function within the story, frequently behaves unexpectedly, for example traumatising Sam, and has become known for using fire to attack and kill.

Moreover, there is no order of occurrence for Carol's archetypal roles – they are not incorporated on a clear path to individuation and wholeness; rather, they come and go, there seems to be no limit to them, they occur simultaneously and it is often not possible to categorise her or her behaviours by archetype: archetypally, Carol is unlimited, indefinable and fluid. This state of being links in closely with the notion of potential. I would now like to postulate that the psyche is driven by unlimited potential via the psychodynamic process of two joining together to create a third, and that we need to re-think the concepts of wholeness and individuation.

J. R. Van Eenwyk (1991) has theorised convincingly that chaos theory and Jungian psychology are analogous, in that the psyche constitutes a self-powered 'feedback loop' wherein content is emitted and re-enters, like sound waves leaving a microphone, entering space, and then re-entering the microphone, and then space, etc. (p.3). A feedback loop is an equation which works on itself "so that the result of any one computation becomes the basis for computation of the next" (1991, p.3). Van Eenwyk claims that the "feedback loop intensifies the interactions between ego and unconscious, in effect 'pushing' the system [and] when the tension between consciousness and the unconscious reaches a certain intensity – chaos ensues" (1991, p.11). Moreover, "just as surely as pushing the system will generate chaos, maintaining the pressure ensures that the chaos will generate patterns that recapitulate the original tension that started the whole thing off" (1991, p.11). Archetypes are analogous to unstable saddle points, which break up linear flow and allow orbits to move around indeterminately (1991, p.22). The ensuing "chaotic systems stretch and fold back on themselves" which means their outcome, though not random, is too complex to predict long-term; "they are feedback loops that build upon themselves" (1991, p.18) and tiny changes effect huge changes (1991, p.19).

Though complex, this theory is simply that, as Jung's theory of the transcendent function shows, two things interact to create another thing. Moreover, that chaos allows the system to power itself and go on unpredictably and infinitely, both in terms of matter and psyche. We have seen that Carol is completing Murdock's cyclical journey, that her archetypal identity is in a constant state of flux and that her actions are often unpredictable (or chaotic) in that she deceives other characters and subverts their expectations, and she does things which seem out-of-character to viewers, such as abandoning The Group. Therefore, she illustrates Van Eenwyk's theory. In the sense that we cannot predict or define her, Carol has unlimited potential. Furthermore, since there is no completion to her development that would imply a linear equation, she does not integrate archetypes – as I said, they come and go. This implies her development is infinite, a feedback loop.

Jean Knox (2004, 2010) has also lent credence to these ideas. Explaining that the brain is a self-organising system, she says:

> Developmental research supports the view that new meaning is constantly being created as a central part of the process of psychological development. For example, some cognitive scientists are finding evidence that information is repeatedly re-analysed and re-encoded into ever more complex forms of representation, in pace with the increasing cognitive capacities of the human brain during the course of development.
>
> (2004, p.6)

Additionally, she points out that "[s]ymbolic understanding is therefore a constant two-way process" (2004, p.11) and that Jung recognised this in the transcendent function – the union of opposites which gives rise to new meaning: "mind and meaning emerge out of developmental processes and the experience of interpersonal relationships rather than existing *a priori*" (2004, p.16). In other words, although meaning is not innate, the potential to construct it is, and since the brain powers itself like a feedback loop, the potential we have to construct meaning is basically unlimited, or infinite. Analyses like this one of Carol from *The Walking Dead* prove that, because there is no such thing as a final interpretation. With regards to two-way systems, Knox reminds us that the brain functions on interplay between the newer neocortex and the more primitive part (2010, p.527), thereby suggesting that even the brain is a sacred marriage bringing forth a divine child: the two parts together produce interplay. We might be bold enough to wonder if the interplay is in fact 'psyche' itself.

These are not the only suggestions that allude to a process of unlimited potential and adding two to get something new, of course. James Hillman has called the psyche "inherently multiple" (1989, p.36), which links the psyche to the number three. Kalsched feels that "Jung would have asked, "How do we keep a dialectical relationship going between the ego and the Self" (1996, p.144). Kalsched points out that "[o]ne of Jung's partial answers to this question was the psyche's natural 'transcendent function,' in which the tension between psychic opposites leads to the symbol, a 'living third thing'" (1996, p.144) and that holding the tension of opposites produces "a symbol which is both a synthesis of the opposites, yet something which transcends them both" (1996, p.145).

Marie-Louise Von Franz has said that the Self is the "organizing center from which the regulatory effect stems [and is] sort of 'nuclear atom' in our psychic system" (1964, p.161) and "brings about a constant extension and maturing of the personality" (1964, p.162), and Edward Edinger has said "the Self is expressed as a union of opposites" (1992, p.275), both of which suggest that the psyche is a dynamic process whereby two opposites create the Self, which is then continuously 'fed back in' and extended and developed, like Van Eenwyk's feedback loop. Clearly, this dialectic concept is something Jungians already accept and understand.

However, I argue that it not emphasised enough to the detriment of the feminine. First, in discussing the dialectal process, the writers I have cited mostly focus strongly on the interaction between ego and Self, understating the potential archetypes have to remove limitations from women. If we consider my comments on Woodman's virgin/whore dynamic in the next paragraph, for instance, we can see that revising and exploring the role female archetypal images play reveals potential for unlimited growth. Patriarchy is not as unshakeable as it used to appear, and those with an interest in equality ought to help shake it by highlighting such unlimited potential. Do not misunderstand – I believe, of course, that all people can be always 'Becoming' without limits, but women have not traditionally been socialised to believe in their potential. On the contrary, they have been raised to view their destiny as lacking in power and opportunity. We must redress the balance by giving limitless potential a female face through the elucidation of feminine archetypal images.

Analysing popular female role models and characters who embody that potential, such as Carol, is a crucial aspect of positive representation of women and who they can be. Marion Woodman has elucidated the poled archetype of virgin/whore which gives rise to a "virgin forever pregnant with new possibilities" (1985, p.76) and who "has the courage to be always Becoming" (1985, p.78), which makes it clear that the feminine has the potential to grow and change infinitely, unpredictably and without limits. Woodman illustrates this with Madonna and Cyndi Lauper, who were famous for continuously re-inventing and fusing their styles (1985, p.76) but Carol, as a character who continuously changes and fuses her archetypal functions, is a better example, since her 'Becoming' is filled with dramatic and unpredictable, or chaotic, new possibilities, such as the meek, abused housewife who becomes an action hero, who becomes a wise woman living alone, away from society, who marries a King and becomes a leader, and so on.

I have argued that Carol's archetypal roles can be understood as indefinable and supple, and lead to seemingly limitless potential. Since the archetype of the Self comprises changing roles and the act of 'Becoming', it could be argued that Carol personifies the Self. In fact, since the Self is multifaceted and transformational, and since I have shown that the process of two creating new repeats ad infinitum and without limit, I would even argue that the Self *is* potential: there is no difference between the two. Our psyche is organised by our (practically) unlimited potential, which I suggest, for the reasons I outline next, is a better term to use.

We must be cautious about the term 'Self' for the same reason we must emphasise the process of infinite and chaotic expansion more. That is, the process of infinite and chaotic expansion is desirable: "systems require a diversity of responses to survive the unexpected [therefore] chaos provides a complexity of response that order cannot" and chaos is normal and healthy (Van Eenwyk, 1991, p.13). This gives rise, therefore, to some concerns over the concept of wholeness and individuation. Although individuation is a process and we conceptualise the hero's and heroine's journeys as a circle, not as a line, it is still implied that the process brings order to chaos; that the wholeness and unity that would come from the realisation of the Self equates to stopping the process. This is a problem not just because it places limits upon us but because it is an internalised patriarchal norm. The feminine way is an infinite lunar cycle, or loop, of birth, pregnancy, death and rebirth, or maiden, mother, crone, descent/ascent, over and over, indefinitely. Although the stages in the cycle are fixed, how they unfold and manifest is unknown each time, and the end of the cycle always brings wisdom one did not have before. Therefore, for something to be truly not patriarchal, it must explicitly recognise and normalise this infinite cycle, its unpredictability and the potential for growth it brings. Consequently, because the term 'Self' implies wholeness and finality, we must be aware that when applying it, we are (probably unintentionally) subscribing to a limiting patriarchal concept. In order for people to have equal and real access to the psyche's organising principle, we need to re-conceptualise it to avoid the norms associated with 'Self'.

Of course, I am not suggesting that women are a hegemonic category who exclusively individuate in a cyclical fashion, only that 'Self' problematically negates necessary chaos, creativity and growth. Carol's continuous changing of internal structure, on the other hand, is a positive representation of a psychic journey because the constant changes in her archetypal identity are indicative of continuous rebirth (Jung, 1976, pp.57–58). The periodic changes in her personality and behaviour, such as from motherly figure to burning people alive, prove her to be unpredictable. The fact that she is unpredictable prevents limits being placed upon her potential. The very setting of a zombie apocalypse further alludes to rebirth in the sense of reanimation from death, and also constitutes a union of two opposites (life and death) to create a third, new thing (reanimation).

It is not my intention to suggest that *The Walking Dead* is unproblematically feminist. It is necessary to mention that the series has received considerable feminist criticism, both online and in academia, mainly for the sexist division of labour and apparent weakness of female characters. However, these observations were based almost exclusively on the comics and early seasons of the television series and they do not consider the theme of change which runs through the series. In particular, Chris Gavaler (2014), Charles Nuckolls (2014), John Greene and Michaela D. E. Meyer (2014), Philip. L. Simpson (2014) and Stephen Olbrys Gencarella (2016), as well as number of non-academic online commentators, have been fixated on the fact that the earlier story is characterised by male characters leading, fighting and hunting for supplies to ensure survival, and female characters meekly being wives, doing laundry, cooking and caring for children, as well as initial attempts to re-install patriarchal social systems. This chapter has hopefully convinced readers that those early criticisms are redundant. Some researchers have started to see that this is the case, in fact. For example, Dan Hassler-Forest (2011) and Katherine Sugg (2015) have written works which concede things are not as simple as they initially appeared, and Amanda Keeler (2016) has discussed how later seasons of the television series depict a radical change in attitudes towards and representation of female characters. I have shown that it is irrefutable that the show's reputation for sexism does not stand up to analysis, and that Carol's story shows women they do not have to live the 'male way' and that they have the potential to grow infinitely and without the limits of accepted structures, be they 'patriarchy', 'individuation' or 'Self'.

Going forward

To finish, I would like us to remember that the 'third' thing which is created by the union of opposites one and two gives us the number three, and if, once we have our number three, we unite the next two opposites: three and another, flipped three, we get a figure eight, the symbol of infinity. This is the empowering image with which we should understand our psyche: infinity and, therefore, potential which is essentially limitless. Indeed, the image Edinger puts forth as a model of the union of ego and self is a small circle on top of a larger circle with a vertical axis running between them (1992, p.5), which is a small step away from an eight, or infinity symbol. Edinger's axis, however, is misleading, since it suggests there exists a linear (masculine) interface between the conscious and unconscious, which is simply not the case (Van Eenwyk, 1991, p.13).

Sometimes those Jungians who work in clinical settings have not had the chance to look at the benefits of exploring cultural products as well as people. I hope this chapter has demonstrated that doing so can both support and challenge depth psychology, as well as support feminism and challenge patriarchy. It can help us to give form to a future with more feminist potential than we have today, helping us to start imagining differently and maybe even creating new, empowering myths for our time.

References

Allen, A., 1998, 'Rethinking Power', *Hypatia*, 13(1), pp.21–40.

Bassil-Morozow, H., 2017, 'Jungians vs. Freudians Gender, Identity and Sexuality on Screen'. In: H. Bassil-Morozow and Hockley, L. (ed), *Jungian Film Studies the Essential Guide*, Oxon and New York: Routledge, pp.136–166.

Bishop, K., 2009, *Dead Man Still Walking: A Critical Investigation into the Rise and Fall . . . and Rise of Zombie Cinema*. Ph.D. thesis, University of Arizona. Available at: https ://repository.arizona.edu/handle/10150/194727 (Accessed 25 August 2018).

Black Kultov, B., 1986, *The Book of Lilith*, York Beach: Nicolas-Hays.

Covington, C., 1989, 'In Search of the Heroine', *Journal of Analytical Psychology*, 34(3), pp.243–254.

Edinger, E. F., 1992, *Ego and Archetype Individuation and the Religious Function of the Psyche*, Boulder, CO: Shambhala.

Gavaler, C., 2014, 'Zombies vs. Superheroes: The Walking Dead Resurrection of Fantastic Four Gender Formulas', *Interdisciplinary Comics Studies*, 7(4). Available at: http://eng lish.ufl.edu/imagetext/archives/v7_4/gavaler/ (Accessed 25 August 2018).

Gencarella, S. O., 2016, 'Thunder without Rain: Fascist Masculinity in AMC's the Walking Dead', *Horror Studies*, 7(1), pp.125–146.

Greene, J. and Meyer, M. D. E., 2014, 'The Walking (Gendered) Dead: A Feminist Rhetorical Critique of Zombie Apocalypse Television Narrative', *Ohio Communication Journal*, 52(October), pp.64–74.

Hassler-Forest, D., 2011, 'Cowboys and Zombies: Destabilizing Patriarchal Discourse in the Walking Dead', *Studies in Comics*, 2(2), pp.339–355.

Hillman, J. and Moore, T. (ed), 1989, *A Blue Fire: Selected Writings by James Hillman*, New York: HarperCollins.

Jung, C. G., 1976, *Four Archetypes: Mother Rebirth Spirit Trickster*, London and Henley: Routledge and Kegan Paul.

Kalsched, D., 1996, *The Inner World of Trauma: Archetypal Defences of the Personal Spirit*, Hove and New York: Routledge.

Keeler, A., 2016, 'Gender, Guns, and Survival: The Women of the Walking Dead'. In: Catherine R. Squires (ed), *Dangerous Discourses: Feminism, Gun Violence and Civic Life*, New York: Peter Lang, pp.235–256.

Knox, J., 2004, 'From Archetypes to Reflective Function', *Journal of Analytical Psychology*, 49(1), pp.1–19.

Knox, J., 2010, 'Response to Erik Goodwyn's 'Approaching Archetypes: Reconsidering Innateness', *Journal of Analytical Psychology*, 55(4), pp.522–549.

Murdock, M., 1990, *The Heroine's Journey*, Boulder, CO: Shambhala.

Nuckolls, C., 2014, 'The Walking Dead as Conservative Cultural Critique', *JCRT: Journal for Cultural and Religious Theory*, 13(2), pp.102–110.

Rowland, S., 2002, *Jung A Feminist Revision*, Malden: Blackwell.

Simpson, P. L., 2014, 'The Zombie Apocalypse Is Upon US! Homeland Security'. In: D. Keetley (ed), *We're All Infected Essays on AMC's The Walking Dead and the Fate of the Human*, Jefferson: McFarland, pp.28–40.

Sugg, K., 2015, 'The Walking Dead: Late Liberalism and Masculine Subjection in Apocalypse Fictions', *Journal of American Studies*, 49(4), pp.793–811.

Tacey, D., 2006, *How to Read Jung*, London: Granta Books.

Van Eenwyk, J. R., 1991, 'Archetypes: The Strange Attractors of the Psyche', *Journal of Analytical Psychology*, 36(1), pp.1–25.

Von Franz, M.-L., 1964, 'The Process of Individuation'. In: C. G. Jung (ed), *Man and His Symbols*, London: Aldus Books, pp.158–229.

Von Franz, M.-L., 1996, *The Interpretation of Fairy Tales*, Boston and London: Shambhala.

Woodman, M., 1985, *The Pregnant Virgin: A Process of Psychological Transformation*, Toronto: Inner City Books.

Part 3

Voices

Chapter 12

Women in war zones

From rupture to repair

Heba Zaphiriou-Zarifi

"If anything is sacred,
The human body is sacred"

– Walt Whitman

Women survivors of war come to therapy seeking support for what has wounded, shamed, or maimed their identity as women and as citizens of the world. They choose the safety of the therapeutic alliance to denounce the sidelining of their experience of war and the use of rape as a weapon of war. This chapter aims at opening a window on women's experience in war zones, to bear witness to their fractured lives, and to the ways by which they struggle and they survive.

Threads from clinical work are woven into the fabric of storytelling, and cross-cultural referencing is entwined to narrative-medicine, to highlight how war impacts women, and how women in return impact war.

Here, the topic of war is approached through the symbolic language to articulate the complexity of war, its abusive relationship to gender, and its exploitation of the body as a site of political inscription. The body in wars is helplessly ensnared in a racist culture constructed on gender and sexuality-based oppression. This is an attempt to lay out the stepping-stones to 'new cultural activities', and to offer an insight on how clinical work can help redirect the instinctive energy toward a "value quantum [which] exceeds that of the cause" (Jung, 1960, p.25).

War is 'a blood sport' to paraphrase the renowned military strategist Von Clausewitz (2008). Although physical struggle with the opponent is no longer dominant in battlefields, war remains an act of force whose essence is violent combat, a description with which Hannah Arendt would agree (Owens, 2007). No longer the instrument of an equilibrium between powers, armies fight private wars for privately owned contractors. The sale of weapons: a highly profitable industry fills coffers and pays dividends. War under the auspices of security is tailored for an aggressive pursuit of economic supremacy and a unilateral control over natural resources, profiting the few and depriving the many. The ethics of inflated heroism on which wars thrive are glorified, and the sacrifice of the innocent disavowed. Diversity is the social zeitgeist of our world today, yet army recruits come mostly from deprived backgrounds. They are the 'other' within one's own, expended to fight wars on others.

As science is exploited to further develop lethal weaponries and nuclear munitions, and military bases encouraged to proliferate across the planet, it is no surprise to see armed retaliation made inevitable as a result. Wars are forcibly imposed on our societies and decreed as the sole means to resolve conflict. From another perspective, war is used to replace politics in the hands of dysfunctional political leaders, and to normalize it as a default position for lack of a global affairs policy. Leaders exploit the emotional susceptibilities and psychological vulnerabilities of their electorates and present war as mandatory. War is sold as necessary. Furthermore, in the pursuit of optimising personal power, leaders present wars as a reality show. The reality is that war never ends well, and it is almost never justified.

Ultimately war is a feminicide. It is a direct attack on the Feminine principle of relatedness and connection as it severs bridges and splits parties apart. War is also an attack on the chthonic and on the sacredness of *matter*: on the human body as well as on the living body of planet-earth. Plundered and exploited, she is poisoned by our unprocessed waste, her ecosystem decimated. Whilst red poppies commemorate the bloody Great War, the earth continues to weep for the blood spilled on her body. Her soil is laid bare, cratered by bombs and torn by mines. She is scarred by artillery fire and calcinated by the crude fires of revengeful rage. Whatever the politics, leaders' decisions ought seriously to consider the damage wars inflict on our planet and on our humanity, and maximum pressure should be exerted by civil societies on politicians to negotiate conflicts peacefully.

Wars have debilitating and long-lasting effects: the body-soul becomes the locus of the battleground, transfixed by events that have no time or age. Captive to the absurdity of war from which few escape, its victims roam aimlessly in a nameless world. Spellbound to a collective psychosis that sees militarism as a solution to conflict, the individual is bereft of meaning. Only death seems to give war some meaning, the rest is about surviving it. The victim's humanity disappears; she/he becomes a number, a despised entity, a no-body. Yet the body carries the burden, and bears the brunt of the unbearable.

"I woke up to the shrieking sound of a blast", Lara, a patient survivor of a bomb attack, narrated. "Thick black dust hovered around me. I was entrapped. Everything was vaporised. In less than no time the world lost its substance: I lost my family. I even lost myself", she added. Lara's memories of war, no longer retrievable, were lodged in her body, invading her inner space like unwanted callers who intrude suddenly when least expected. They hijacked her body parts with somatic symptoms, and her soul with disconnected images and flashbacks. "The eviscerated building, the books burnt to ashes, the sheet music scorched, the disemboweled cat" incessantly troubled her. Sleep deprivation, renal insufficiency, asthma, and heart palpitations were her symptoms. Various skin disorders erupted unexpectedly as though to mirror the "blast that came from nowhere". Body organs held the split-off memories like severed fragments of a whole poem; each segment now compulsively repeated autonomously as though in a house without a Master. "Flames devour the people you love; the people you love are devoured by flames" she continuously repeated, reminding me of Neruda's poignant poem: *I'm Explaining A Few Things,* in which he repeats "… and through the streets, the blood of the children ran through the streets; like the blood of children"(Neruda, 1958/2005, p.10), as though Lara was trying 'to explain a few things' to make sense of the senseless deaths. The human cost of collective war has no meaning and no equivalent, except in the revulsion its absurdity evokes. Amputated from a sense of self, victimisers amputate their victims from their sense of self.

Although war has destructive consequences for men, its gendered crime must be fully exposed. Compacted by the absence of women's rights in some countries, women are also victims of disproportionate inequalities. Excluded from decision-making processes against sexual violence; they are often threatened if they dare to speak, denied their rights to public communication, or included only as an afterthought. Plagued by war-induced poverty, women are sexually exploited especially when their meagre income is dependent on their locus or nature's renewables, both under threat. Often overlooked, sexual violence and rape of women as a weapon of war used to ethnically cleanse or diminish a population must be condemned, and its perpetrators brought to justice and convicted.

War on women: war of the sexes

Ars Requirit Totum Hominem ('The Art Requires the Whole Man') is an alchemist's dictum, which Jung refers to in his introduction to *Psychology and Alchemy* (1953). He reiterates that the 'work' requires the sum of the total being (*homus totus*), which is what the seeker seeks. The effort of the therapist and the patient are directed toward that hidden and as yet unmanifested 'whole', which is the greater, more integrated, and the future human being. But the path toward wholeness is made up of suffering pain and of many detours (the *longissima via*) costing an enormous amount of effort, as we see in the case now discussed.

Josée is a French-Rwandan young woman who had trained as a Drama-Therapist. She came to me a few years ago seeking "support and inspiration for a welfare project" she was setting up for a small group of women survivors of rape during the 1994 genocide in Rwanda.

Women's stories in Rwanda have changed history; for rape, considered 'a thing men do', is now proscribed as a crime against humanity, and in its most powerful legacy condemned as genocide. "But it is not enough to expose the gender crimes against women, what is needed is to help women heal from torture and rebuild their lives", Josée argued.

Attuning to Josée's emotional and imaginative self, we established that integrating traditional music, dance and storytelling from the Rwandan culture with dramatised scenarios from another culture's pool of stories might facilitate the crossing of a threshold toward healing. Narrative is restorative. It pays heed to personal anguish, as well as to collective societal distress. In this case rape is not just a personal trauma but also a collective crime. Rita Charon argues "only in the telling is the suffering made evident. Without the telling, not only treatment but suffering too might be fragmented" (Charon, 2012, p.211).

Images from 'foreign' stories may be easier to bear than highly charged inner images imbued with traumatic memories. Equally, uninfected images from a culturally different background can become a source for newly constructed memories. Ultimately, fixed and rigidified traumatic memories may have a chance to soften and to be integrated, and the body slowly to restore its integrity. The gift of magic Jung discovers in his active imagination process in *Liber Novus* (2009) is the 'art' of integrating darkness as part of the image of the new god. Like Christ's descent into the underworld, preceded by Persephone's rape by Hades, and the much earlier surrender and denuding of Sumerian goddess Inanna, the only redemption possible if we are to grow out of the darkness rape inflicts is to include hell.

Josée described the war on women as a 'war of the sexes'. Violence took on a gender-defined form when, in 1994, over the course of a hundred days, up to half a million girls and women were raped, sexually mutilated, or used as sex slaves, if not murdered. The UN Special *Rapporteur* René Degni-Segui stated "Rape was the rule and its absence was the exception". He also added "rape was systematic and was used as a weapon of war" (De Brouwer and Ka Hon Chu, 2009, p.11).

To reverse the defeat of women victims of sexual violence, Aristophanes's *Lysistrata*, the ancient-Greek-play came to mind, where women turn the tables of power and impose a sex-strike as a protest against male-driven wars. This struck a chord, and Josée invited a small group of women-participants to meet weekly. Guided by the work Josée had done with me, they were invited to witness each other's telling of their stories, and to mirror in movement, voice, or image each person's reaction to the story told. Their first response was to acknowledge: "despite the unbearable pain they would have to face, they would not feel alone".

To see one's shadow mirrored positively in a story opens a passageway for potential to be assimilated. Equally, to imagine different outcomes from the known reality allows an exploration of the internal freedom of becoming. A focus on money, power and sex may be explored through the lens of another culture exposing different yet intersectional issues.

Stories have an archetypal structure with a beginning, middle and end, thus forming a safe container, similar to the sacred *temenos* where the darkness of the chaotic de-structuring trauma is held. The trauma timeline, which seems to weigh endlessly, is incarnated into a frame of the here and now. Josée conveyed her participants' feedback, recognising "trauma like all bad stories should also have an ending. Even when trauma seems to be overwhelmingly present, it cannot hold women hostage". A healthy boundary against the timeless effect of trauma seemed to emerge as the group engaged with the timeline of the Greek play. The energy of the group shifted from archaic survival impulses to a gradual attunement of a co-created project. Through the embodiment of 'all the arts' a safe and grounded experience was forged. Listening to the body-sense experience was essential for self-regulation. Movement, song and drama reconciled the victim-ised with one's own limitations, enhancing a self-acceptance. Creativity through the arts provided the crux of the *opus* ahead.

But there is no creativity without the destruction of the old. Destroying stag-nating beliefs, obsolete adaptations, ideologies, or false identifications requires a death of sorts. "He who wishes to conquer new land brings the bridges down behind him", says Jung in *Liber Novus* as he calls for the destruction of the brain's "entanglement" for liberation (Jung and Shamdasani, 2009, p.321). The brain is not the instrument that will solve the conflict of opposites. The 'fizzing life' implies destruction, enacted to serve the purpose of life. We are the agents of destruction in the service of the divine, Jung reiterates. But the destruction he calls upon is not the destruction of 'the other' but of that within oneself that obstructs the evolution of our relationship with the divine. The old 'story' has to die for it to be renewed in a new vitalised form. All the 'arts of the alchemist' are required for a successful outcome.

Myth, fairytale, or stories evoke the chalice-like feminine container where the traumatised split-off parts of the collective psyche can be held. The liminal meta-morphic space is conducive to reconciling the fragmented parts through paradox, so that unconscious suffering is transmuted into conscious suffering. The way to a higher level of consciousness is symbolic, Jung asserts through his own experi-ence of dis-integration and re-integration as enacted in *Liber Novus*. Symbols are transformers, channeling libido from stagnation to movement, from lower to upward pathways. Symbols birth psyche on her path to wholeness in cyclical, spiraling rhythms.

Initiating the anchorite to the numen and to the mysteries behind it through symbols connects body-soul to spirit. The dis-joined body, raped women felt was reconnecting to the battered soul, and an inner spirit of reconciliation was devel-oping. Warring opposites, polarised in fundamentalist opinion in the outer world, were being met and transformed through the power of symbols of the inner world. Concrete events of outer reality were gradually transfiguring into inner psychic experience.

Trauma "constellates an archetypal landscape highly charged with affect" (Wirtz, 2014, p.17). As women were able to describe the political landscape of their trauma, songs of longing for lost integrity erupted, and the frozen muted body moved the deadening silence to experiences of grief and the suffering of psycho-logical wounding. Women wove their stories, each in their own time, into a fabric of meaning thus plaiting-in what had been disregarded. This process increased the cohesive identity-structure of the group enabling a more fluid condition of play and laughter, teamwork and the exploration of the art of healing. Memorial cer-emonies were put in place, which helped ritualise pain and continued the release of the more throbbing affects that afflicted these women.

The symptomatic 'illness' of our fragmented world is like the "shoot above ground, yet the main plant is an extended rhizoma underground" (Jung, 1938/1960, p.26). We can reach the roots of the dis-ease through the symptom acting as a symbol, which offers a point of entry to the unconscious complexes surrounding history. These unconscious 'historic' complexes of the collective nature are formed around an archetypal magnetic core of magnified energy that can ambush our world with demonic powers of destructiveness (Zaphiriou-Zarifi, 2017). The Rwandan genocide is but a tragic and dark manifestation of such power-full dynamics. Rwanda, like other African countries, was raped by colonialism, leaving the country empty, with a deep spiritual bleakness, cut-off as it were from its mytho-poetic roots. "A view of the world or a social order that cuts [man] off from the primordial images of life not only is no culture at all but, in increasing degree, is a prison or a stable" (Jung, 1968, p.93).

Here are some of the narratives explored in the group. Extensive propaganda through print and radio had incited assaults on Tutsi women labeled as untrustworthy, if not evil, accusing them of acting against the Hutu majority. Ordinary civilians were pressured by their leaders to take up arms and encouraged to maim and rape their Tutsi neighbours. Hutus who had married Tutsis were considered 'traitors', and those who did not join in the massacre were executed all the same. Hutu women who were perceived as moderate, or who had protected Tutsi women were also raped.

Western countries such as the United States, the United Kingdom, and Belgium were criticised for inaction, and France for allegedly supporting the Hutu government after the genocide had begun. The Hutus' violence was fed with self-righteous inflation, and they were brainwashed with the ideology that their Tutsi compatriots were dangerous enemies and unbending to authority. Tutsis as a minority had been persecuted and had been made stateless for decades. Supported by Uganda, the Tutsis were previously promoted by Belgium's colonialist regime favouring them over the Hutu majority. To rule, colonialist powers divided and reproduced on African soil a westernised class system of superiors and inferiors. Now Tutsis were being ruthlessly massacred for it. The goal was to kill every Tutsi living in Rwanda (Prunier, 1999, p.248). Husbands murdered their wives, and boys raped older women who had been their teachers at school. Sexual mutilation after rape was common whereby the victims' vaginas were mutilated with machetes, knives, boiling water or acid. Many of these women were infected with HIV from HIV-infected men, recruited by the genocidists to form 'rape squads' (Elbe, 2002). "Rape was a death sentence," the women added.

There is no consensus on the overall number of victims of the genocide as the authorities made no attempt to record deaths. But "during the first six weeks, up to 800,000 Rwandans may have been murdered, representing a rate five times higher than during the Holocaust of Nazi Germany" (Prunier, 1999, p.261). An estimated 250,000 to 500,000 women were raped during the genocide (Nowrojee, 1996).

As the meetings went on, the younger women of the group uncovered new layers of narratives. Not considered to be orphans – as many of these raped young girls had lost their parents – or as widows – those girls had no husbands, yet some found themselves pregnant with child for which they were treated as outlaws. The women were plagued with the worst taboo in their society. They were ostracised, relentlessly facing discrimination, then buried under shame. The number of children-of-rape, according to research, amounted approximately to 20,000 (Torgovnik, 2007). Some of the raped mothers insisted their babies born as a result of rape were 'animals'. Others tried to kill these offspring who were condemned as 'terrorists' by the community.

Tutsi women were accused of being 'sexually seductive', the participants shamefully confided. "But men were possessed by 'spirits'", they added and "accused women of witchcraft". War gave an outlet to men's repressed fear of women's power, and expunged shame over being 'possessed'. Ethnic annihilation was enticed by collective paranoia, and it developed as a result of the deepest injuries to the collective psyche. A frenzy of unprecedented barbarism was unleashed. Inclusion or exclusion of certain traits that make up identity is extremely volatile in times of war. One trait can flip to its opposite, and what had been included becomes radically excluded. The purification of an ethnic-faction from the 'infectious' ethnic-'other' legitimises violence between the sexes, with higher risks of women being raped (Baron and Strauss, 1988).

As the work proceeded with frequent meetings, participants drew from the African landscape and culture images of a 'deep and wide cave' for the *Akropolis,* and Rwandan dances and songs for the *chorus* developed organically. A witness/ dancer dyadic relationship was trustingly established so that a group of movers attending to their body-sense and inner images could be 'witnessed' in silence by the rest of the group, and vice versa. Women were encouraged to draw and paint mandala images of African trees, birds and lakes. The body-imagery articulated a language pregnant with meaning that spoke louder than words.

Lysistrata was now ready to be explored as a scenario conducive to a safe formation of other values. Sharing in the imaginal realm cemented the isolated back into community, Josée acknowledged. More significantly, it revealed 'the way of the women' in re-owning their body and their sexuality. Far from dismissing the issue of violence, the play addresses it specifically, not by bloody massacres, but in a structured, ritualistic approach pertaining to the feminine way of resolving conflict.

I should like to note that although the play relies on outdated gender essentialism, it was beneficial as a necessary passage rather than a final station. *Lysistrata* is a comedy that awakens the hidden tragedy behind the scenes, but like most comedies it conjures the impossible, and the fantasy, as in dreams, provides a denouement: a *lysis*.

Spartan and Athenian women belonged to the warring 'ethnic' clans, but they relied on gender-solidarity to unite their forces for their common good. Men's power over women was toppled over as they surrendered to women who took into their hands control over their bodies and their city. The Rwandan women belonged to different clans, yet they too discovered solidarity could bring healing to the imposed artificial divide.

Athenians and Spartans were opposing forces in Hellenic times, but were pulled together in conscious relationship, held by Lysistrata as the still point of the turning wheel. Her capacity to hold the centre axis between polarities, supported by efforts from both communities of women, produced the necessary force for change. The creation of a new condition was established where no one community was destroyed by the other, giving the Rwandan women hope for the future, and courage to persevere.

Other 'opposites' were equally constellated and became 'partners' in the dance of transformation, bringing forth a new level of consciousness with a new peaceful *modus vivendi*. But this evolution is never acquired once and for all. A continuous separation and uniting of opposites enables a constant renewal of life force and the development of human consciousness.

In the Greek play, we discover traditionally women are confined to household duties for the private, domestic affairs of the home οικος (*oikos*). But Lysistrata claims the right to exert authority in the public management of the city πολις (*polis*) and in political affairs. Love and power are opposites, paralleled by the private and the public confronting one another. Significantly, the *Akropolis* was the locus for the meeting of the opposites: whereby public money of the *polis* was managed as household economy of the *oikos*.

In the absence of personal ego strength, the community of Rwandan 'actors' provided a window of tolerance to stabilise anxiety and hyper-arousal. The humiliation of the injured women shifted from the entangled and traumatised psyche of a victimised politicised group to the safety of attachment to a familial group. Toxic shame that "pervades the core experience of the self" (Mollon, 2005/2018, p.110), is a kind of shame that affects the body 'like a paralysis' Josée acknowledged, and is usually concealed when it needs to be openly exposed as a collective political issue.

Josée and the women she worked with elaborated on the symbols in *Lysistrata* that spoke to them. And far from being obvious, they struggled to challenge their content and meaning, and to find their uniqueness as they sought an opening of a gateway into women's empowerment, and a gradual ownership of their own sexuality.

Lysistrata: make love not war

The Battle of Two City-States (*Poleis*)
The Battle of the Sexes

Lysistrata is the last of Aristophanes 'peace plays', produced in 411 BCE at a time when Athens was going through the most desperate crisis, when there was seemingly *no way out* of the Peloponnesian War, fought between city-states, which lasted 27 years (431–404 BCE), *no way out*, that is, other than via the un-thinkable and the un-imaginable which only a woman like Lysistrata could bring about.

Together with Josée, we looked at this play as though it was a dream, where the 'characters' expose energy-based dynamics of psyche, where 'men' and 'women' are not looked at in terms of gender but as inner dynamics, whereby the opposites are constellated, and where the instinctual is confronted by the spiritual. It is also where the collective is challenged by the personal, and where the instinctual body manifesting the soul of the Polis is the locus where the politics of war and peace are played out. There are many layers and many symbols to this play, but we chose to work with those most relevant to the issues brought up by the members of the group.

There is an understanding in Ancient Greece that peace is better than war, but war presents itself as the *only* way to protect the safety or honour of the warring cities. But wars are fought mainly to provide *un-equal* opportunities for men and city-states to gain and display, what Marion Woodman called: "PPFF: Power and Prestige, Fame and Fortune" (Woodman, 1985, p.16) the lynchpins of patriarchal power.

In Ancient Greece, women, it might be thought, were uninterested by these temptations, and whereas the worst that could happen to a man in war was a glorious death, for women it would cost them decades of misery due to the death of their protector, or they would become bereft of their chance to be a wife and mother in a society where unmarried women had no place or position.

Lysistrata perceives exactly this condition and uses it as a strategy to unify women across the divide. "There is an oracle that we will triumph if only we don't fall out among ourselves," (Aristophanes, 1973/2002, p.171) she exhorts. With moral and political authority Lysistrata assembles and organises the women together, and makes them agree to use the most potent weapon they have to thwart their men's belligerent potency by imposing a sexual boycott until their men stop warring and agree to a compromise. No longer deferring to men, chastity signals women's sovereignty and self-empowerment. The withdrawal of sex is an intelligent way for women to force their men to think, but it is also a way for women to become conscious of the power they have over men which, if misused, will equally betray the feminine archetype of relatedness, and reinforces the duality they set out to resolve in the first place.

But Lysistrata makes her intention and attitude clear. She calls upon the power of Eros and obedience to the Self by taking on the figure of a priestess to serve the highest value. She binds the women's oath with a religious ritual, not in a written contract, but in words and wine as though in flesh and blood, to seal it. The wine is used instead of animal sacrifice, representing the sacrifice of ego-desires in order to serve the Self. That is not all. Lysistrata exposes the co-dependence between sex and money. We can relate this to the libido energy symbolised by wealth or lack of money in dreams but also in waking life. Lysistrata calls upon the women to literally occupy the Acropolis where the treasury is kept. Women block the men from accessing the money, without which the financing of the navy is doomed, lest funding it be to their ruin and that of the City.

It is clear that Lysistrata's initiative could not have succeeded without the *mediation* of the Feminine values she calls upon to counterbalance those of Patriarchy. From Athena-Polias she gathers wisdom, justice and strategic-skill, and reminds the warring parties that Athena is venerated by *both* Athens and Sparta, and that therefore they have more in common than what separates them. Athena-Polias is not only *the* warrior goddess, she is also the reconciler-unifier, presented as the connector-mediator, uniting both sides, and offering the possibility of transcending the split, through spiritual worship and the offering of sacrifices.

As the play unfolds, we discover Lysistrata, which literally means 'the liquidator of armies', is Lysimache herself, 'the liquidator of battles' which is the other name of Athena-Polias. Lysistrata-Lysimache, in effect, stands for what dissolves the previously coagulated, as in the alchemical process: *solve et coagula* ('dissolve and coagulate' – referring to the breaking down of elements, and their coming together) so that the possibility of a new rapport, 'a reconciling-third' element between the two warring sides may emerge. In a final twist, Lysistrata turns into Athena herself and summons the divine personification of Reconciliation, the neutral Goddess, who stands beyond the conflict.

But what does the feminine realm provide to dissolve the war and coalesce a new form?

It is from the female domestic sphere that Lysistrata finds agency to face the broader workings of the Polis. She calls upon women's household-finances to manage the city as a whole.

In the course of heated negotiations, men vow to burn all the women who have ignited and pursued this plot. But women's organisational skills and quick-call to action outwits their men: they pour out their 'water-pitchers' onto the men's 'inflamed logs'. Water puts out fire. And if this was not a strong-enough metaphor to reveal the way of the women, Lysistrata goes on to describe the untangling of the knots that tie men to war, using an extended wool-working metaphor.

There is a notion in the play that men entangle and women weave; that men fight whereas women spin. Weavers link left and right brain together, whilst those who divide split their thoughts from their hearts and tie their thoughts, hands and actions in knots. This is the kind of entanglement Jung the Magician decides to sever with a strike of a sword. In one of his paintings (see Jung, 2018, p.142, 'The Artfully Tied Knot'), Jung is dressed in a ceremonial robe woven in rich silk-like fabric, ornamented with gold threads to indicate the feminine attitude is of the highest moral value. He carries a ritualistic sword to cut free what has been entangled in his brain in order to release and set his feminine soul free. The Cartesian *Cogito, ergo sum* ('I think, therefore I am'), does not enable any dissolution let alone a resolution to the entanglement. It is not in the brain that the transcendent function is birthed.

The play insinuates men rush to spill the blood of others whereas women bleed cyclically out of their wombs. Men bond in war games for heroic solar outcome, women attune with one another through synchronous menstrual cycles in accordance to moon phases. They know there is time for action and another for inaction, a time for outward activity or sexual intercourse and another for seclusion and creative power. However simplistic the assumptions about men are, the participants agreed that women's bleeding asserts their autonomy as it accentuates an idiosyncrasy pertaining to their sole feminine nature, intrinsically denied to men.

Taking in hand the weaving cloak, Lysistrata demonstrates how to separate and dis-entangle the administration of the state with discrimination and discernment:

> It's rather like a ball of yarn when it gets tangled-up. Well, consider how we deal with a tangled skein of wool. We take it like this, and with the help of our spindles we pull it gently, now in this direction, now in that, and it all unravels. That's how we'll unravel this war, if you'll let us, unpicking it by sending diplomatic missions, now in this direction, now in that.
>
> (Aristophanes, 1973/2002, p.163)

Transformation in alchemy is effected by discerning, then paradoxically reconciling what seem to be irreconcilable opposites. The goal is to produce an incorruptible wholeness transcending oppositions. Jung refers to alchemy to amplify psyche's transformative processes. The art of political diplomacy resides within the feminine art of relational opposition as manifested by the *separatio* and *coniunctio* processes forming the nexus of feminine power. They are characterised by the alchemist as the *albedo*, or the whitening phase of transformation. In other words, the extraction of the *quinta essentia* follows a process of separation, then further purification, before it can be united with its opposite. To purify is to refine the darkness of the *nigredo* out of which light emerges.

Instead of resolving conflicts with splitting wars, warmongers could use the art of weaving by dis-joining then joining forces. There are spaces between the woven stitches. A multitude of infinitesimal spaces where silence exists enables the re-threading of the politics of war into spaces of reflection. These spaces are like a replica-memorial, a cosmological repetition of the great womb out of which our common humanity is born. The *nigredo* of war is transmuted into psychic spaces, a dis-entanglement of the brain, to refer to Jung's *Liber Novus* affirmation. Every era of human evolution has seen its illnesses and plagues. Our era today seems to indicate the human brain is at stake with more mental illness and brain tumours appearing at younger ages. The entangled brain of man is destined to connect to the disentangled brain of the universe for the dawn of a new cosmology of awakening, like the eight-headed star of consciousness. Feminine paradox joins together opposites that are usually dis-jointed by separating the entanglement whilst bringing the opposing threads together into a new design.

The negative father complex amputates the maiden's hands, and negative power amputates women out of the Polis. But Lysistrata evokes another plan: the entire Polis must be cleansed from negative power, and the infectious knots of corruption that tie men together must be severed. The clots and lumps of exploitative ambition manipulated to snatch important posts and positions must be washed out. Politicians conspiring to get each other elected must be beaten out like clogs of wool, and the money behind the power that pulls the strings of elections, must be tied up in knots. Men's abuse of power is but a disconnection from the feminine and from Eros.

If the Goddess Athena is Lysistrata's twin sister in battle for balance and equilibrium, Aphrodite, the Goddess of love and sexuality is her ally. Aphrodite's epithets define her as: 'the sea born', 'ally of war', 'she upon the graves'. Aphrodite, among the Olympians, is the 'other', the one who comes from the Orient, or the Middle East, yet she is integrated in the Greek pantheon. She was born in Paphos on the shores of Kypros, and her identity was largely derived from the Phoenician-Canaanite goddess Astarte, the Egyptian Isis, and rooted in the Sumerian cult of Inanna. The other prominent temple where she is worshipped close to her birthplace is in the region of Gaza in Palestine. In effect, she embodies sexual union, symbolic of the union of opposites, and that love is the love of 'the other', constellated by the opposition.

There are many women who serve patriarchy and are ruthless patriarchs. *The Devil Wears Prada* (Weisberger, 2003) is an example of how the power principle runs over the Feminine principle of relationship, cooperation and friendship, and how young aspiration is put-upon by driven success. Unconscious mothering, disconnected from the instinctual body and from feeling, maintains daughters in a power-system of perfectionism by colluding with it. Perfectionism dis-inhabits the body. Perfectionism dis-connects reality into black or white, good or bad. Marion Woodman called this inner split an "inner civil war" (*Parabola Conversations*, 2019). I would add there is nothing civil about such wars, for they only split life further from the necessity of inner death. Instead, these delusional wars feed soporific idealisms, whose real enemy is the simplicity and the humanity of life itself. Warding-off the consciousness of one's dark shadow leads to projection onto 'others' of our own evil, to the extent of exterminating 'them' in order to maintain our idealism intact. Patriarchy worships illusions. The reality is that there is no good without bad, or white without black. This is a complexity war tends to avoid, which reinforces its addictive nature: war is used as substitution, and as avoidance. To avoid the 'inner civil war', external wars on the evil 'others' are concocted with perfect lies.

There are men who serve the feminine principle and are more in touch with their souls than women. But when women are raped, the feminine in men is also raped. The rape of women remains the most pervasive crime of our modern world whose values have also raped the *anima mundi*. The stigma of rape inflicted on the personal must be read within a collective context of violence, which directly or indirectly condones these crimes. In colluding with an endorsed societal violence, rape frequently remains unpunished. Rape must be addressed as a symptom of our sick society, for below and above our civilised humanity lurks the un-civilised and ruthless urge to rape with violence. However, discussions between the members of the meeting-group attempted to uncover the structural violence of gender relationships at home, which was spilled on the streets. Underexposed, the culture of rape, they agreed, remains one of the most insidious, gender-biased crimes of our times: a perverted instinctual urge weaponised for political encroachment.

Lysistrata manages to bring opposites together, to unite women through social solidarity: the elders and the young, the widows and the married, the Athenians and the Spartans, to bring about what unites rather than what separates, and to successfully impose a negotiation leading to peace. Peace indeed is better than war, and Love dissolves Power. Jung would add: "the factors which come together in the *coniunctio* are conceived as opposites, either confronting one another in enmity or attracting one another in love" (Jung, 1963, p.3). To the *coagulated* war, a *solutio* by another equally power-full instinct must be constellated.

For Jung, libido was not limited to the sexual instinct as Freud emphasised. He rather saw it as the creative impulse encompassing the totality of psychic-energy. Jung borrowed the concept of *élan vital* (vital force) from Henri Bergson to describe libido as life-instinct energy, a creative power existing everywhere and in everything. Instincts are drives. They are compulsive, fixed, and have an invariably inherited organisation. Plants know how to grow, and animals follow a set pattern of behaviour. In his *Liber Novus Red Book*, Jung defines these drives as a "primordial form of creation" (Jung and Shamdasani, 2009, p.368). But he goes on describing these *"first dark urges"* as "the new dark god" (Jung, 2009, p.368). To this he adds that these forces are *"the very secret teacher(s) of nature"* which combine opposites and are "the mother of all abominable deeds and all salutary symbols" (Jung, 2009, p.368). Evil is not simply the absence of good, evil is a god in its own right, and is in need of salvation. The healing can firstly happen in the creative *ars* of fantasy. Fantasy is the beginning of all human creativity, whereby the gods in need of transformation can become moral in us. Through the individual suffering of each of us nailed on the cross, we come to accept we are evil as we are good and to hold the tension of the opposites, so a new level of consciousness arises. "I bring you the beauty of suffering" (Jung, 2009, p.553) says Shade, for there is no heaven without hell. When we look at what humans inflict onto each other in the dark rooms of torture, and in broad daylight on bloodstained war-grounds, we succumb to the inevitability of evil and the struggle this fateful condition provokes.

Instincts are "ectopsychic determinants", writes Jung later on in *The Structure and Dynamic of the Psyche* defining the relationship of the subject to the world (Jung, 1960, p.118). Jungian psychology does not limit the instinctual impulse or desire only to sexuality. Instead, it manifests in *"five main groups of instinctive factors",* all equally powerful, which may in turn suppress or serve one another which Jung names hunger, sexuality, activity, reflection and creativity (Jung, 1960, p.118) which can also be collated as CRASH: Creativity, Religion (reflection), Aggression (activity), Sexuality, and Hunger (nutritive instinct).

Rape experienced as a physical and psychological trauma calls upon a strict understanding and treatment of trauma and its effects on body-brain-psyche. Yet this approach requires comprehensive engagement: the urge to symbolise beyond the symptoms is an unequivocal attempt to unite the known with the unknown and the knowable with the unknowable, thus compelling a radical mutation of the victim's personality as a whole. "Because this work takes place in an archetypal-laden field, a religious attitude is called for, one that seeks to unite ego and Self, as in the Latin *religare*, 'to bind together'" (Wirtz, 2014, p.183). Balancing the inflated instinct by constellating another opens a doorway toward a harmonious inter-dependence, and a path of non-adversarial relationships. God and humanity, as John Dourley remarks, float in the same bathtub, and a "move by either affects the other" (Dourley, 2008 p.13).

To offer a contemporary version of *Lysistrata*, I introduced Josée to Nadine Labaki's film whereby the instinct of war is confronted by the religious instinct.

Where Do We Go Now? (Nadine Labaki, 2011): do you think we exist simply to mourn you?

We explored the film *Where Do We Go Now?* as a modern re-visioning of Aristophanes's play: a dreamlike tale about war and peace whereby the nutritive/hunger instinct and the reflective/religious instinct are constellated to balance the overwrought destructive drive. The female voiceover at the beginning says (in colloquial Arabic):

> *This is a tale of a lonely town*
> *With mines scattered all around,*
> *Where women fast and pray,*
> *But are caught in endless waves*
> *Of wars between men who cannot love or hate,*
> *But for peace women defy*
> *Law, gender and the divine,*
> *And form an understanding:*
> *The whole cannot be at peace*
> *If its parts are at war.*

The film is directed by a woman (Labaki is a Lebanese actress, now also a director and activist) highlighting women's resourceful and ingenious methods to side-track men from war. The country where the film takes action is not named, pointing to the archetypal and symbolic level of the message. The film takes place in a rural village where Christians and Muslims have lived harmoniously together for centuries. Now they coexist in a fragile peace as though it is hanging on a thin thread in the face of absurd sectarian violence, financed and exploited in part by those who seek money and power.

The village itself is ringed with landmines, and its cemetery filled with the bodies of too many men who died senselessly, leaving behind bereft and grieving mothers and wives, sisters and daughters. Slights and ridiculous misunderstandings explode into incendiary provocations, which are met with heated retaliations. The men from both sides, in effect, do the same jobs, eat the same food, like the same music, speak the same language and supposedly pray to the same God, yet they are on a constant verge of exploding into fratricidal warfare, infected by the wider context of violence. In response, the women of the village band together to form a tightly knit female community intent upon keeping peace by any means.

The women's solidarity is viewed right at the opening scene in which a choreographed procession of a black-clad corps of women of all ages march solemnly in a subdued dance to the cemetery. "Where do we go now?" they ask as they file off in different directions, suddenly baffled by the segregated cemetery, yet they mourn their deceased men alike. Heart-stricken and eyes haggard, they clutch the photographs of their killed fathers, husbands and sons, beating their chests with sorrow as they sway with grief to a destination beyond their comprehension. "Do you think we exist simply to mourn you?" they cry out their painful sacrifice to the remaining men.

Throughout the film, the women plot and conspire. They stage fake miracles, sabotage the radio and TV to block bad news and dampen inflamed tensions. But at their most inspired, they solicit a drive in men stronger than the so-called religious drive. As in Aristophanes's play, the instinct of war is confronted by the sexual, as well as by the hunger instinct. In a Dionysian-like set up, entranced with drink and dance, the women manage to divert the testosterone-charged men's urge for retaliation, whose hungers and weaknesses they know well, by serving them drinks and feeding them food, baked with sedatives and tranquilisers, maybe even Hashish, all served with an entertaining troupe of foreign showgirls.

And the outcome was as simple as laughter. It is said that laughter is the beginning of prayer, and that God who sits in Heaven laughs (Psalms 2:4). A Middle Eastern saying announces 'Laugh, and the Cosmos laughs with you', and 'Laugh and the Gods enter in'. Laughter cracks complexes open whilst uniting people in a common experience. It releases endorphins, decreases stress and boosts the immune system. Laughter warms up relationships and creates an emotional bonding between members of a given group. Similar to yawning, laughter is contagious. By laughing together, we attune to one another. It dissipates anxiety and fear of the other and brings people closer to intimacy. It facilitates a *coniunctio* of heart and mind. As a result, the lethal tension that could have led to another bloody strife among the men was halted by the laughing geniality of the women.

This dissipation was aided by the women who formed a garrulous female regiment who 'dug deep' to unearth a cache of buried weapons, hiding it away from their men who had been hyping-up for possible combat. But the ultimate *lysis* to the religious strife was when the women agreed to swap religions, and embrace the other's religion, and the religious rites of the 'other' side. Their men were dumbstruck, and halted any attempt to carry arms, now against their own!

Women demonstrate that hopelessly complex knotted situations, similar to Gordian knots, can only be undone with creative thinking, or thinking 'outside the box'.

With women facing adversity we discover that, unlike the theories of social Darwinism, which emphasise competition and the survival of the fittest, it is rather the mutual aid, mutual cooperation and reciprocity that helps women survive. Feminine structures, like that of the beehive, or, as in the flight of geese who take turns in leading over long distances together, rely on collaboration and team work, and we find that sociability is as much a law of nature as mutual struggle. The

Guilds were an example of how skills and knowledge were passed on to the next generation. Feminine forms of mutuality and collaboration need to be rediscovered, re-owned and reinstated as a balance to a goal-oriented, unilateral achievement-based society. Mutuality is a form used to support one another within a community and, when abided by, could develop into altruism as one community comes to the aid of another struggling community. The voiceover ending the film says:

> *The tale is now ending*
> *For those listening,*
> *Of a town where peace was found*
> *While fighting continued all around,*
> *Of men who slept deeply to awake*
> *To a newly found peaceful way,*
> *And of women, still in black,*
> *Who, despite the guns and flares*
> *Have fought with flowers and prayers,*
> *And did everything they could to tell their children*
> *About a tale of strife transformed by love.*

Josée's welfare project continued for a number of months. The use of story as metaphor to the inner struggles enabled the participants to identify with its healing symbols, and in parallel process, to allow the story to resonate with and amplify what lay within. The story awakened women's curiosity and willingness to think and feel. It helped contain the trauma and unravel discourse toward a more integrated outcome. It allowed laughter to erupt again.

Empowered by the new-found meaning, participants went on researching how other African women dealt with 'rape war-crimes'. They discovered Congolese women, who were equally victims of a pandemic of sexual violence, were threatened when they distinguished rape from sex. They also discovered there are literally no words in local languages to identify rape as a criminal act. The word *ubakaji* was borrowed from Swahili and brought into the Congolese lexicon. "Rape is not sex!" was firmly confirmed by the participants.

They continued their comparative research to discover men can also be victims of war rape and by the thousands in some neighbouring countries such as Uganda or the Congo. "Men too dare not speak for fear of being disrespected", Josée clarified, thus enabling the women to identify with the suffering of male victims of rape. In a patriarchal society where gender roles are strictly demarcated "men are expected to be strong, not victims", a participant interjected. "Men are also abandoned by society and often by their wives who can no longer trust their husbands are manly enough to protect them", a participant explained. For these reasons, a conspiracy of silence prevails over the issue of male victims of rape, forcing men to collude with their perpetrators.

A variety of research projects by Lara Stemple at the University of California (see her faculty homepage for details) revealed sexual violence against men is a component of wars all over the world. She also suggested international aid organisations are failing male victims.

To ignore male rape is to neglect men. It also reinforces a patriarchal view of men, reinforcing their machismo and denying their vulnerability. More critically, it equates women with victimhood, hindering their resilience and empowerment.

The alienation of women-participants and their journey to wholeness resembled that of Nietzsche's wanderer. Speaking of a return to home he invokes the return to oneself of the exiled parts: "It is returning, at last it is coming home to me – my own Self and those parts of it that have long been abroad" (Nietzsche, 1969, p.173). For these women the return home meant the re-valuing of their "female bodies".

Together we set up a ritual of a 'washing of the hands', as a way of expressing an acceptance of being 'touched', but this time with respect and honour. It is through careful sensing that the body feels what it wishes to think and to imagine freely. With reverence for the present moment, the participants washed each other's hands to symbolically purify their bodies from 'disturbing memories'. This enabled them to move toward the recognition of the sacredness of womanhood, and for the stigma of oppression to be countered, if not healed. The body parts 'that had been abroad' were called to re-inhabit the safety of home, and to experience a 'whole-embodiment' of sexuality.

The sacredness of matter is a new paradigm whereby the feminine in both men and women is redeemed. Through the feminine the instinctual-spiritual body is redeemed. Living in the present moment, here and now is also redeemed. The Feminine stands as a witness to the metamorphoses our feminine self yearns for to move from rupture to repair.

References

Aristophanes, 1973/2002, *Lysistrata and Other Plays*, translated by A. Sommerstein, London: Penguin.

Baron, L. and Strauss, M.A., 1988, 'Cultural and Economic Sources of Homicide in the United States', *Sociological Quarterly*, 29(3), pp. 371–390.

Charon, R., 2012, 'Narrative and Medicine'. In: N. Jecker, A. Jonsen and R. Pearlman (eds), *Bioethics: An Introduction to the History, Methods and Practice*, London: Jones and Bartlett Learning, pp. 210–213.

De Brouwer, A.-M. and Ka Hon Chu, S. (eds), 2009, *The Men Who Killed Me: Rwandan Survivors of Sexual Violence*, Vancouver: D & M, Publishers.

Dourley, J.P., 2008, *On behalf of the Mystical Fool: Jung on the Religious Situation*, Hove: Routledge.

Elbe, S., 2002, 'HIV/AIDS and the Changing Landscape of War in Africa', *International Security*, 27(2), pp. 159–177.

Jung, C.G., 1938/1960, *Psychology and Religion: Based on the Terry Lectures Delivered at Yale University*, New Haven and London: Yale University Press.

Jung, C.G., 1953, *Psychology and Alchemy*, Hove: Routledge & Kegan Paul.

Jung, C.G., 1960, *Structure and Dynamics of the Psyche*, Hove: Routledge and Kegan Paul.

Jung, C.G., 1963, *Mysterium Coniunctionis: An Inquiry into the Separation and Synthesis of Psychic Opposites in Alchemy*, Hove: Routledge and Kegan Paul.

Jung, C.G., 1968, *The Archetypes and the Collective Unconscious*, Hove: Routledge & Kegan Paul.

Jung, C.G. and Shamdasani, S. (ed), 2009, *The Red Book: Liber Novus*, Translated by M. Kyburz and J. Peck, New York: W. W. Norton.

Jung, C.G. and the Foundation of the Works of C.G. Jung, 2018, *The Art of C.G. Jung*, New York: W.W. Norton.

Mollon, P., 2005/2018, *EMDR and the Energy Therapies: Psychoanalytic Perspectives*, Abingdon: Routledge.

Neruda, P., 1958/2005, *Spain in the Heart*, New York: New Directions.

Nietzsche, F., 1969, *Thus Spoke Zarathustra*, London: Penguin.

Nowrojee, B., 1996, *Shattered Lives: Sexual Violence during the Rwandan Genocide and Its Aftermath*, A Report for Human Rights Watch. Available from https://www.hrw.org/sites/default/files/reports/1996_Rwanda_%20Shattered%20Lives.pdf (Accessed 19 Februrary 2020).

Owens, P., 2007, *Between War and Politics: International Relations and the Thought of Hannah Arendt*, Oxford: Oxford University Press.

Parabola Conversations, 2019, 'Worshipping Illusions: An Interview with Marion Woodman'. https://parabola.org/2019/04/13/worshipping-illusions-an-interview-with-marion-woodman/ (Accessed 9 March 2020).

Prunier, G., 1999, *The Rwanda Crisis: History of a Genocide*, London: Hurst.

Torgovnik, J., 2007, 'Rwanda: Legacy of Genocide', *The Telegraph*. https://www.telegraph.co.uk/culture/3668387/Rwanda-Legacy-of-genocide.html (Accessed 9 March 2020).

Von Clausewitz, C., 2008, *On War*, Oxford: Oxford University Press.

Weisberger, L., 2003, *The Devil Wears Prada*, New York: Broadway Books.

Wirtz, U., 2014, *Trauma and Beyond, the Mystery of Transformation*, New Orleans: Spring Journal Books.

Woodman, M., 1985, *The Pregnant Virgin: A Process of Psychological Transformation*, Toronto: Inner City Books.

Zaphiriou-Zarifi, H., 2017, 'Violence, Analytical Psychology and Imagining the Peace in Palestine/Israel'. In: S. Carta, A. Adorisio and R. Mercurio (eds), *The Analyst in the Polis: Conference Proceedings from the Second Conference on Analysis and Activism: Social and Political Contributions of Jungian Psychology*, Rome, Italy: Stefano Carta, pp. 157–194.

Chapter 13

The role of a grandmother

MJ Maher

Introduction

As a child, my when-I-grow-up dream was to become a grandmother like my grandmother, the most powerful feminist in my entire little world. Although a cultural outsider within a patriarchal society, her soft voice nevertheless commanded respect. This was my grandmother, my *gogo*, whose skirt was so wide that it sheltered us from the misery thrown at us by social stereotypical discriminations. This was my *ambuya*, who fought for our rights and would gather us, her grandchildren, her walking sticks, in her thatched hut, semi-lit by a home-made lamp and dying fire, and open our eyes to who we were through folk stories, proverbs and metaphors. Laced with moral values, these were the cultural and traditional hand-me-downs that were passed on from generation to generation. So, the logic for the future was to become a grandmother and command similar respect.

Fast forward. I am now a grandmother in Surrey in the United Kingdom and a cultural outsider, but am I as powerful as the feminist old lady in the thatched hut in Chivhumudhara Village of Mutemachani Kraal? That is the question I plan to explore. Will you relate to my old feminist grandmother and recognise your own imagoes of strength that you internalised - grandparents, uncles, aunts, teachers or any other forceful personality that crossed your path? That is the question for you to explore. In this chapter, I will also explore issues raised in two articles. The first was covered on the Zimbabwe News website which reported that "Children of Zimbabwean families resident in the UK are being seized by social workers on an astonishing scale. Most are taken never to be seen again" (Zimbabwe News, 2017).

It states that if parents discipline their children and the school is informed, the family home is raided and the children, all of them, are bundled out of the house and taken to live with total strangers. In most cases, the problem arises from cultural differences. The reported consequences for one Zimbabwean woman was 10 years in prison for disciplining her daughter: she lost her job and her future. Her daughter was placed into care.

The second article, 'Children are not safe in the UK', was written by Dr Masimba Mavaza and published in *The Patriot: Celebrating Being Zimbabwean*, where he states, "Data published by the Department for Education (DfE) shows there were 646,120 referrals overall to councils" children services during 2016/17, equating to 1,770 referrals every day – a rise of four percent compared to the previous year" (Mavaza, 2018). He reports that most of the children taken away are Zimbabwean.

It is my intention in this chapter to reflect on the role of a grandmother in such a situation. Hopefully some lessons will be learnt, because this is a serious problem.

My grandmother, my heroine

My grandmother, my *ambuya*, my *gogo*,
The most powerful person,
In my entire tiny little world.
An ever-giving breast yet a *mutorwa*,
A cultural outsider,
A bearer of the lion totem,
Handed to her through her paternal lineage.

Hers is a timid voice that does not roar,
Yet her patriarchal tribe tremble and bow
To her presence,
And her soft voice.

Her son, my beloved father,
A beautiful striped beast of the forest,
With its masterful hind leg kick,
A believer in spare the rod and spoil the child,
Would humble himself in her presence.
His long arm of discipline,
Touched us not,
In the presence of my *gogo*, our lioness.
Coz, hitting your child in her presence,
Is as good as hitting her royal highness.
Unotanda botso meaning walking around,
In a sack and covered in ash.
Followed by little children laughing and mocking,
And spitting at the offender.
So, no, no to punishing the offspring,
Not in front of their grandmother!

My *ambuya*, my educator,
Scoops all her walking sticks,
For school holiday in the country.
Where most things are done in circles,
Eating, story time,

All in circles.
In her thatched round hut,
Semi-lit by a home-made lamp and a dying fire,
Folk stories about *Sekuru Gudo*, Granddad Baboon,
And *Muzukuru Tsuro*, Grandchild Hare,
Are told.

What hits itself then cries?
A cock crowing!
Ah, that's a proverb!
I like proverbs that test one's observational skills,
And stretch the mind's creativity and imagination.
Metaphors laced with cultural and moral values,
And cultural and traditional hand-me-downs,
Flow,
From generation to generation.

My *gogo,* my educator,
Her curriculum covers every angle,
Sex education for all approaching puberty,
Is taught by the river banks of Nyamatsanga.
Amidst giggles of innocence.

Beating drums herald the approaching full moon,
And teenagers follow their beat,
To a place where waistlines are wiggled and thrust about,
As they dance *chipisi* and *jega.*
And ripe firm breasts pop about,
As they dance the chicken wing style,
To the rhythm of the beating drums.
Young men respond to the shaking bottoms,
By whistling and clicking their fingers to the music,
Working a cloud of dust with their feet,
Like bulls about to charge,
As they compete for a space in the dancing ring.
Yes, that's life in Chivhumudhara Village,
Where we felt safe under the watchful eye,
Of my *gogo,* my grandmother, my *muchembere.*

My grandmother, my protector, my advocate,
Whose skirt is as wide as a tent,
My safe haven,
Sheltering us from the misery thrown at us by life,
Like confetti.

Being a serial trouble brewer,
When in the city and in trouble,
I waited for her visit to confess my crime to my father,
Because,
Her visit was similar to the Pope's visit,
Marking a time for confessions.
Any crime that would attract the lick
From a stick would be confessed then,
Coz once confessed in front of the pope,
No parent would hit you for it.
No, not even after the old lady has gone.

Crystal clear are the cultural rules of disciplining,
No disciplining a child,
When your vision is clouded with anger.
No use of a bare hand,
As the offspring might consider it a fight,
And with time will fight back.
No use of a wooden spoon on boys,
Any cooking utensil on a son,
Marinates them to be hen-pecked,
By their future wives.

My grandmother, *my gogo, my ambuya,*
Commander of respect,
I salute you.
So, when I grow up, Commander Grandmother,
I dream to be like you!

Children of the state

A Zimbabwean grandmother,
Settles on the leafy side of Surrey,
Commanding respect and admiration,
Yet a cultural outsider is she.
But is she as powerful,
As the old lady in a thatched hut,
In Chivhumudhara Village,
In Mutemachani Kraal?

As school holidays and weekends descend,
This *gogo* collects all her walking sticks,
To stay with her in leafy Surrey,
Where this educator teaches them,

How to survive racism and discrimination.
They learn about totems and proverbs,
And she speaks in colourful metaphors,
Laced with moral and cultural values.

This *ambuya* serves cultural food,
Often cooks *sadza,* thick maize porridge,
Served with pumpkin leaves in peanut butter.
She pounds roasted dry maize,
Into *mbwire mbwire* powder,
And walking sticks lick it and chuckle with delight,
Filling their leafy garden with sheer delight,
Because it's great to be in grandmother's den.

The walking sticks recite,
What to do with unfairness.
Go to grandmother,
Run to nan,
Phone or text *gogo.*
Their parents who were brought up,
Under spare the rod and spoil the child regime,
Get rehabilitated,
Not to use implements,
Because that's child abuse.
But if necessary, to smack gently with a bare hand,
Thus, divorcing from their cultural teachings,
Where use of stick is permitted,
But smacking with bare hands is taboo!
Parents are confused about how to discipline their children.

Will a walking stick threatened with a stick,
Dive under nan's skirt like we did?
When a bare hand threatens to smack,
Will the walking sticks run for cover,
Behind their *gogo* like we used to?
Will they trust their *ambuya* to protect them?

No! because they are taught to …
Call the police,
Who ring the social worker,
Who engages the Children's Guardian,
And employs a barrister,
Who recommends expert witnesses.
But no one thinks of calling the best expert,

Their grandmother, their nan.
They forget their *gogo,* their *ambuya,*
Because they are now children of the State.

They forget their grandmother.
Their nan, the educator,
Their *gogo,* the narrator,
Their *muchembere*, the wise old lady.
They forget their pounder of problems,
Because they are now the children of the State.
Without roots and clear boundaries,
The walking sticks are lost,
And little monsters are born.

Mum says wash the dishes,
They call the social worker.
A parent gets angry when they disrespect others,
They report to the school.
Parents fear upsetting their sons and daughters,
Because they are now children of the State.

When the call is made,
The walking sticks are removed,
And are handed over to strangers.
The wise advisors,
Recommend that blacks be placed,
With black families.
But skin colour doesn't determine their culture,
Black Africans and black West Indians,
Chalk and cheese they can be.
Enslaved minds and colonised minds,
Cheese and chalk they can be.
A colonised descendant,
Is more likely to find common culture with a coloniser descendant,
Even though in the past one was oppressed by the other,
They share a similar history and culture.
So, a black African child is likely to be better off,
With a white family,
As a West Indian family,
Might prove to be an unsafe placement.
The old lady knows that,
And refers them to Maher (2012) publication,
But nobody listens to her.

No one listens to their nan,
Nobody involves this enormous shade,
That protects them from the scathing, scorching heat.
Their *ambuya* needn't know, social service whispers,
Because of data protection.
They must protect her grandchildren from her,
Because they are now children of the State.

Gogo weeps,
Ambuya cries,
Grandma laments and shakes her head,
As she discovers that she is naked.

Her skirt is shrivelled and redundant.
It cannot protect her future generation,
Because there is no recognition of grandma's role.
There is no place for a *gogo*, in this society.
Grandmother is left in the cold, in the dark,
Because they are now the children of the State.

Nan fights for her walking sticks,
But social workers say she can't be trusted,
Because her bond with her child is too strong.
Too strong,
That she can't protect the sticks from the perceived evil,
Of the breast that fed them.
Social service set a challenge,
For *ambuya* to prove her strength of character,
By killing off her relationship with her child.
She must choose a side,
Her walking sticks or her child, their mother?
She can't sit on a fence.

What nonsense!
What rubbish!
For nothing can shake her bond with her walking sticks.
Her wide skirt is a strong, protective shield,
No child born in this culture,
Will disrespect a parent.
No child born in this culture,
Will be left at the mercy of a cruel parent,
Because nan always steps in.
But social service says nan's sitting on a fence.

Social service's fence runs between mother and child,
Forcing the old lady to take a side.
But *gogo*'s fence runs around the family,
Forming a boundary,
That keeps everyone inside and together.
No sides, no divisions.
Sitting on this fence,
Means grandma can have a clear view of everyone,
Because inside the fence,
There are no sides, just one side, same side.
But social service wants a division marked,
Because they are now children of the State.

Grandmother refuses to take sides,
That's a foreign culture, not hers.
Demands keep being made,
To prove her love for her walking sticks,
By killing off their mother,
Her own child.

A psychotherapist is hired by social service,
To help open her eyes,
Ambuya sees the psychotherapist,
Her eyes are open wider to hold onto what she believes in,
Gogo's internalised culture insists,
Never forget your culture,
Never trade your beliefs,
Never lose your own identity.
With eyesight sharpened by the psychotherapist,
Grandmother refuses to take sides with confidence.
The law warns her of the risk she was taking,
The risk of losing her walking sticks forever,
To strangers, to the carers,
For they are now the children of the State.

The old lady's heart is torn,
She fears losing her walking sticks,
And she fears losing her own child.
She remembers the dreadful state,
Her walking sticks came back from care in,
Socially, psychologically, physically damaged.
Being in care had changed and damaged them,
They now speak slavery language of addressing family,
By the tone of their skin colour,

Black, white and maroon.
What's maroon?
The wise old lady wonders in her ignorance,
And recognises a division,
A division never experienced before going into care.
Gogo weeps.

Nan laments,
As she recalls the damage the separation has had,
On their mother, psychologically, emotionally,
Physically and socially.
The light in her child's eyes had gone.
Mother nature says if you touch a bird's eggs,
Mother bird is likely to reject them.
What happens to the eggs touched by social service?
Grandmother worries about that.
Her family is falling apart,
And she's caught in the bureaucratic web,
Helplessly surrendering.

Surrendering,
To the pressure to pick a side.
But what side?
Both sides are very vulnerable.
Even if she rejects their physical mother,
What will happen to the mother they internalised?
The one they carry within their bosom?
That is a dangerous mother to ignore,
For if not allowed to heal,
Will influence and sabotage their future relationships,
So, taking sides is not an option,
Coz they both need her,
And they both need each other to heal.

Fighting for both is hard,
Social service focus on the mother/child bond,
Believing that the strong bond is toxic.
Nan feels that social service's health and safety assessment,
Tries to control unreal anxieties they created,
So, she refuses to consider it.

Ambuya looks at the environmental inspection report,
She shakes her head in despair,
She observes, in her humble opinion,

That racial attitudes and prejudices lace the report,
But she will not let that side-track her,
So, she just disregards it.

She goes through the report by the school counsellor,
Which states that many moons ago,
One walking stick,
Expressed suicidal thoughts with intent.
He wants to die,
So that,
He can go and look after his deceased baby sister.
Feeling her pain,
A pain only her big brother could end,
He reasoned and concluded,
That he has no choice but to join her,
To go and protect her.

A knife shreds *ambuya's* heart,
Silent tears meander through the contours,
Of her aging sagging cheeks,
As the pain her walking stick carries,
Gets transmitted into the ribbons of her heart.

Nan kisses her teeth in shock.
This is serious why was the mother not told?
Why was the family not informed?
Because of data protection!
She is told.
A minor child is left to carry this burden!
Data protection my foot!
Grandma kisses her teeth again and again,
And again.

She studies the expert witnesses' reports,
Gogo feels that experts focus,
On their perception of her 'misuse' of her wisdom,
She is scared,
Because their perceptions carry a lot of weight,
As experts the court heavily relies on them.
They recommend that the walking sticks,
Should go into full time care.
The noise in nan's head is getting louder.
Grandmother knows she now needs a miracle,
She prays to Virgin Mary,

For strength, courage and wisdom,
And for Virgin Mary to speak to her Son for a miracle.

The noise is getting louder and louder,
The sticks are now scared of losing their family,
Coz, no one is listening to their wish to return home.
Desperation to be within the family again can be smelt,
But their noses are clogged,
No one is paying attention to the stench.
Frustrated, angry and scared,
The walking stick's last cry of helplessness,
Is delivered loud and clear, signed in blood,
And the noise stops.

Suddenly grandmother is recognised,
The health and safety,
And environmental concerns are overridden.
The walking sticks' safety becomes a priority.
They are taken out of care immediately,
And placed with their nan temporally,
Grandmother is given a chance to fight for them.

Nan rolls up her sleeves for the fight,
But she still holds tightly to her principles,
Her strong cultural upbringing,
Her identity as the root holding her family together.
A daughter of *Mazvimbakupa* clan,
Of the zebra totem,
Prepares for the biggest fight ever.
Maintaining her dignity, beauty and brains,
Anyemba, a true zebra warrior ready is she.

With every strength in her body and soul,
She fights for her walking sticks.
For they are now children of the State,
Needing to be reclaimed and rescued.

Their *ambuya* calls upon her psycho-ancestors.
First call is to Foulkes,
Who tells us that we are penetrated to the core,
By the culture of the environment we grow up in.
So, you can take an African child from their culture,
But you cannot take the African out of them.

Their grandma then texts Winnicott,
Who teaches us that no child exists
Without the mother.
Winnicott stresses the child's need,
For a good enough mother.
Nan develops this further.
There is no mother without a family, a community or a society,
And she argues that a mother's failure is a family failure,
Therefore, her failure too.
There is no individual in a family,
And the only way toward healing,
Is staying and working together as a family.

The walking sticks are deeply rooted at the centre of their family,
Which is why providing them with a new family,
Failed and damaged them.
A new family can only be the last, not first resort,
And it can only work in the absence of a good enough family.

Their *ambuya* then summons Melanie Klein,
Who marches in waving a banner,
Of togetherness.
She shouts that splitting never contains a child!
Good and bad dwell in us all.

Nan believes that a family traumatised by the splits,
Needs to march hand in hand,
Together through the depressive position,
Reflecting on what went wrong,
Bringing the splits together,
And accepting collective responsibility,
Of the actions and inactions that contribute to this mess,
Then, and only then,
Can healing take place.

The old educator then skypes with John Bowlby,
Father of Attachment Theory.
Bowlby plays his guitar to the tune,
Of Attachment Theory.
Highlighting the importance of consistency, responsiveness,
And proximity with the primary carer in building a secure attachment.
That separation from primary carer needs to be handled carefully,
As it influences their attachment styles in future relationships,
And their ability to tolerate separation anxiety.

Gogo demonstrates skilfully,
Bowlby's theory using her drawing of an African village,
She explains that no one can explore anything,
In the presence of a threat or danger.
She points at a bird of prey hovering in the sky of the African village,
As a symbol of the threat,
Linking it with the unbearable fear mothers experience,
Fear of losing their children to social service and to strangers.
Such strong feelings can become so overwhelming,
That some women regress to the age they first experienced those feelings,
Of fear, helplessness, hopelessness, separation, abandonment,
And so on.
As a result, some regress even further to a preverbal age,
Where they can't find a language to describe,
Their experiences.
Yet in that regressive state,
Mothers are called perpetrators of their children,
And they listen in silence,
As they get dressed in their new robes,
Identifying them as abusers and perpetrators,
Through floods of boiling tears.
At worst they are crowned as criminals,
Facing years in prison.

Yes, years in prison,
Because in that moment of traumatising reality,
They are unable to respond cooperatively and logically.
No one can reason or reflect when overwhelmed with emotions,
Coz when emotions are high,
Thinking flies out through the window.
Doubting Thomas can have a quiet word with Bion,
Bion, another psycho-ancestor,
Who blows his trumpet producing a melody,
About how when emotions run high,
The ability to think logically is attacked and blocked.

Click!
Like a delicate hand into a protective glove.
Pieces of this jigsaw puzzle fit into place.
Hezvo! Hezvo!
Whaaat?
Cries of surprise are heard,
But complaints that *ambuya* is being too clever are heard,
In the statement that the old lady is being a psychotherapist,

Instead of being a grandmother.
The expert witness bellows out,
Grandma deserves to be struck off,
By her professional body.
What for one might ask?
For using her professional skills to make sense of this mess,
And clarify her position?
For challenging the expert witness with skill and logic?
For doing what the professionals failed to do?
Coz if they do their job,
Then nan wouldn't call upon her psycho-ancestors!

Should the wise old lady be ashamed of her wisdom?
Of her identity?
Well, you cannot take the psychotherapist,
Out of this grandmother,
Because the psychotherapist and *ambuya,*
Are all rolled into one,
Making her a super grandmother.

Grandma is forced to take a different route,
She calls upon her psychiatric knowledge,
To clarify a claim by social service,
That a walking stick hears voices,
Coz if not clarified and cleared,
Her walking stick,
Could be labelled psychotic,
When the stick is just an ordinary child,
With a creative active mind,
Not a genius,
Not a schizophrenic,
Just boring ordinary with a clever creative mind.
His *ambuya* needs to claim him back,
And the expert witness agrees with grandmother's observations,
He's not psychotic!
But social service,
Please don't throw mental health diagnosis like confetti,
No,
Not on this old goat's walking stick,
Because the stain of the stigma lasts forever,
So no, grandma says no.

It's time to conclude,
By smoking out her family ancestor,

So, she calls upon her own superheroine of a grandmother,
Who now lives where the wind blows from.
What say you, *Shava*, daughter of a lion?

One of her metaphors descends upon us,
She says when mother hen eats her own eggs,
You must burn its beak to stop it from cracking the eggs,
Because a blunt beak will not damage the shell.

Should children report to the school, police, social worker?
Categorically yes,
But the authorities need to listen carefully,
And consult with the family members,
Instead of leaving the family out in the cold, in the dark.
Zimbabweans do not have extended families,
No cousins, no aunts and uncles.
Your cousins are our brothers and sisters,
Your aunts are our big or small mothers.
Your uncles are our big or small fathers.
The loss of family when the children go into care is significant,
Because theirs is a very big close family.

The walking sticks might want help for whatever reason,
They might want mother hen's beak burnt blunt,
To stop hurting them.
But in the absence of physical evidence of abuse,
A holistic approach is needed.
In the presence of trauma, a careful ear is needed,
To detect any re-enactment of the trauma.
These walking sticks watched their baby sister die,
And they were taken by Social service,
A week before her birthday,
So, they really needed to be listened to,
To trace where their pain is coming from.
If children can't be angry with their primary carer,
Who can they be angry with without fear of rejection?

Their *gogo* understands that,
Their grandma would burn that beak,
Burn the beak blunt,
But never kill mother hen.

Nan understands the pain around anniversaries,
And that children get traumatised by witnessing their mother,

Their pillar of strength,
Crumble,
As she is losing her baby to SIDS, to cot death,
Killing a part of her.
At the tender age of 3, 7, and 13,
These walking sticks ride in the back of an ambulance,
Watching the paramedics fight,
But fail to resuscitate their baby sister.
They witness their mother,
Too broken to protect them from the intensity of this trauma.
And that's the beak that needed to be burnt blunt.
Witnessing their mum in severe distress,
Cuts deep into their tender little hearts,
Producing unbearable pain.

Now,
A week before the baby's birthday,
The children don't want to re-witness their mother's distress.
The distress often resuscitated back to life by flashbacks,
Flashbacks intensified by the approaching anniversary,
Her birthday,
A reminder of how old she would have been,
Unbearable pain for any mother to bear,
Unbearable pain for any child to re-witness,
So, the walking sticks want that pain stopped,
Mother hen's beak burnt blunt,
So, burn the beak but please don't kill mother hen.

But Social services want mother hen dead,
And fail to look at the significance of the trauma,
The significance of the approaching anniversary.
Instead,
They allocate a very pregnant social worker,
Reminding mother of her loss.
Mother already on her knees,
Weakened by the approaching anniversary,
Is called a bad mother,
An abuser,
A perpetrator,
Who doesn't deserve to have children.
So, her children are swallowed,
Taken by the pregnant social worker,
Destination unknown.
Mother is left in an empty nest,

That holds the ghosts of her baby stolen by SIDS, cot death,
And living children now gone,
Yet their laughter continuously mocks her ears,
As she is left in an empty cold nest,
Where God claimed her youngest baby,
And a pregnant social worker,
Waddles in to claim her remaining minor children.
Leaving her holding her intestines,
In her now empty hands,
Alone,
Ripe to suicidal thoughts,
Which promise her the comfort of a peaceful sleep,
No more cutting pain,
No more judgments,
Just perfect peace,
All on her own,
Alone.
The temptation to follow the beckoning finger is high,
Peaceful perfect sleep is better,
Than pondering about being a mother,
Yet children has she not.
What is the point of living,
When she can be reunited with her baby girl?
Temptation, tempting temptation.

A piercing cry from her older daughter wakes her up,
From a world of fantasy,
A world of untold silent peace.
The piercing cry tags at her umbilical cord,
You are a mother,
You have other children who need you,
And the strength of mother's milk gives her no choice,
But to live on,
Giving up is not an option,
No.
Don't give up on your babies!
Can't give up on your children!
But what's the point?
Her mind battles on,
Swinging between the two options like a pendulum,
Tick! Tock!
Tick! Tock!
All on her own,
In the empty, cold nest.

Social service fails to involve her family,
Tick! Tock!
Tick! Tock!
All on her own,
In the empty, cold nest.

Social service fail to consider a risk assessment to see how safe she is,
Tick! Tock!
Tick! Tock!
All on her own,
In the empty, cold nest.

Didn't she deserve any compassion?
Apparently not.
On the other hand,
The walking sticks struggle in care with strangers for a year,
While authorities are busy investigating a point to prove,
Only succeeding in creating further losses for the children,
Loss of their entire family in its extension,
And loss of their beloved dog, Miracle,
They're not allowed to see Miracle,
And that kills them.
That kills the walking sticks.

The noise stops.
Their mother weeps in disbelief,
This is not happening!
It's a nightmare I am failing to wake up from!
And their grandmother's heart breaks,
Helplessly witnessing her daughter's pain.
Silence.
If nan had not found out through the grapevine,
She could have lost her daughter to suicide.
Grandmother shakes her head,
Not keen on carrying on with that thread of thought,
Too scary, too painful.

With grandma's clarity of events,
And her analysis still ringing in his ears,
A tall American barrister rises like the sphinx,
With a rich distinct, thick, soothing American accent,
He stands as the barrister of Children's Guardian.
Capturing the court's attention,
And aligning himself with one other barrister.

He amplifies the walking sticks' cry,
To return to their family.
Three other barristers seem to soften too,
But will the expert witnesses review their position,
After recommending that the sticks go into full time care,
For they're unsafe with their grandma,
Who refuses to let go her daughter, their mother?
Will the softness in this giant from America be significant enough?
Enough to change the direction the wind is blowing?
Those are the questions,
For the judge to ponder over!

In leafy Surrey the peace is destroyed,
Making the depressed squirrels come back to life,
Leaping from branch to branch
Of the huge oak tree.
Chirping blue tits, now the princesses of the garden,
Retreated up the yew tree to watch,
As the garden monsters scream and shriek,
Chasing each other round the garden.
The word was out,
The walking sticks are back!

References

Mavaza, M., 2018, 'Children not safe in the UK', *The Patriot: Celebrating Being Zimbabwean.*   https://www.thepatriot.co.zw/old_posts/children-not-safe-in-the-uk/ (Accessed 18 October 2019).

Zimbabwe News, 2017, 'Zimbabwean parents lose children to UK social service at alarming rate'. http://webcache.googleusercontent.com/search?q=cache:cm9z38aUwTIJ:https://www.zimbabwenews.co.uk/zimbabwean-parents-lose-children-to-uk-social-services-at-alarming-rate/&client=firefox-b-d&hl=en&gl=uk&strip=1&vwsrc=0 (Accessed 18 October 2019).

Recommended reading

Ainsworth, M.D., Blehar, M.C., Waters,E. & Wall, S., 1978, *Patterns of Attachment: A Psychological Study of the Strange Situation*, Hilldale, NJ: Lawrence Erlbaum.

Allen, J., 2005, *Apartheid South Africa: An Insider's Overview of the Origin and Effects of Separate Development*, New York: iUniverse.

Balint, M., 1968, *The Basic Fault: Therapeutic Aspects of Regression*, London: Tavistock.

Bion, W.R., 1961, *Experiences in Groups and Other Papers*, London: Tavistock.

Bollas, C., 1995, *Cracking Up: The Work of Unconscious Experiences*, London: Routledge.

Bowlby, J., 1969, *Attachment and Loss: Volume 1. Attachment*, New York: Basic Books.

Bowlby, J., 1973, *Attachment and Loss: Volume 2. Separation: Anxiety & Anger*, New York: Basic Books.

Bowlby, J., 2005, *The Making and Breaking of Affectional Bonds*, London: Routledge.

Brewster, F., 2017, *African Americans and Jungian Psychology: Leaving the Shadows*, London & New York: Routledge.

Crockenberg, S., 1981, 'Infant irritability, mother responsiveness, and social support influences on the security of infant-mother attachment', *Child Development*, 52(3), pp. 857–865.

Donald, M., 1978/1987, *Children's Minds*, Belfast: Fontana Press.

Fanon, F., 1952, *Black Skin, White Masks*, London: Pluto Press.

Foulkes, S.H., 1983, *Introduction to Group Analytic Psychotherapy: Studies in the Social Integration of Individuals and Groups*, London: Karnac Books.

Foukles, S.H. & Anthony, E.J., 1965, *Group Psychotherapy: The Psychoanalytical Approach*, London: Karnac Books.

Grinberg, L., 1992, *Guilt and Depression*, London: Karnac Books.

Kilgore, J., 2011, *We Are All Zimbabweans Now*, Athens, OH: University Press.

Klein, J., 1987, *Our Need for Others and Its Roots in Infancy*, London: Tavistock.

Maher, M.J., 2012, *Racism and Cultural Diversity: Cultivating Racial Harmony through Counselling, Group Analysis and Psychotherapy*, London: Karnac Books.

Maher, M., 2018, 'Response to 'World in motion—the emotional impact of mass migration' by Elisabeth Rohr', *Group Analysis*, 51(3), pp. 297–303.

Miller, A., 1995, *The Drama of Being a Child: The Search for the True Self*, London: Little, Brown Book Group.

Robertson, J. & Robertson, J., 1971, 'Young children in brief separation: A fresh look', *The Psychoanalytic Study of the Child*, 26(1), pp. 264–315.

Rohr, E., 2018, 'World in motion—The emotional impact of mass migration', *Group Analysis*, 51(3), pp. 283–296.

Segal, J., 2004, *Melanie Klein*, London: SAGE.

Seinfeld, J., 1996, *Containing Rage, Terror, and Despair: An Object Relations Approach to Psychotherapy*, Northvale, NJ: Jason Aronson.

Winnicott, D.W., 2006, *The Family and Individual Development*, London: Taylor & Francis.

Winnicott, D.W., 2012, *Deprivation and Delinquency*, London: Taylor & Francis .

Zetzel, E.R., 1970, *The Capacity for Emotional Growth*, New York: International Universities Press.

Chapter 14

Alternative visions – polysemy/art[1]

Frances Gray

Land, air, water, fire make us and fills us. Together, they give us place and space, solidity, movement, shape, colour, liquidity, resilience, the foundation of our senses, our imagination, some of the elements of artistic practice. We need to rest in this knowing. But we also need to engage, actively in envisioning ourselves *in* the world and the world in us. What we see, how and why we see what we do and what we are, our vision, are fundamental to our being in the world; where we locate ourselves, in our own subjective privacies, or in a world beyond our small selves, or both, can change, and indeed, must change …

In *Pilgrim at Tinker Creek*, Annie Dillard wonders:

> Can I stay still? How still? It is astonishing how many people cannot, or will not, hold still. I could not, or would not, hold still for thirty minutes inside, but at the creek, I slow down, center down, empty. I am not excited; my breathing is slow and regular. … There! I am saying nothing. If I must hold a position, I do not 'freeze.' If I freeze, locking my muscles, I will tire and break. Instead of going rigid, I go calm. I centre down wherever I am; I find a balance and repose. I retreat – not inside myself, but outside myself, so that I am a tissue of senses. Whatever I see is plenty, abundance. I am the skin of water the wind plays over; I am petal, feather, stone.
>
> (Dillard, 1974/2013, p.203)

Annie Dillard's text was written in 1973, forty-four years ago, and well before the current capitalist, social and work-place infatuation with mindfulness. She is here giving us an alternative vision, a way of being in the world in which she alludes to the experience of standing outside herself. She is speaking not of the presence of a self that grabs at, and hyper-reinforces individuality; rather, she speaks of a kind of pure consciousness of being, a phenomenological alternative to our everyday focus on me, my, I. This deep awareness is not directed at herself, her interiority, but to the other, exteriority. And that exteriority takes her up, as it were, transforming her being into that which she observes, and in a sense, becomes.

The apparent movement from the personal pronoun, 'I', to the external reality of a wonder-filled world, with both its pleasures and disasters, is one instance only of alternative vision. Alternative to what? We rumble along in the world, doing what we need to do, very often not even present to ourselves. The visual/auditory/sensual worlds we inhabit certainly change as we move, as time passes. We travel through these worlds, and take a form of attention along with us which doesn't sit in a kind of pre-set focus on the task or tasks at hand. Alterations to this pre-set focus occur only, it would seem, when we are pulled out of focus either through disaster or in an epiphanic moment. Borrowing from Edmund Husserl, we might think of this pre-set focus as the natural attitude. Hence the 'alternative' in 'alternative vision' implies either actual or metaphorical change in space and time, a change in the everyday, habitual, attitudes with which we are familiar and comfortable.

'Vision' is itself polysemic: there are many meanings, some concerned with eyesight, some concerned with mindsight, and some concerned with a kind of propulsion into an imagined future, or past. Vision, as we know, is not used always within the context of sight: it acts as a trope for emotional/mental/psychic endeavour or projection. All modes of vision, all alternatives, represent something we may not have noticed and now see, or something we *re-see*, or *re-notice*, or even see beyond the previously imagined. The meanings we bring to, or discover in the phrase 'alternative vision' depend to a large extent on whom and where and what we are, our world experiences, and the stories we tell ourselves and that are told to us by others. Staying still to let ourselves just be, brings with it an opportunity for alternative vision, either in the moment or as a consequence of that moment. Alternative vision lifts us out of the natural attitude, the everyday, the habitual. Alternative vision take us to places that are unfamiliar and uncomfortable, or, contrariwise, to the unfamiliar, the pleasurable, the deliciously transformative. An aspect of this which I note in passing, lies in the idea of *metanoia*, or change of heart with its potential for moral transformation.

We should not be fooled into thinking, however, that the movement from the first person pronoun, 'I', to an external reality is an entirely one-way move. Already, when we make this movement, we have internalised aspects of the world to which we are drawn. In my view, we have been made by this world through our birth, our childhood and adolescence. The confluence of socio-culture, physical psycho-neurally charged embodiment and situation produces us as individuals. The moment we become ourselves as individuals is the moment when we begin to reflect, that is to say, when we become self-aware. Becoming the person we are, the development of our selves and our experience of those selves as our subjectivities involves always, and as a necessary condition, the ability to reflect, to stand back from the natural, everyday attitude. This means that our vision is in flux, and consequently, that *we* are in flux, that we are not fixed and determined, but that we move and change, stop, and then move again.

Many of us will identify with this process of polysemic, dynamic, change, where our meanings seem to be fixed, then are altered either by circumstance or deliberation. This latter brings us to an important distinction: between the accidental or what happens to us beyond our control, and the intentional or deliberate. Think of an art project in which you are involved. Let's imagine for the moment, that you are painting or drawing or sewing or sculpting, or photographing. See yourself in the scene. You have all of your equipment, you have thought about what you want to do, or maybe you don't even know, but you have decided to experiment. You begin, you feel instantly engaged, or instantly restless. Whatever the case, there is something going on in your mind and your body that draws you to this project, *now*, a sense of urgency or a desperate, frustrated need to make art. This is an element of the creative process, of which vision is an integral part.

The distinction between knowing what you want to do, and not-knowing is important, tied as it is to the accidental and the intentional. How often have we wondered just where has *that* come from? How often have we intended one thing, only to come up with something else? How often have we spilt or broken, or over-heated, or lost a bit of equipment and have had to improvise? How often have we been interrupted, drawn away from the heightened moment of invention and creativity? How often has the world been lost as we focus totally in our minds/hearts/heads on what we are doing? And how often do we realise that we have been 'carried away' into some place we inhabit in a kind of unintentional, but isolated solitude? When we realise the latter, our vision and its meaning, changes.

Of course, this is not an experience unique to artists. But it is important to artists precisely because, in my view, the ubiquity of this experience is an element in what draws artists to the world and the world to artists. The reciprocity of inter-subjectivity, and the intertwining of the nonhuman other and selves, ground multiple *visions*. Vision belongs to the everyday, to particular ways of being in the world (think of the taxi-driver or the plumber), to the visually impaired, to the scientist, to the parent, to the young child. Our awareness that 'vision' in each of these instances has same and different meanings, suggests that vision is not entirely in the domain of the sighted, that vision is not the same as the visual. Vision can be tied to illumination, to insight, to the absence of sight. Nor is vision tied only to what we might think of as the everyday world.

In his book *Confronting Images,* Georges Didi-Huberman begins his discussion of the visible, the invisible, the visual realm and the virtual, with an exploration of Fra Angelico's *Annunciation* found in Cell 3 of Convent San Marco in Florence. He examines different ways in which we might explore this image, and the light in which this particular image is situated. At one point he proposes that knowledge and not-knowledge interplay as we gaze at an image. In his discussion of the gaze, and the ground between knowledge and not-knowledge, he says that:

> the efficacy of these images is not due solely to the transmission of knowledge – visible, legible, or invisible – but that, on the contrary, their efficacy operates constantly in the intertwinings, even the imbroglio, of transmitted and dismantled knowledges, of produced and transformed not-knowledges. It requires, then, a gaze that would not draw close only to discern and recognize to name what it grasps at any cost – but would, first, distance itself a bit and abstain from clarifying everything immediately. Something like a suspended attention, a prolonged suspension of the moment of reaching conclusions,

where interpretation would have time to deploy itself in several dimensions, between the grasped visible and the lived ordeal of a relinquishment. There would also be, in this alternative, a dialectical moment – surely unthinkable in positivist terms – consisting of not-grasping the image, of letting oneself be grasped by it instead: thus of letting go of one's knowledge about it. The risks are great, of course. The beautiful risks of fiction.

(Didi-Huberman, 2005, p.16)

The idea of letting oneself be grasped by the image, echoes the moment when Annie Dillard becomes as a tissue of senses, when she is grasped by the visual world that transforms her vision through immersion in the visual. She moves from self to other, letting go, it would seem, her cognitive world, moving to the not-known of experience other-than-herself as if she were it. She moves from the everyday to another plane, lost, or maybe found, in her flesh, in the sensibility of the senses. By this, I mean that her awareness of her senses is full, is complete. It is her abundance.

Not-knowing is the risk. But trying to write the not-knowing *after* the risk of admission, is yet another risk. Writing-after is the challenge that emerges when one's natural attitude is suspended, and when one has gone, momentarily, elsewhere, where one is compelled to abandon one's status as knower. A trace of the experience of knowing is what remains and, writing in these circumstances, perhaps an extraordinarily difficult task, becomes, itself, a transformation. In that transformation, a refiguring of the not-known, what has transmogrified the known is central. Such writing can express an attitude of openness, and, paradoxically, even of closing with the temporary suspending of the rational and the cerebral. It is the risk one takes when one writes about one's own works of art: how does one write one's not-knowing? Does one indeed do this? Does one write fiction, beautiful fiction, a point of view, an expression of something tangible, yet not so? Does one write *away* from the factual, the empirical, the provable, the testable? Is one's writing about one's art fiction, in the sense that one is creating form in words that arise out of one's art? Does one find, express and embody a vision in words, in this spatio-temporal space that lives through the art work? I think so …

French feminist philosopher Luce Irigaray, in her critique of the phenomenologist, Maurice Merleau-Ponty, remarks that:

We co-belong to this living world and we exchange, indeed sometimes reverse, the roles between us. That a tree looks at us is not at all strange, that a table does would be another matter. Similarly, we give water to the plant which gives us air. In multiple ways, for the most part invisible, we exchange with the life which surrounds us. Thus claiming to perceive a living being simply with our eyes which, moreover, are mirror-eyes, and then to give it for others to see seems a little naïve.

(Irigaray, 2004, p.401)

The co-belonging to this world in the manner in which Luce Irigaray suggests, takes us to the deep mystery of the arts: writing, visual art (as if writing were not a form of visual art), music, movement, stillness. We are situated, and from our situation and its expansion, we create with words, with paint, with clay, with steel and wool, with the still and moving image. We do not simply imitate, we do not simply use our eyes as a touch upon and into the world. We begin with perhaps an idea, a vision that as yet may not have form, but maybe has intuitive impetus. Juhani Pallasmaa quotes Cornelius Castoriadis: "The body creates its sensation; therefore there is a corporal imagination" (Pallasmaa, 2011, p.29). This needs the rider, I think, that we need to acknowledge that it is *the body as sentient, self-conscious creature in the world*. The world gives the body its ground as corporeal imagination. Specifically, the female body is this very first ground. Without the world, and a healthy one at that, natural or built, we are nothing.

Yet imagination does not give itself over to full disclosure. Indeed, the activation of our imagination as the not-knowing is an integral part of the creative process. Juhani Pallasmaa writes:

> As I begin to express an argument, I do not have the idea or sentence verbally formulated in my mind. I feel an embodied pressure to express something valid in relation to the situation at hand and the words emerge to shape this embodied reaction. ... I speak as an ingredient of the flesh of the world, and speech is fundamentally an existential mode of communication in the same way as artistic expression.
>
> (Pallasmaa, 2011 p. 29)

In my view, vision in all of its complexities, in the seen and unseen, in the visible and invisible, in the known and the not-know; in other words, in all of its meanings, samenesses and differences, subtends the processes about which I have been speaking. The polysemy of vision and art expressed in and through our tissue of senses should fill us with wonder and with dread: wonder for the immensity of beauty and creativity; dread for the potential of our own and the world's self-destruction.

So remember, just occasionally, to retreat outside yourself, to be still, to be silent, to let yourself be grasped. As they said in the sixties, 'Turn off and tune out'. Be assured, you will come back.

Thank you.

I would like to thank Ruth Waller, Raquel Ormella, Anne Masters, and everyone else involved in securing funding from the Australian National University for my conference travel and expenses.

Note

1   This is the modified text of a keynote address I delivered at the Graduate Student Conference, School of Art and Design, at the Australian National University, Canberra, in May 2017.

    I would like to acknowledge the traditional land on which I stand and affirm my great respect for the Ngunawal people whose traditional land this is.

References

Didi-Huberman, G., 2005, *Confronting Images: Questioning the Ends of a Certain History of Art* (J. Goodman, Trans.), University Park: Pennsylvania State University Press.

Dillard, A., 1974/2013, *Pilgrim at Tinker Creek*, New York: HarperCollins.

Irigaray, L., 2004, 'To paint the invisible', *Continental Philosophy Review*, 37(4), pp.389–405.

Pallasmaa, J., 2011, *The Embodied Image: Imagination and Imagery in Architecture*, Chichester: John Wiley & Sons.

Chapter 15

Let's talk about our mothers

Introduced by Leslie Gardner

Feminism is as much about individuation (Jung's term for 'becoming oneself as distinct from others') as it is about a collective effort with other females. Particularly, mothers and daughters regard each other sceptically and often conflicts among feminist commentators are often generational, reflecting this designation metaphorically.

We had a series of exchanges on a forum on the site 'IAAP-Politics' (International Association for Analytical Psychology), which elicited passions – several of the postings warrant appearance here in the 'Voices' Section.

The topic proposed had two aspects: first, what our mothers' expectations were of us as females; and, second, how did they communicate to us what they thought a female should be. Stories of mothers' reactions of crucial moments in their daughters' lives were elicited: as an example: the mother of a friend, a former soldier, told her to shrug off a rape, and get on with it – what female/narrative theme did she imagine her daughter should engage in? Should she channel Joan of Arc and valiantly weather the story (but look where that got the saint!).

And the Oedipus narrative, foundational in Freudian depth psychology where Jocasta plays out her loyalty, in an intimate albeit initially unknowing attachment to her child, to maintain power, and then kills herself when she discovers it – is it about consent? Is it about shame?

Carolyn Steedman (1992) recounts stories of specifically working-class mothers in her research, that reveal another aspect, providing "a corrective ... to accounts that seek to define the mother/daughter relationship as one of nourishment and support" (p.125). Her work is a salutary reminder we only tangentially touch on in this book: that class circumstances alter psychological cases, as well as the global cultural distinctions we entertain primarily in this volume.

The stoical response to life speaks to the hardship working-class, or poverty-stricken, mothers grinding on through lives of oppression. It also provides, in some women's minds, a kind of behavioural get out: a 'rationalisation of oppression'. In Kathleen's mind (a patient in one of Steedman's case studies) the "façade of endurance cracked, and [her mother] expressed herself in extreme violence towards her children" (Steedman, 1992, p.126). In Steedman's study of Kathleen's psychological damage, she tells us that the daughter accepted the physical violence 'calmly, but she violently rejected the dreary stoicism of her mother's vision: "shut your mouth and go on"' (Steedman, 1992, p.126).

Her work reveals an "ambivalence [and awareness of the] … restrictions of the relationship between mother and daughter, about mothers no longer split into good and bad, as in fairy tales and psychoanalytic theory, [but associations that are] … 'powerfully integrated, terribly confining'" (Steedman, 1992, p.125). The figure of Jane Eyre (Charlotte Brontë, 1847/2009), abandoned and left in heartless surroundings, growing up, becomes for Steedman a romanticized creature of the industrial age – growing up to be redeemed in the literature, exploding the dire necessities of modern life in the nineteenth century, where their harsh treatment and reactions were emblematic of the processes of the 'inner life': pure unconsciousness. The psychological results of deprivation by mother and/or by culture are the themes of her work superseding the Romantic, Wordsworth-ian, depiction of childhood where the child is a potential 'rescuer or reclaimer' of 'corrupt adulthood' – especially of the mother.

In our call for stories of their mothers, we did not expect judgemental responses but simply looked for explorations of the myth/narratives which are invoked as a way on to explode cultural patterns: a kind of 'exemplary deviancy'. A fellow member observing our conversation, reminded the forum of Susie Orbach's comment that 'we all marry our mother; especially women' – and many of the greatest learning experiences, both difficult and pleasant, are with that carer functioning as mother in our lives. Mothers and sons have different themes and issues, so we are not including comments from sons, that also appeared on the forum.

Here is a sample of the responses.

Gretchen: Maybe I'm too interested in the topic! For me, gender formation is profoundly personal, and political. I think some steer away from the topic with a sense their gender excludes them. The conversation is definitely not gender binary. My own family was/is a matriarchy. Mother steered all choices she could reach. My father was/is more a cipher – seldom speaking and ever in opposition to mother. Because of my childhood, I often hold women more responsible – see them as more capable. This has nothing to do with reality, but with my own childhood with no substantial memories of my father. My mother was the only woman in her Master's in Agriculture program at Cornell, a missionary before she met my father. They were both committed to whatever 'being missionary' meant. Either mother gave up too much in the process of marriage and children, or she always lacked the capacity for emotional connection. Two pivotal moments stand out – the first when I was five and attended the local mission school for first grade. The female teacher decided to punish a boy who had done nothing wrong. I tried to tell her that she made a mistake. The boy who did nothing wrong was black. The boy who set him up was white and the teacher was white. The teacher refused to listen to me, whipping the wrong boy. I ran away. Mother brought me back, said this was just how the world was, and I would have to grow up and get used to it. I said I did not want to live in that world, and spent days against the wall, refusing to return to school until a year later. Was mother telling me what she told herself? Was her lack of emotional capacity linked to a passive acceptance of the unacceptable?

The second moment I have mentioned before. I was ten, attending the local girl's secondary school. English and books gave me advantage, and I knew this. I also knew the other girls at school (aged fourteen and up) were among the lucky ones as they were not already married off for goats or land. I knew girls about my age were sent off to the Bundo bush and came out as women. I did my best to hide everything I knew, deliberately answering wrong on exams. I also openly and vehemently challenged my parents' missionary vocation, pointing out the serious faith of those around us with their Muslim prayers four times a day, their shrines in the bush, their rigors of Ramadan. I said – don't you see, they don't want us here. Mother's solution was to send me to boarding school. She kept my siblings with her, and home schooled them. The boarding school was a day's ride through the bush. I reached home for break before my letters. There was no phone. At school, all we had was Jesus – Jesus in the morning and noon and night and all day on Sunday. Shakespeare was unheard of. Russians were the antichrist – with books on shelves to prove it. I once asked if Russians knew they were the antichrist – that maybe we could all be antichrist and not know it. I was told that I was the devil. At times I believed this.

Did mother not want my mind because I was female? I think it was more that she just did not want my mind. I was the only one in the family who challenged, and this was unacceptable. It is my mother who enforced the patriarchy. I was into adulthood before realising that reacting in opposition to her was not a form of freedom.

Often on this list we touch topics of feminism. For me, feminism is not about male/female. In my family, my mother was the enforcer of patriarchy. In the African cultures where we lived, it is women who did the clitorectomies of girls. It is women who have screamed at me that because I do not like to cook, I will not 'get a husband' and that 'getting a husband' is the job of women. It is women who have been the most vocal in telling me not to speak.

Carola: I don't know what to say about mine [mother]. I haven't seen or spoken to her for years. She was traumatised by the death of her brother when he was three years old. He was subsequently idolised by their parents. She married my father; they were ill suited and separated when I was six. She systematically denigrated him [my father] to me so I too disdained him. Much later I realised how disturbed she is, she has such a good persona [Jungian term for a person's social presentation]. She's really only interested in men. She used to talk more to my husband than to me.

She was mostly unhelpful when I was growing up but at least she didn't pressure me into anything. She didn't get on with her mother, who I loved, who was a GP in Austria and used to take me on visits to her patients. My choice to study medicine was influenced by my holidays with her.

Loralee: I just returned from working with a group of women in Lisbon. Some of the stories shared resonate deeply with what we've been saying here. ... there was a collective solidarity around commonality of deep wounding, and the chasm that often exists between mothers and daughters. The dynamics are complex. I don't think we can separate out a cultural complex relative to feminine oppression from the relationships of mothers and daughters.

... I think ultimately individuation is about liberation ... liberating our authentic selves, from the self we've been told by our mothers, and by the culture at large we *should* be. As daughters, this journey of individuation often has to be done in spite of rather than because of our mother's influence. To the degree that we can make this journey, I think we are freed to see our mothers from a place of compassion. ... As the mother of a young adult daughter, I have watched and tried to support her own struggle to separate out, to carve out, her own unique identity, independent of mom. In some ways, the closer the bond the more fierce the struggle.

As daughters, I don't think we can rescue our mothers. I think we can commit to healing ourselves by first naming and then accepting the wound, and to liberating ourselves by affirming ourselves authentically, regardless of cultural projections and in spite of a legacy of unlived revolutions handed to us by our mothers.

Carola: So hard to generalise! My young adult daughter as well as being her own person also wants to *understand* me which I find intrusive! Probably connected to my reticence with my own mother; I wasn't close to her and I don't think I wanted to be. But as for trying not to be her ... sometimes when I hear myself speak, I shudder inwardly. ... I have her tone of voice and even phrasing – all so complex!

Leslie: ... it's just that the form the personal takes is so locked in step with cultural expectations, with underlay of mythic shapes to behaviour and thinking. The notion of the 'individual' and subjectivity (and 'interior') is interrogated in this miasma of cultural/primordial feeling, tone, hierarchy – not being able to open to Mom ... 'intrusive' is an interesting way to put it, Carola. Think of Demeter hovering, powerless, at Hades portal, anguished while her daughter Persephone descended yearly to the underworld, where she stays with her husband. ... I suppose Persephone might have felt *her* to be intrusive ... after all it was Demeter's negotiation that established the condition of seasonal rhythm associated to her control of earthly fecundity that sealed the deal. Demeter is of course diverted by the transgressive figure of Baubo, as she wiles away the months without her daughter.

Loralee: ... the interwoven tapestry of cultural oppression, also embedded in how we interpret mythology, is something to work with. Relationship between Baubo and Demeter is a critical one on many levels. Baubo is key to Demeter's transformation from a grieving, disempowered mom who is disenfranchised from her own power. Baubo is the only one who convinces Demeter to cross a key threshold that starts her own healing, and even then we find a mythological female trying to project her power on to the young male (placing the baby in the fire). The angry mother is another transformative feminine in Demeter's life who forces her to come to terms with it for herself.

Leslie: ... but I am pointing at consent: listening to reports of testimony from women in Harvey Weinstein trial, for example, many were in years-long abusive relationships with him, in which their willingness to be there is deemed problematic by his lawyers. Consent was in the spotlight – why did they 'stay' so long.

While Demeter and Persephone are not figures with interiors, and don't have 'psychologies', they nevertheless participate in formula of human relations, cultural narratives. Psychological observance and performance plays out in formal, *tropic* modes for mythic figures. How are we to regard those females who stay in abusive relationships?

Persephone is let out every six months: that was her mother's deal, bargaining with Zeus, she would kill off vegetation – permanent winter – otherwise – unless her daughter was freed. Is Persephone on board with this? Demeter is no feeble player, there was a price – did Persephone want that? Did she want to leave her underground home?

Catriona: This discussion calls to mind for me Marion Woodman's 1990 book *The Ravaged Bridegroom: Masculinity in Women*. I might take issue with her use of masculinity and femininity attached to male and female, preferring perhaps less obviously gendered terms *Logos* (rationality, intellect) and *Eros* (empathy, relatedness), but Woodman points out that: "Feeling is not valued by the industrial and post industrial macho machine that drives Western civilisation. Women as often as men hand over to their inner or outer patriarchal judge the power of evaluating their own feminine worth and end up dismissing their authentic feelings as 'naïve, illogical, stupid'. This is profound self-betrayal" (Woodman, 1990, p.171). It struck me when I read this originally, that the second wave feminists, in their struggle for women to take their place in the public sphere, may have inadvertently ended up devaluing the 'feminine' or 'eros' in themselves. They were warriors, amazons, fighting for justice and fairness and a place at the table, and so giving into empathy (responding to the needs of others) might be seen as a failure, because that's what women have always done. My grandmother was a domestic servant who had been denied schooling past primary school by her own mother, but was determined her own daughter would have every opportunity. My mother gained a grammar school scholarship and a place a university in the 1950s and she in turn was very supportive of my own educational ambitions. But as a daughter of a second waver (and perhaps unlike some of the stories in the discussion), the fight was not so much to be out of the domestic sphere, or a fight for independence, but rather a struggle to understand relationships and relatedness are not necessarily weakness, and that home making can be a valuable art form, requiring skill, craft and accomplishment too. The second wavers brought us some choice in the matter (though there are still too many who have no choice), but when it comes down to it, there must be a place to value Eros as well as Logos, in ourselves, in our sisters and daughters and mothers (not to mention brothers, sons and fathers too).

Marilyn: I must have been four the first time I overheard my mother (a parent of two girls and a good enough mother in many ways) say to a friend: 'Well, you certainly don't want a kid who is too smart'. I was young enough to have only a literal understanding of language so I feared that there might come a day when my mother didn't want me. Was I in danger? And what would she do with me if she didn't want me?

The next time I heard her say this, I was a little older, maybe six or seven, and this time I knew I was physically safe, but I wanted to be wanted, so I tried hard to figure out what it was to be smart, and how I could avoid crossing that deadly line of *too* smart. Turns out this wasn't just an early childhood misunderstanding. Consciously or unconsciously I worked hard never academically to exceed my sister who was three years older. One time, as teens, we were taking a summer course in typing and shorthand together. We had to take the same quiz at the same time and I was terrified (but by now I'd forgotten why). I felt a HUGE sense of relief when she got 99% and I got 98%. If I'd gotten a higher grade, the whole family would have been put off kilter, and I could not have borne the guilt.

Leslie: So competition – is that a component of maternal/filial envy – issues of self esteem? Or is it power relations? My mother advised me, like other mothers mentioned here, to be conciliatory: her own alcoholic, abused mother (abused by her husband/my grandfather) necessitated my mother's taking independent measures to evade settling into midwestern US life. She went into the army to escape but also to fulfil patriotic sentiment – insisting on higher education and career – she created an employment agency for women returning to work after having had children – she was a politician (following her mother's footsteps too – who worked as public relations for presidential hopeful Hubert Humphrey in Midwest) ... but my mother created competition unknown to me with my sister who now feels that my success (in her eyes) because of my ability for one thing in negotiating my mother's demanding personality has harmed her in her endeavours – is that a Cain and Abel contest?

Carola: ... the Cain and Abel allusion is not quite right ...

Anne: I think the corollary of envy is scarcity. Envy is a moralistic word implying something nasty in the one who envies. The common theme in the unloved, scapegoated child is lack. There is a certain amount of affection or approval that is doled out, and withheld. The poor kid tries and tries and maybe one day gets it ... this realisation is very difficult in small nuclear families or indeed systems which advocate power – capital as a *modus operandi*. There can be change personally or intergenerationally the catalyst can be politics or therapy or luck or a partner with different values.

My mother had a nasty mother who preferred her son. They were born in the snobbish British Raj system. Eventually came to Australia, political awakening my uncle a GP was a very early activist for Indigenous land rights.

My mother [was participant] in anti-Vietnam war and other stuff. They were in the communist party back then but essentially fellow travellers. So not taken up by cult phenomena. My mother read endlessly, including Jung and wrote a book about boarding school, the loneliness, snobbery and poor food, the covert lesbianism and shaming.

In fairness I would have to say my grandmother was a good enough grandma. Yes, she did splitting amongst cousins and horrible to her daughter in law and nasty to my mother

She was a narcissistic product of Victorian Edwardian England. Her entitlement was an object of mild inspiration and much hilarity to us grandkids "what did grandma say today?" she said "I could, should, must be a ... and she will ensure it." Endlessly aspirational and hierarchical, a FOMO of giant proportions. Poor grandma. Her son loved her and I was upset when she died. She left stuff to me that had always been left from mother to daughter, thus excluding my mother.

Jean: My mother's family was matriarchal, with a grandmother who ran businesses in the 1850s, where my father's family was equivalently patriarchal.

Carola: Some of our mothers were literally soldiers in the Second World War, something I often forget.

Carolyn: The first murder in the creation story of Genesis (other than the murder of innocence for which Eve is perpetually blamed) was Cain's murder of his younger brother Abel. It wasn't over property, unless one considers being favored by God as a kind of thing to be possessed. I would say it was over envy – not unlike the murder of hope that Cinderella's step-sisters and step-mother kept creating in her life. Cain was a farmer, Abel was a shepherd. And apparently Yahweh was not vegan. In preferring Abel's sacrifice of a lamb over Cain's offering from his harvest, the elder brother became enraged (shame? envy?) and did in his baby brother. So yes to sibling rivalry, right there from the get-go of that saga.

    Gretchen, thank you for your story, which so underscores the role of the mother in sustaining patriarchy. I was a father's daughter, growing into a mother's daughter in my later life, but so fortunate that I was able to have a mother who kept growing as she entered her great agedness. She was forever curious about what I was learning in my Jungian training. We talked about dreams and death and dying and life, both inner and outer. Growing up, she was a daughter of the patriarchy, but at some point in the last twenty years of her life, she set that all to one side and entered into a long and deep internal conversation with Sophia.

    I'm touched, Carola, by your note that your interest in medicine was influenced by this and reminds me never to lose sight of the reality that even the most difficult of our experiences may contribute to some of the best choices we ever made.

Vreni: My case is different: we lived in Switzerland, but of course being a close neighbour of Germany there was fear everywhere, among Jews and non-Jews. I was born during the war, my mother being pregnant with me and my first two years during a period of intense fear. Of course, it affected me.

    My mother grew up in Basel. Her father's family lived in Alsace. Her cousins/friends were murdered. She was about seventeen then. She never got over this completely. We were not allowed to be aggressive or talk badly about other people. We always had to be 'positive' in speaking or thinking this was how she could live with the trauma. But I grew up in a surrounding of love filled with mother's livelong gratitude that we were alive and happy.

References

Brontë, C., 1847/2009, *Jane Eyre*, New York: Penguin Books.

Steedman, C., 1992, *Past Tenses*, London: Rivers Oram Press.

Woodman, M., 1990, *The Ravaged Bridegroom: Masculinity in Women*, Toronto: Inner City Books.

Index

For Product Safety Concerns and Information please contact our EU
representative GPSR@taylorandfrancis.com
Taylor & Francis Verlag GmbH, Kaufingerstraße 24, 80331 München, Germany